Over the top with Jim

Hugh Lunn is an author and journalist who has won
many awards for his writing. His previous memoir
Vietnam: A Reporter's War was an *Age* Book of the
Year in 1985, and in 1986 was published in New York.
His first book, the unauthorised and still definitive
biography *Joh: The Life and Political Adventures of
Johannes Bjelke-Petersen,* was a national bestseller and
has appeared in many editions.

Three collections of his newspaper feature stories
have been published: *Queenslanders* (UQP), *Behind the
Banana Curtain* (UQP), and *Four Stories* (published by
the Aboriginal Treaty Organisation). His journalism
won him five national awards for feature writing including three Walkley Awards.

Born in Brisbane, Hugh Lunn began his career on
the *Courier-Mail* before going to Fleet Street, via China
and Russia. He worked on the London *Daily Mirror*
and then joined Reuters. From London he was sent to
Vietnam as a correspondent, and later worked for
Reuters in Singapore and Indonesia. He was for many
years assistant editor of the *Australian* and also its
Queensland editor.

Over the top with Jim

Hugh Lunn's
tap-dancing , bugle-blowing <u>memoir</u>
of a well-spent boyhood

University of Queensland Press

First published 1989 by University of Queensland Press
Box 42, St Lucia, Queensland 4067 Australia
Reprinted in paperback 1990, 1991 (three times)

Printed in Australia by The Book Printer, Melbourne

Distributed in the USA and Canada by
International Specialized Book Services, Inc.,
5602 N.E. Hassalo Street, Portland, Oregon 97213-3640

This work was assisted by a writer's fellowship from the Australia
Council, the Federal Government's arts funding and advisory body

Cataloguing in Publication Data

National Library of Australia

Lunn, Hugh, 1941–
    Over the top with Jim : Hugh Lunn's tap-dancing,
    bugle-blowing memoir of a well-spent boyhood.

    1. Lunn, Hugh, 1941–   . — Childhood and youth.
    2. Brisbane (Qld.) — Social life and customs —
    1945–1965. I. Title.

994.3'105'0924

ISBN 0 7022 2255 0

Contents

1
A Russian called James

You couldn't get much further away from international politics than to be a child in Brisbane in 1951 but, although I was only nine years old, I knew enough to know that you just don't get Russians called James. I don't know how I knew this. But I did.

Perhaps it was because the nuns said the government was going to ban the iron heel of Communism in Australia. Or maybe I was just suspicious of all foreigners because of the number of non-Catholics and State School kids who were living at Annerley Junction in those days. Or maybe, after six years of religious instruction by the nuns at our Saint Joseph's Convent, I knew that the name of an apostle didn't sit well on a Red. Not even Judas, let alone James. For, despite what he had done by telling on God, Judas was still a Catholic and he could well have made an Act of Contrition just as he passed away and thus could have died in the State of Grace (barring any last-minute impure thoughts) and gone straight to Heaven.

And I knew from our religious instruction that no Communist like this new kid in the class could go to Heaven or even get past Limbo, even if he did somehow find out about our secret of doing the nine First Fridays so that Saint Joseph would make sure we went to Heaven.

I knew a lot about Saint Joseph because the convent was run by the Sisters of Saint Joseph. They named themselves after him because he was God's Dad and it was their job to teach us about God and how he made the world and Catholics. In fact the first line in our most important study book, the Catechism, was "Who made the world?" I was

1

pretty stupid when I started at the convent when I was only four years old and so, because the next question in bold print was "Who made me?", for a long time I said my prayers to "Who".

But that was before we learned the answers off by heart: "God made the world", and "God made me, giving me a body and a soul". After that I worshipped God.

Then the answers got much longer and more complicated like some of the prayers after you learned off by heart the simple ones like the Hail Mary, the Our Father, and the Act of Contrition. These were the three main prayers other than the "Glory Be": the first one admitting that I was a sinner; the second asking God to deliver me from the evil that was everywhere; and the third begging forgiveness for my sins and promising never to sin again.

Not that there was much chance of risking a sin at the convent with all those nuns around, at least twenty of them, I reckon. They were sort of like God's policemen, dressed in black and able to predict sins before they were even committed. Think of cheating and you would be warned; consider swearing and one would appear; throw something and your name would be called. Impure thoughts were just far too risky. Boys seemed to be their main target, which perhaps explained why there were so few of us and so many girls at the school: outnumbered probably four to one.

They often referred to a boy as "his nibs" and if you did something tough, like pulled a girl's hair, they said you were "looking for notice" yet if a big girl hurt you they said "we should put you in a glass case and throw sugar at you".

The Sisters liked the same things as the girls—especially Holy Pictures—even though the nuns were almost all incredibly old and often had men's names: like Sister Vincent, Sister Damian, or Sister James. They wore large crucifixes stuck into a black belt around their waist like a dagger. Giant black rosary beads hung down from their waists to near the ground, rattling a muffled warning when they glided into a room like moving statues.

Apart from their hands, the only visible human parts of these nuns were all the holes in their face: the eyes, nostrils and mouth. This made them look like non-human creatures who could only talk, breathe and see. Particularly as the face was framed tightly by a stiff white material which hid their foreheads, ears, and necks. Their hair was hidden beneath a black veil pinned to the stiff white material with long pins which they often removed and replaced while talking to the class so it seemed they were sticking long sharp pins deep into their heads. The white material folded down over the bosom, reflecting light up into their faces from below.

It was this lit-face look and the stiff-headed effect which made them seem like the life-sized statues we prayed to in the huge red brick church in the school grounds—a church so sacred and holy it was called Mary Immaculate after "Our Lady": which is what we Catholics called the Virgin Mary to show she was no one else's but ours.

Not that I knew the meaning of "virgin" or the other words we used every day in prayers about her, like "womb" and "immaculate"—but I guess I knew enough about them to know not to ask any of the nuns what they were.

And I knew enough to think it strange that the nuns dressed in black, because it was not a church colour: it was the Devil's colour.

What I didn't know, as we lined up in our grade five class at assembly, was that one of these black figures was watching me, realising I was about to sin. Standing in the row in front of me was the new boy, the Russian, James, whose family had just arrived in Australia. The nuns said he was a White Russian, but he didn't look very white to me. Everyone who came to Australia was supposed to be white before they could get in, so it was obvious he and his family had slipped into Brisbane one night in the dark. We were all white—even the State School kids—but this Russian's skin was brown and his hair was as black as our school shoes. He had an ugly scar down the length of his nose in the middle of his round face. He also had a funny name the like of which had not been heard at the convent before—"Egoroff".

And, something even stranger, although he claimed his

first name was James someone had checked the roll book and his initial was "D": which proved I was right. Even I knew enough to know that James did not start with a "D".

One of the smart girls found out that the D was for Dimitri, another foreign-sounding name like Stalin and Egoroff.

"You Communist pig, Dima," I sneered from behind him: shortening Dimitri because it was long, as was our custom. Confident in the knowledge that none of the boys around me wanted anything to do with him, and convinced that he was too scared to answer I continued: "You Russian dog, Dima." At last, after nearly six years, I had found a way to be popular with the rest of the boys—the girls didn't matter: the only thing that interested them was homework and Holy Pictures. Particularly new Holy Pictures, which seemed to arrive every week to be held up triumphantly before the class by a nun so that the girls could cry in sickly unison "Oooohhh Ssssisterrr". Which was their girls' way of saying they liked something a lot.

Just as I was about to give the Russian another one Egoroff turned around: "You Australian donkey," he said, in English. Donkey? Of all the animals he could have picked this was the last one I had expected. Rat, dingo, grub, snake, yes ... but donkeys were friendly like kangaroos or horses. And how could they allow a foreigner, a dark New Australian, a banned Commo, to come to our school in Brisbane in broad daylight and call Australians names? "You Red worm," I answered just before Egoroff lunged his palms at both sides of my head saying "I rubber your ears", "I rubber your ears".

It was like torture, Japanese torture at its worst, and this smart-alec Russky added a whole new threat to my already awful existence. If ever an example of Red aggression was needed this was it: the Cold War they talked about all the time in Dad's cake shop was really starting to hot up. Forget the Berlin Blockade and Korea, where the Cold War was being fought in snow, and which filled the *Telegraph* every day. In the fights behind the immaculate church during Big Lunch or with the State School kids on the way home headlocks were applied by the winner. No-one had ever yet resorted to rubbing ears: not even in the serials at the flicks on Saturday afternoons. It wasn't our way of doing things. Our society—Protestants included—boxed or wrestled.

We didn't grab hold of protruding pieces of the body and try to destroy them, or, worse still, rub them off.

Only recently had the Russians got the same bomb the Americans beat the Japanese with when I was four ... a real humdinger of a bomb my older brother Jackie told me could blow up the whole of Annerley Junction in one hit. And now this alien had arrived: not only from Russia but after having lived in China, a country full of yellow people, which had suddenly turned Communist a few years before and was fighting against us in Korea. Right into my own class. What they said on the wireless all the time was so right: there was no place to hide from Communism. Egoroff got into our convent, and he wasn't even a Catholic.

Two things struck me about this Egoroff as he rubbed my ears—he stank of garlic and he was much stronger than me. Jackie always claimed that you could beat anyone up if you were determined enough about it but, try as I might, I could not get past Egoroff's arms to apply my winning headlock, let alone Jackie's favoured Full Nelson. And I could not get him away from my ears. Luckily the young nun who had just been appointed our teacher—Sister Veronica—came to my rescue and pulled the ugly, dark, scarred Russian off me.

Then she took me up onto the hall verandah to talk to me alone.

Unfortunately, Sister Veronica had heard everything I had said to Egoroff and, being new and young, she stuck up for Dima. She was nowhere near as tough as the other nuns. There was no way Sister Vincent or Sister James would have copped any nonsense from foreigners. They had both told us of God's warning that one day a dark cloud would spread from the north across most of the world—and they waved their hand across the map from Russia down to Australia. And on other days they had also warned of the Yellow Peril from the north ... until I didn't know which to fear the most: the black peril or the yellow.

Poor young Sister Veronica was too pretty and soft for

5

her own good. The peril had arrived, yet for hours and hours she lectured me about this poor Commo. How would I like to be driven from my homeland and forced to live in another country and speak a strange language?

How would I feel if people there called me names and wouldn't be friends? He couldn't help it if he looked and spoke a bit differently. English was not his mother tongue. What would God think looking down from Heaven and seeing me abuse one of his children? What would Saint Joseph think? What would my Guardian Angel think?

I must admit she stopped me there. I was so impressed by large pictures on the classroom walls of men with wings guarding children near cliffs that the one person I particularly respected was my Guardian Angel. Life was so dangerous in Brisbane in those days that I always left room on my form for my Guardian Angel to sit next to me.

Sister Veronica must have noticed the effect this had because she announced in triumph that she was going to sit me next to Egoroff in class all day every day—like a human Guardian Angel so that I could help him adapt to our way of life.

That was all I needed.

I was enough of an outsider with the other boys as it was without becoming friendly with a Russian. I couldn't run fast, I couldn't fight much, I was down near the bottom of the class in all subjects, and I had a funny name. So there I was in class sitting next to a Communist who stank and who was so far behind in his work he couldn't even help me. I sat as far from him as our single form allowed and every time I looked across at him I wondered how he got that big scar down the middle of his nose.

Although we knew the Communists didn't allow churches, Egoroff claimed he belonged to some Russian church which had some relationship with us because their bishops were also—unlike the Protestants—what the nuns called "apostolic": able to trace themselves back in an unbroken line to the apostles and Saint Peter, who was the rock God built his church on. Not much of a foundation mind you, a man who had denied God three times in succession when he was in a lot of trouble with some foreigners. But you didn't criticise saints—it was too dangerous. What size sin criticising saints was I didn't know, but certainly it was even worse than impure thoughts, though perhaps not as bad as that most unmentionable of sins: "impure actions".

So Sister thought life was tough for Dima—well it wasn't being too kind to me either. Here I was forced to spend my days pursued by a posse of angry nuns, stonkered by the piano, the mouth organ, the theory of music, analysing sentences, writing compositions, spelling, doing fractions and long division, answering questions like what grows in Africa (I got into big trouble when I replied "elephants"), parsing words, and saying the Ten Commandments and the Apostles' Creed, when all I wanted to do was play marbles or stay home and play with Jackie or hang around Dad's cake shop watching everyone come and go.

That was the best—so long as you could avoid having to serve the shop or sort the soft drink bottles.

Long division got me into trouble a few days before this Russian run-in when Sister Veronica tricked me by asking those in the class who could do it to put up their hands. I knew better than to admit to ignorance of anything to a nun so I put up my hand: along with the five smartest girls in the room, including of course Imelda Holyoak—whose very name gave her a big advantage with the nuns—and, naturally enough, Carmel Sherman, who knew more than the nuns.

I also knew not to confess to a lie, and, being new and young, Sister Veronica believed me where no other nun in the school, or anyone in our class, would have. Anyone with any brains would have known I could never have learnt anything as complicated as long division.

In her ignorance, Sister divided our class of more than forty into six groups so that each of us who completely understood long division could teach the others. You can imagine the disastrous result. I was given one side of a blackboard, some chalk, and six classmates with absolutely no idea what to do and twenty minutes to go until big lunch.

For fifteen minutes I pretended, I faked, I cleaned the

7

blackboard perfectly, I drew mathematical signs, I created numerous sets of figures, I questioned each of the six as to what they knew and what they didn't, waiting desperately for the school bell, or divine intervention, until even Sister Veronica woke up that I didn't know how the trick was done. But I got away with it because, unlike most of the nuns, she didn't give the cuts.

In fact, Sister Veronica didn't even have a cane she was so new and weak.

But now that she had seen me in action Sister Veronica realised that I wasn't any good at schoolwork. Not only couldn't I parse words and analyse sentences but I couldn't write a composition to save my life.

Every year the choice of composition topics was always the same, and every year I just couldn't think of anything to say about "A Day in the Life of a Penny" or "The Bushfire". While the nuns would read bits from essays by the girls about a penny being dropped by the tram conductor into a bag full of nasty pennies or being dropped in the rain and nearly drowning in a puddle, I could only see the penny as a round piece of copper that you could buy things with ... things like conversation lollies that you were able to read in different colours, and tram rides clear across town, and marbles and small ice-creams. These precious pennies were like flat Queensland nuts and about as hard to come by.

They were dead things. Not things like people.

After all I had seen a lot more pennies than anyone else in our class from serving in the shop. And, as for bushfires, I knew nothing of the fiery horizons and frightened animals the girls wrote about: but I did know what it was like to be caught in a fire.

Egoroff had his scars but I had mine: a burnt ear.

I had spent three months in Brisbane's Mater Children's Hospital when I was six years old after setting Mum's house on fire during the night. But I wasn't going to tell anyone at school about that—the less said to the nuns the better. Children weren't supposed to play with matches, and I had. But once again it was a case of me sinning by accident.

It happened just after the War finished and there wasn't

much of anything around in Brisbane: probably because the rest of Australia wanted to save themselves by giving Brisbane to the Japs—"the Brisbane Line" grown-ups called it.

There were even ration cards for tea and Mum used to look forward to Jackie's ninth birthday because he would be eligible for the tea ration, and she planned to drink it for him. Fags were rationed and kept in brown paper bags under the counter at our shop with the name of the man they could be sold to on the packet. Even if you had the money to buy a comic it didn't mean the paper shop had any for sale—maybe one torn second-hand action comic. When they did get some comics in, Jackie—who was two-and-a-half years older than me—used to get very frustrated because my young sister Gay and me would always try to buy whatever comic Jackie bought.

To try to stop us, he would take us out of the paper shop and sit down in the gutter and explain how we were all in the same family and, if we each bought a different comic, it was like the family buying three comics which we could all read. It was, he claimed, sheer stupidity to own three comics which were all the same.

We did what he said, but I would still have preferred to buy the same comic as Jackie.

There mustn't have been much paper around after the Japs had been defeated because when I arrived at the convent we wrote on pieces of black slate with thin grey sticks half wrapped in red-and-white or blue-and-white checked paper. These were called "slate pencils". They broke very easily and were difficult to write with, but the marks they made washed easily off the slate with a wet sponge each of us kept in a bottle.

To help teach us to count, Sister instructed that we should each have a collection of dead matches: since there was nothing much else around to use. Which was a problem for me since no-one in our house smoked, and Mum wouldn't allow me anywhere near matches. So, when I was at the shop, I pinched a couple of boxes from behind the counter— it wasn't a sin because Sister had asked us, and Sisters were somehow married to God and even wore wedding rings to show it. I then hid the matches on the ledge behind a door leading from the breakfast room to the verandah in our house.

I remember clearly what happened, though the doctors didn't believe my story: they claimed I lit a match and put it under my pillow because the pillow was badly burnt. But that wasn't it at all.

When I awoke in the dark that night I went and got the matchboxes and got back into bed. I knew enough about matches to know that when they were thrown on the ground they went out. I had watched cigarette smokers outside the shop do it hundreds of times, and it looked great fun: which I supposed was why only adults could do it.

So I lit one and threw it on the brown lino floor: and it went out.

So did the next one.

The third one just touched the side of my mosquito net where it reached the floor and a small semi-circle of fire formed as big as a shoe heel and I decided to get up and hit it with a shoe to put it out.

But I didn't get time.

Before I moved there was a sheet of red instead of white around me—and that was the last thing I remembered until Mum was cuddling me in the lounge room as my left ear dripped onto my burnt left shoulder.

I didn't feel any pain at all. I vaguely knew I should be in lots of trouble for being naughty but I knew I would be all right because Mum had her arm around me and was talking softly about how I was so important to her. But still the lounge room was just too quiet. Jackie, Gay, and the street were too quiet.

Everyone was waiting for something in that lounge room, and somehow I knew they were all waiting for me to be taken away.

When I arrived at the hospital a nurse covered a piece of cloth with white zinc cream and slammed it on my dripping ear ... a terrible mistake because it was so painful for them to scrape it off the next day. The doctor said I had third degree burns which, since I was only in grade one at the convent, sounded pretty high. Jackie and Gay could only wave to me in my hospital bed because children weren't allowed in because of diseases. And, for three months, I did my penance with only visits from Mum, and green jelly on Sundays, to look forward to. I cried everytime Mum left and everytime she was late arriving because she had to serve the shop. And I cried everytime I thought of home.

For the first time I found out that there were places like Hell and Purgatory and Limbo where they could keep you from going home.

The nuns were right.

People could easily be punished with isolation forever. And God was also right to punish people with fire in Purgatory and Hell because, as I now knew, burns hurt so much that you wished your body did not belong to you.

Thus I left the Mater Hospital more determined than ever to stay out of Hell.

2
Doctor Mum

Mum kept a really close eye on us when we were born, and as soon as she spotted something wrong she immediately fixed it up.

Jackie, she told women in the shop, had been born with his head tilted to one side and the doctor said only a special daily massage by an expert would fix it up: and a few months later Mum—to the amazement of the doctor (and the women on the other side of the counter)—had him right as rain herself. Then I was born with one of my feet pointing upwards, so Mum got me leg irons to fix it up.

Mum was big and strong but she still had to get various grown-ups to help hold me down on the kitchen table to strap my legs into this long steel-and-leather contraption which I had to wear all day and which hurt. When it was on I couldn't walk properly because I had to swing each leg through as though it were made of wood. My feet were in special boots and bits of iron ran up the outside of the leg, strapped with three buckles around the knees and joining more steel around the waist. On the table I cried and screamed and fought, but Mum was never impressed with present grief if she thought it would lead to some future happiness: even after you were dead. And she took no notice of my complaints as I staggered around all day looking forward to night-time, when the iron legs would come off. But I knew there was no use telling her I wished I didn't have to wear them or I wished they could come off, because she invariably replied: "Wish in one hand and spit in the other—and see which one fills up first."

Mum told the ladies in the shop we were born with defects

because she had to work so hard all the time to keep the shop going seven days a week until late at night.

Gay was bandy, Mum noticed, but instead of getting leg irons she was sent into town to a place where she climbed ladders and walked straight white lines and other easy stuff like that. Then Mum's last baby, Sheryl—whose head was covered with long red curls—had a turned foot and had to have a plaster cast fitted which made her cry and scream until Mum worked out that the hospital had put it on the wrong way round.

Because of these leg problems, before we were four years old we were all packed off to the local dance studio in the Annerley Junction RSL Hall—the boys to learn tap dancing and Gay and Sheryl to do ballet. It was most embarrassing for me, and a sissy thing to do, but Mum didn't know so much about boys and Dad was always in the shop. Anyway Dad didn't know very much about what went on, being from an orphanage in Western Australia.

Mum said the dancing would strengthen our legs.

That was how she was: quick to solve any problem as it arose.

When Jackie started to choke on some cabbage at dinner in the kitchen she frightened me because I didn't know that she could move so fast. My impression of Mum was that her sheer size would slow her down, but, as soon as Jackie started spluttering and gasping on the other side of the kitchen table, she was out of her cream wood chair and around the other side before you could say Jack Robinson. She didn't ask him what was wrong or anything like that. She just went straight down on her big knees and reached under the table and pulled Jackie out and up by one ankle with her left hand as easily as if he were a dirty apron. She held him upside down with her left arm raised high above her head and started belting him on the back with heavy blows from her right as if she were dusting a blanket on the clothes line. She must have been hurting him but Jackie couldn't say anything because his mouth was open facing the floor. And she kept hitting until he coughed up a piece of cabbage as long as a pencil. Then she put him back down again, gave him a glass of water, wiped the floor, and explained that we all had to chew our food properly.

I was not reassured, and preferred it when Mum solved our problems in a more gentle way.

I liked the way she would sit Gay on a stool in the kitchen and light the ends of her fine white hair with a match to make it grow thicker—"singeing" she called it.

I liked watching the matches being lit and the way the fire burnt in spurts and killed the hair by turning it black and brittle. But, best of all, was to see the way Mum held the hair between her fingers so the fire couldn't get past her.

I also liked to watch Mum when I got ear ache. She would go into the kitchen and light a match by ripping it across the side of the box and then hold the fire beneath a teaspoon full of oil. Then she would drop the warm oil slowly into my ear while talking to me softly, immediately bringing a delightful feeling instead of the pain.

The kitchen was where Mum kept all her cures. If anyone had a splinter that wouldn't come out with a needle (which she also heated in the fire of a lit match), Mum would get some bread and butter and other ingredients and mix it up in a white basin and put the contents into a white rag and make a poultice which she applied to the splinter to suck it out overnight.

If I had a sore fingernail with swollen red flesh around it—Mum called it "proud flesh"—she would get a bottle and some brown sugar from the kitchen. She would put the brown sugar in a rag and roll the bottle over it until the sugar was a fine dust: and then she would wrap the rag around the finger. And the sugar killed the proud flesh.

Nothing was ever left to chance.

Practically every week, Doctor Holmes would arrive in the middle of the night with his round leather bag to treat one of us for something—usually with an injection. Sometimes he even arrived with a coat over his pyjamas, but you could tell he didn't mind coming because he was so nice to everybody. He was so keen to be able to come if you were sick that Mum said he had two Austin cars so that if one didn't work he could drive the other one.

Even if you had nothing wrong with you Mum would still take action.

Every night we each had to eat a teaspoonful of Hypol, a foul-tasting white mixture which she said would do us good. If we got a cold it was a teaspoon of Kays Compound essence, which at least tasted good, and a chest rub with Vicks Vaporub, which felt really nice.

One horrible ritual was the enema on the kitchen table where she would pump warm water into your bum until, as soon as she finished, you had to make a terrible dash down the back stairs to the corrugated-iron room under the house.

She hated us being dirty or having worms. At night she would arrive unexpectedly at any hour in the dark with a torch to search our bums for worms. And sometimes, after Jackie and me went to bed, she brought a basin of warm water to wash our pogeys because we hadn't had the skin removed like all the other boys.

That was an embarrassing thing Dad had inflicted on me. I had to be different there because he said he had suffered in front of hot ovens in Mt Isa where even an apron of wet flour bags gave no protection.

Other mothers were so impressed by Mum's reputation for fixing up her kids that they not only brought their failed Christmas cakes to the shop for her to repair by filling in the sunken middle with a piece of her own cake or cutting off the burnt bits and icing them, they also brought their babies into the shop for help: which made Jackie hide because, whatever was wrong with the baby, Mum would point at Jackie and offer a solution, like: "Jack's ears used to stick out like that but I stuck them back with elastoplast."

But no sooner did Mum get us all right for school than other things went wrong.

Soon after starting school Jackie caught rheumatic fever and was put in hospital. Not just for a couple of days but for a lousy ten months. As if that were not bad enough he wasn't allowed to have a pillow. And, even worse, he wasn't allowed to have salt on his food. Mum thought he could have caught it when he jumped into our flooded air-raid shelter down the back of the shop to help another boy who had fallen in.

It cost Dad a lot of money because just to stay in the Mater Hospital cost three guineas a week—not counting medicines: half a man's wages.

I hadn't started school then and I stayed home with Mum, watching her whip cream into butter so we didn't have to always have dripping on our bread because of the War rations. The only way to make the bread and dripping taste any good was to put plenty of salt on. Mum and I had lots of fun in the kitchen, particularly when she was making up a food parcel to send to Britain or when she used to put milk on an arrowroot biscuit in a saucer so I could watch it magically grow bigger and bigger until it filled the whole plate.

Mum seemed to spend most of her time, when she was at home, in her kitchen and I liked it the best because the gas stove made it warm in winter, and the breeze and the light poured in from the breakfast room next door in summer because the breakfast room was like a verandah with the outside wall all windows, each with small coloured pieces of glass at the bottom and top and a big sheet of plain glass in the middle.

After the kitchen I liked under the house best because it was so cool sitting in the dirt and there were so many different places to see. There was the lavatory room—made of roofing iron with a wooden door and concrete floor—and the shower. There was the laundry with Mum's gas copper and the big stick she poked the clothes with, and its cement floor for hitting things on. There was under the old tank stand where the tap dripped and Mum grew her mint. One of my regular jobs was to get some mint for the mashed potatoes.

Behind the laundry there was a tap and a drain where we kids used to make tea in our red elephant tea set, and another dirt area behind the room: where I used to bury my money.

The cool dirt led straight out into the hot garden where Uncle Les had grown white daisies and pink gerberas and

16

we had a patch of potatoes and some beans between the big rose bushes and the monstera deliciosa patch where you could hide among the big leaves and no-one could find you— but you could watch them through the holes in the leaves.

Out the front were palm trees as tall as lamp posts which dropped red berries like marbles. Red gladiolis grew wild and at the very end of the back yard there was the big mango tree where Mum saved me from making a mistake when I had my grub collection in a jar.

Mum was in the kitchen looking out the small window over the tank stand just as I spied this big brown grub. She wasn't the type of person to scream, but she came running down the back stairs saying it was a snake. It stopped and watched us so Mum put her apron on the ground because she said it was an old bush trick to make the snake watch it while we raced back under the house where she got a bucket of boiling water out of the copper, and threw it over the snake as he tried to escape up the mango tree. It was the most exciting thing that had ever happened to me, but Mum wouldn't take the dead snake upstairs.

Mum was always saving us.

Once she saved us from an awful tram driver who didn't like Jackie pushing me up the tram tracks along Ipswich Road in our toy red pedal car. The man was even threatening to get the police because he said only trams were allowed on the steel tracks. The car had pedals inside which you pushed with your feet and this made the wheels go around. But it wasn't as fast as a real car, even with Jackie pushing. Mum saw what was happening when she reached into the shop window to put a newly iced sponge cake on display, and she raced out of the shop to tell the tram driver to be on his way.

She even saved us that time I set the house on fire.

After my mosquito net caught fire, apparently the flames spread to Jackie's and Gay's mosquito nets because we were all near each other in the one bedroom of the timber house. The smell of the smoke woke Mum up and she rushed into the room but in the dark kicked the heavy panelled door and broke two of her toes and fell over.

17

Dad had already gone to the shop, as he often did at 4 a.m. to cook cakes, so Mum got to her feet again and wrapped us in blankets and shoved us out of the room and put out the fire which had turned the walls black. By the time I came home from hospital the room had been painted and there was no evidence of the fire. And she never brought the subject up again.

Mum, whose name before she married was Olive Rose Duncan, loved to tell us stories about what a wonderful man her father John "Jack" Duncan was, and how he fought snakes and giant trees as a timber-getter behind the Gold Coast and how his father, William Doig Duncan, was the first white man to settle on the Gold Coast—and how he used to carry a huge bag of flour on his back in an all-day walk through the bush from Nerang to Gilston.

Olive was the type of person who sang loudly at sing-songs around the piano and recited poetry about the Kelly gang she learnt from "Pa", as she called her father. She would not just recite poetry, she would carry on like an actor—pointing her finger, rolling her eyes, extending her arms. It was good fun if no-one else was there but it became embarrassing when she did it in front of visitors.

Pa knew all these poems off by heart, even though he couldn't read and write properly: but Olive said that was a family secret.

Her voice would rise and fall dramatically to emphasise the lines she liked in these poems: such as how Ned Kelly was forced to turn to crime "all for his sister's sake", or how his brother Dan Kelly was so unafraid of the police that, while they were searching the countryside for the bushrangers, "Dan, the most religious, took the Sergeant's wife to Mass". Another favourite was what poor Ned said when he was cornered in his armour by a score of police, after being betrayed by a man he let go to tend his sick wife: "I will not surrender to any coat of blue; nor any man that wore the Crown belonging to your crew." What a brave man. Such courage was difficult to comprehend and could only be rivalled by another bushranger, Ben Hall. When Olive recited Pa's version of Ben Hall, in just one sentence I could see the most powerful man in the world, a sort of cross between Tom Mix and Captain Marvel: "It took ten men to take Ben Hall, when he was fast asleep."

From what Olive said, Pa—who sometimes made damper in the ashes of the fire in our garden—was pretty tough himself. He carried his brother, Uncle Hughie, for miles after Hughie cut his big toe off with an axe in the bush; he survived a fall over a cliff after being attacked by a giant snake; and he scored ninety-six with a broken finger in their Nerang team of ten Duncan brothers and one Guinea cousin: hitting six sixes off one over.

These timber-getting Duncan brothers discovered the natural arch behind the Gold Coast and stored their meat there because it was so cool inside. Some of them were such big men that they ate a dozen eggs for breakfast, Mum said. But not her Pa. He was a thin man with a moustache— the thinnest, but strongest, of all the brothers and he hated gluttony so much that once he kept taking bucket after bucket of food to the family pig, explaining "I'm gonna bust the bugger."

All of Olive's stories made me glad I wasn't born when she was, especially when she said Gilston School actually started in the Duncan house with seventeen children and a teacher—because there was no school in the area. I couldn't have stood having teachers in the house. But Mum claimed she loved school, where she won a book prize she still kept and where, she said, the headmaster had recommended that she alone of all the children should be kept on at school. But her Pa couldn't afford it.

After school she worked as a housemaid at an exclusive private boys school on the Gold Coast where she was the servant of young men from rich families who were being prepared and educated. This was another one of her stories she described as "family secrets".

Perhaps it was because her Pa was so tough that Olive had one quality which I greatly admired: she was never afraid. Not of anything.

While I was scared of bogeymen and the dark and hospitals and the future, she faced doctors, policemen, nuns, priests, and drunks as if she were in charge. And when I needed her she was always there.

When my first teeth went rotten I had to have all fourteen out at once and I went under chloroform gas—with that terrible feeling of choking to death, as numbness took over my whole body, pulling it around and around while my brain swelled like a balloon and travelled into space until it seemed it would burst as I struggled for air and couldn't get it. And my body started to lift off the bed and spin clockwise, faster and faster, making me dizzier and dizzier as my mind expanded and expanded like an explosion and I shot ever upwards and upwards like a skyrocket trying to call out for Mum and yet unable to ... but she was there when I came to, and she sat for hours next to the bed and rubbed my back as I vomited and bled into a bowl. I just couldn't tell her about the chloroform experience because it was too bad. All I could say was "keep rubbing".

As she rubbed she told of her own operations and how things were soon right and that they were all for the best. If something had to happen then it had to happen and you had to put up with it, she said.

When anyone got ear ache in Brisbane in those days you went to the hospital at 8 a.m. and queued up with the other sixty or seventy people with ear ache and waited to get inside to see a doctor.

There were so many people it was impossible to get a seat on the long low polished timber forms in the waiting room. Sometimes Mum and I waited for five hours at the Mater Hospital, but at least at the ear place you didn't have to roll up piles of bandages for the nuns as you did when waiting in casualty or other parts of the hospital. Mum said we had to wait so long because the government had made the hospitals free.

Once inside, three doctors sat in different parts of one big room with a wooden chair in front of each of them for their patients. They wore round mirrors on their heads and squinted into ears through a torch-like thing. Every time I went there the doctors would order that my ears be syringed by a nun with a giant silver plunger as big as a rolling pin.

This would inject a hard stream of warm water into the ear to force out the wax that was growing inside. This water would be trapped inside by the wax which would tear at the ear drum with a pain which made the dentist's drill hitting a nerve seem like a tickle. Not surprisingly, I couldn't hold the kidney bowl under my ear, and water would go everywhere and I would start to faint: but they wouldn't let Olive come in—she had to wait outside. When this failed, as it always did, one of the doctors would stick a crochet needle or a pair of bent tweezers in my ear to try to tug the wax out.

God could not have made anything worse for Hell. The pain made me cry out and I would get into trouble for nearly fainting off the chair. "Sit still, we will never get it out if you don't," the doctor would warn me. "You're going to have to wake up to yourself sonny and sit still." Finally the exasperated doctor would give up and I would be given ear drops to soften the wax (which they said was like black concrete) and told to come back in a week for the same treatment. And Mum always came and queued up for the five hours with me—even though she was needed in the shop.

The ear ache was so bad that eventually I begged them to use even the chloroform, but they wouldn't. Sometimes the pain was so great that at night I saw big green spiders coming in the window. Luckily I got to know a Sister at the Mater, Sister Emmanuel, who used to let me come in the back entrance to be syringed very gently with her own hands. I used to bring her a big apple pie from the shop and eventually she talked the doctors into an operation, and they got the wax out.

When we went up to see the specialist a week after the operation he could not get out the long cotton wicks he had put in my ears after the operation had finished. While the outer few inches of the white wicks hung outside my ears, the rest of them were inside—stuck by dried blood to the damaged sections of inner ear. When he tugged at them it was like the crochet needle treatment all over again.

This specialist was a much gentler man than the hospital

doctors and he made no second attempt. He said the wicks were stuck and would be too painful to remove, and he would have to operate again to remove them. I was sitting on a chair facing his desk and cried at the prospect of returning to hospital to face the dreaded chloroform again just when I thought the nightmare was over. Mum walked over behind me and rubbed my head and spoke to me in her usual soft, soothing way.

When I awoke, my head was on the desk in front of me. The doctor looked shaken, but Mum was beaming her best blue-eyed beautiful smile from beneath the two plaits she tied over her head. Her soft pink cheeks glowed and in her two hands she held up the long, offending red and white wicks for me to see. She had whipped them out of my ears and, though I'd fainted, I hadn't felt a thing. "Come on, we can go home now," she said.

3
Waiting for the iceman

Mum walked me to school on my first day in January 1946—the year after the big War ended—up along Ipswich Road which carried the frequent silver trams, past the high wooden fence you couldn't see through where they said the nuns lived, past the brick convent school fence with rusty vertical iron rods like prison bars, and down underneath the huge red brick church to a classroom full of girls in dark blue dresses and white collars and a big old nun called James who had hair on her upper lip.

Mum left me with this woman called James and I panicked.

James wanted me to sit with about fifty kids I had never seen before in my life. So when I spotted Jackie in his class on the other side of the big room I raced in and sat between him and his mate Terry Puey and refused to shift. Jackie knew everything about school because he had been going there for two years and he promised to look after me.

James looked unsure what to do but she gave in as she was running late because before school could begin on any day everyone had to say: "Good morning Sister, and God Bless You", and kids were yelling it out in desperation to be seen to be good.

Jackie and his mates called these kids "goody goodies".

Sister James was teaching Jackie's class from a big sheet of brown paper hung on the wall and covered in big black numbers written with ink. She pointed at them as the class recited over and over again "seven plus five equals twelve", "seven plus five equals twelve", until even I knew it: though I didn't know what it meant. But it must have been very hard because Terry lent across and said: "Jack, I don't know

23

how Hugh is ever going to learn all this stuff." And Jackie backed me up, as he always did, by saying he didn't know how I could ever learn it either.

Sister James went on to another large sheet of brown paper, this time covered in words, and pointed at the letters and everyone recited a hundred times "a..r..o..u..n..d .... around", "a..r..o..u..n..d .... around". And this went on all day except for two breaks for what they called Little Lunch and Big Lunch.

Even though it was very hot you couldn't leave the class for a drink or keep one with you at your desk, and I found myself dreaming of a steel milkshake can full of cold water from our shop. And you couldn't go out for a pee either, no matter how bad it was, unless you were game to put your hand up in front of all the girls and ask for the wooden pass which anyone who went to the lavatory block had to take with them. This stopped two people going out at the same time so they could play. And you couldn't take anything with you in case you wanted to eat something while in the lavatory, which wasn't allowed.

Sister James said that to eat in the lavatory was to eat with the Devil.

At Big Lunch we were locked in under the school to eat our sandwiches before we could go out to play. Sister James checked to see if we had eaten them all—even the tomato sandwiches, which were sloppy and awful and stank by lunch-time because of the summer heat.

So, was I glad to get back home to 40 Ekibin Road where it was so cool sitting in the dirt under the front verandah or out under the big mango tree, where you could pee anywhere whenever you liked.

On the second day James got tough, just as I thought she would, and forced me away from Jackie's desk back to my own class with Sister Damian, and there was nothing Jackie could do about it. It was unfortunate, because I had just begun to enjoy Jackie's class and my class was very boring. We recited things all day from a book with little drawings: an apple and a little letter "a" and we said: "a is like an apple on a twig, a says uh", and "b is like a bat and ball, b says ber", and "c is like a cake with a bite taken out, c says ker" and so on for the rest of the alphabet. As if we didn't know already.

I wanted to start on words because Jackie—who could read like a grown-up—used to read me a poem out of one of the School Readers about how this Roman soldier, Horatius, defended a bridge against 90,000 State School kids and escaped by jumping into the creek. I thought this was such a great story I tried to learn to read it myself. Once I tried to read it to some other boys in the class, but I couldn't recognise the words.

I never could seem to catch up to Jackie.

Jackie might have missed a whole year in hospital with rheumatic fever but he was the only boy in the school who was as smart as any of the girls. For example, I bet he was the only person in Annerley who could spell ornithorhynchus, which was another word for platypus. This made it difficult for me because his former teachers were always disappointed when I arrived in their class. According to them "the Lunns" (meaning Jackie) had a great "general knowledge". But I didn't.

However, I knew how Jackie got it.

He got it in hospital when he had to lie still on his back and everyone showered books on him and he had nothing else to do but read them. He got in the habit so much that he couldn't break it, even when he got out of hospital. So he used to catch the tram all the way to the South Brisbane Library just to get books to read. He often made me go with him but I was more like Dad and didn't read books, except a book we had at home we got in 1949 called *Stories of King Arthur*. I read this because it was about a kitchen scullion called Gareth who defeated the Green, Yellow, Blue, and Black knights and became a knight of the Round Table.

Other books didn't interest me. I liked playing, whereas Jackie often stayed in his room to read books. Actually I don't think he read a lot of them at all and just pretended to, so he could show off. I could tell because he skipped through the pages far too fast.

Not only was Jackie always a deadset cert to pass any

test he ever sat for—even the piano—but, despite instructions by doctors that he should not run or exercise because of the fever, he was also such a good fighter that it was safe to say no-one could bash him up: not the toughest bloke at the convent, Neil Fallon, or any State School kid. Which was more than you could say for me. It seemed that just about everyone could beat me, including even some in my own class, like the bloke who grabbed both of my shoulders in the boys toilet and finished me off with a knee to the balls.

Because he was so smart, Jackie was chosen to be an altar boy to help the priest at Mass. He was given a white and red uniform to wear and got to stand up the front with the priest on the altar like an angel and shake smoking incense from a gold can. He tried to teach me the Latin words he used to have to recite in answer to the priest but I could never remember them and, anyway, no-one ever asked me to be an altar boy—probably because you had to be very very good. And, by the time I was old enough to become an altar boy, the priest knew I wasn't a good boy at all.

It was when we were seven that we made our First Confession so that we could make our First Holy Communion in what they called "a state of grace", with a soul washed clean—like the black slates we used in class—of all the sins we had committed since we were born.

Although I didn't want to tell the priest all of my sins, because they were much worse than anyone else's, I had no choice because the alternative was worse: to receive Communion without confessing a mortal sin was the biggest sin of all, a "sacrilege" they called it and it meant Hell forever for sure, unless you were game enough to go to Confession and tell the priest you had been to Communion while your soul was not in a condition of sanctifying grace.

There was no way you could duck out of Communion either, because the priest actually put the little round white wet thin Host that was God's body and blood on your tongue which you poked out while kneeling in a long row with other kids in front of the altar. And you had to hold a heavy silver tray under your chin, just in case you tried to drop the Host.

The First Holy Communion in particular was no time to try anything. It was a big dress-up day with the Mary Immaculate Church full of parents watching as you walked back from Communion up at the front of the church wearing a First Holy Communion medal on a red ribbon around your neck. By the time you got back to your seat, the Host was well and truly stuck to the roof of your mouth. And before Mass was over it was gone.

The First Confession was one of those days—like all Confession days—when I wished life would stop. The embarrassment of telling the priest who knew me about how I had once tried to pull down the pants of Sheila and Bubby across the road to have a look and how I had sworn at Mum and stolen a slate pencil and coveted my neighbour's blood alley marbles, and even my worst thoughts in daydreams in class—because wanting to do something was as bad as doing it—was a nightmare which made me want to run out of the church as I knelt in the pews outside the twin-doored Confessional waiting for my turn to enter and carry out the instructions of the nuns by starting "Bless me father, for I have sinned. I accuse myself of ..." The only thing I had going for me was that the nuns had told us lots of stories about how priests had died rather than reveal what had taken place in the confessional: so I knew he wasn't allowed to tell on me.

It was the one place where I couldn't get any help from Jackie, who seemed to know how to handle any other situation.

One of the reasons for his power was that, unlike me, he knew how to fight. This made him confident about turning up at school or walking home by himself or telling people it was his turn to bowl or be captain. Other boys listened to him.

It wasn't just that Jackie could fight like everyone else did by relying on strength—he knew the proper way to fight and win. And I was the only one in Annerley Junction who knew how he knew.

Mum always found someone in the shop who needed a dinner or even a place to stay, so our third bedroom nearly always had a stranger living in it—while all of us kids lived in one room or, in summer, on the verandah. The first of these men I can hardly remember, an old bald cove called Mr Dyer who had taught Mum's young brother, Uncle Cyril, how to be a carpenter. As far as I could tell, Mr Dyer never worked and had only one interest in life: listening to the boxing from the Stadium on the wireless on Friday nights and reading boxing magazines with men on the cover in shorts and gloves with their dukes up.

Because I was too young, he got Jackie interested in his magazines and gave him a book called *The Gentle Art of Self-defence*. Mr Dyer taught him all the things about the way to stand in a stoush and to lead with the left hand and keep the legs apart and where to look and lots of other tricks. And this famous method they used in the pictures suited Jackie because he was only thin, but he had long arms and his left arm—the one these boxers hit with first—was his best.

Mr Dyer's lessons helped Jackie so much that he could easily hit a boy three times on the nose with his straight left arm—his best arm, since he was what Mum called a mollydooker—and they thought he still had his powerful right arm in reserve and quickly gave in and became his friend.

Jackie told me the main thing he tried to achieve was to inflict pain on the other boy so the next time he would pick on somebody who didn't hurt him.

Mum said Mr Dyer also taught Uncle Cyril boxing and she reckoned Uncle Cyril had beaten blackfellas in the ring at Southport.

But it didn't help him against Jackie.

At a birthday party one day, long after Mr Dyer and his magazines were forgotten, Uncle Cyril sat on his haunches with half a hand-rolled cigarette hanging stuck on his bottom lip and invited Jackie, who had our boxing gloves on, to throw one at him. Jackie declined and all of us kids urged Uncle Cyril—who could get pretty angry and was always warning kids "don't fool"—not to do it. But he smiled confidently and urged again in his croaky voice: "Come on Jackie, throw one at me", as he raised his two hands. Jackie did, and hit him right in the gob and the cigarette finished all over Uncle Cyril's moosh. I started to run because he had come such a gutser but Uncle Cyril, who was normally so serious that I was scared of him, just laughed and laughed and congratulated Jackie.

By the time I was old enough to learn about boxing Mr Dyer had been replaced by a man who wanted to teach me chess, so I learnt to be as inconspicuous as possible at school—which is the lot of the boy who is neither strong, nor fast, nor a boxer.

But this was impossible because of the fighting reputation of my brother and because of my first name which was so unusual boys couldn't even say it: they all said "youie". It wasn't like being called John or Jim—it immediately marked me out for special attention. I had a first name that rhymed with poo and a middle name, Duncan, which so easily became dunnycan—the black cans Hunter Bros used to take everyone's shit away in.

Either I would have to fight someone for calling me Youie Pooey or I would get bashed up in the playground by a bigger boy who didn't like someone called "you", or who hated Jackie.

Sometimes I would play the dangerous game of having to avoid some boy all day.

After school I would not be safe because we had to get through the State School kids on the way home. They used to yell out "Catholics Catholics sit on logs, eating the bellies out of frogs" and they used to say our knees were always dirty from kneeling down. And we used to answer "Catholics Catholics ring the bell while you State School kids go to Hell".

I was never sure what these State School kids were, except that they were some sort of enemy of our religion who were always looking for fights. We wore school uniforms with a tie, while they dressed like the rubbish men, which made me feel I was from a better tribe.

When they got too close to us we had a good system where we would offer to let them fight Jackie if they wanted to and mostly they turned it down because they had heard about him: just as we had heard about a bloke called Wheeler from their school, who had to be avoided.

When fighting did break out it was usually Jackie against their best man. But once there was an all-in struggle outside the Fellnaw private hospital where young Gay joined in and knocked one of them rotten with a double-storey wood pencil case, though she waited until he was looking the other way.

Sometimes I was caught alone and on various occasions slapped across the face, knocked over, or held in a head-lock. Once hit, I found it best to cry and kick out while lying on my bum, because I was then hard to hit. Though I was too scared to get up and be knocked down again, at least I didn't give in and I kept on taunting them from ground level.

After all, I wasn't the fighter, Jackie was. And I always told them how lucky they were he wasn't around.

Thus I stuck close to Jackie, and his friends became my friends so that all my mates were from his class, not mine. The best of these was Kenny Fletcher whose house was on Ipswich Road a street away from our shop. Although Kenny was in Jackie's class, and a year older than me, he was more like me in that we were less studious than Jack, and less adventurous.

Because he was an only child poor Kenny was forced to lead a terrible life even though he got lots of presents we would never get: like a fishing rod, a train on tracks, and a tennis racquet. But he wasn't allowed to climb trees or ride bikes in case he hurt himself. He couldn't even go down to Ekibin Creek—though sometimes he did—and every night he had to be home by dark or his father would come looking for him. His father was so careful that Kenny couldn't even have a drink of milk from the fridge unless it was put in a warmed-up glass first.

Kenny used to like to come and play with us, or help us help Dad make the meat pies in our shop. And he used to like to threaten the State School kids that he would get Jackie to bash them up. Kenny thought we were really lucky that we had such an easy-going Dad. But I thought he was lucky because his father drove a train and wore a uniform with a big blue cap and carried a big leather bag around Annerley Junction. Also, Kenny had a tennis court in his back yard and he was learning how to play. Kenny said he was going to become world champion, which made me laugh so much I fell through a big hole in the slab timber fence next to his house.

I knew he wasn't much good because the woman next door, Mrs McQuinney, used to collect the tennis balls that he hit over the high court fence into her yard and give them to us. I had never played tennis but I knew that if he couldn't keep the ball inside that big fence he was never going to be any good.

Kenny used to read comics with us and play under the back of the shop or we used to go to his place to play with his Hornsby train set which ran all around the room.

Kenny's parents, Norm and Ethel, thought he was too young to do what we did—catch the tram into town by ourselves. Mrs Fletcher used to take him on the tram to Ashgrove for his tennis lessons while Mum boasted that Gay, who was nearly three years younger than Kenny, caught the tram to town by herself, aged six, to dance on stage at the Theatre Royal. Though when Gay and Sheryl got lost on the way home once and ended up being brought home by a shopkeeper at Stones Corner Mum told us this was another family secret.

For an outing away from the shop on a Sunday, Mum would put us all on the tram and, for a penny each—and with Jackie in charge—we could go all the way to Chermside on the other side of Brisbane and back. It was a great trip, smooth and cool and interesting all the way. The highlight, if we were lucky, was to see the railwayman walk across the Gabba Fiveways in front of the train waving a red flag and ringing a big brass bell to warn the cars and trams.

There were times though when even Jackie needed help, like the time the iceman deliberately tripped him over and gravel-rashed his arm. Worse still, it was when he was on his way to a piano exam. That was the year Aunty Vera and Uncle Bill came back to Brisbane with their three

31

children—John and Gem, who were older than me, and Mel who was younger. They lived with us for months while they got a house in Annerley and we ganged up on everyone—including even the grown-ups when the four of them were sitting in the kitchen laughing and telling stories and they locked us out. We had bamboo bows and arrows we made like in the pictures and we fired arrows in through the small window in the kitchen.

When Olive and Uncle Bill came after us we shut ourselves in the front kids bedroom and all seven of us leaned against the door to stop them from getting in. But, just as Uncle Bill announced he was about to knock it down, everyone ran out the double French doors and over the verandah rails. But I jumped under a bed and got caught and copped the hiding.

Shooting arrows through windows was one thing we were particularly good at. We used this technique when Lindsay Graham, a State School kid up the road, called me "patch pants". It wasn't my fault that I always ended up wearing Jackie's old clothes and shoes and getting his old school books because I was younger.

From the road outside Lindsay's house you could see the kitchen window high above the fence. Sitting on the window ledge were some milk bottles. So we shot at these bottles to knock them inside to smash on the floor. But we didn't know his father was at home and, a few minutes later, Mr Graham came down the stairs to the fence with four arrows in his hand.

We were in big trouble, we thought. But he was a nice man who used to push us around his yard in a wooden wheelbarrow when we were very small, and he held his right hand up and open and, as if he were an Indian Chief in the pictures, said: "I want pow wow talk peace." And he gave us back the arrows and we went home.

Another man we used to gang up on was an ugly old goat who used to take his horse and cart up and down every street selling clothes props. Mum already had about three of these straight branches with a forked end to lift her long wire clothes lines high off the ground after she had hung out our washing, so she didn't need any more. But every couple of weeks he would go past yelling in a long, low voice as he passed each house "clothes .... props", "clothes .... props". So we used to hide behind the fence and, just as he was about to yell out, we would call in unison: "What do you feed your horses on?", and then he would say "clothes ..... props". Then we would yell: "No wonder they are so skinny!" And it was true. The horses that pulled the carts that brought the bread to our shop from Websters Bakery opposite Boggo Road jail looked big and healthy —like Uncle Ray's horse that he sometimes rode over from Windsor on to see us. But you could see the bones in the clothes prop man's horses, which, to us, seemed unfair on the horses.

However we saved our biggest assault for the iceman who had tripped Jackie. We knew when he would arrive to deliver the ice for Mum's ice chest—a green tin chest on four legs to keep food cold in the kitchen. It had a plughole in the bottom to let the water out after the ice melted. These had replaced the old meat safes grandpa had—tin boxes full of holes to let cool air in and keep flies out.

My cousin John was the oldest so he placed us in our positions. He stood behind the big rose bush with a handkerchief tied to the end of his spear. Gem and Jackie were the same age and they hid behind the hydrangea bushes under the verandah with bows and arrows. Me, Gay and Mel were up the cascara bean tree with my bow and arrow and gibbers. This particular tree was Mum's favourite because the long black beans tasted nice, but always gave us the runs.

The idea was that the iceman would come up through the open double gate and turn right to walk along the side of the house to the back door. As he walked past the house he would be caught in the ambush.

As the iceman turned the corner, John dropped the handkerchief from the end of his long spear and we all opened· fire, raining arrows, spears and rocks on him. What a great feeling it was as he realised he was trapped and dropped the block of ice and ran out the gate under a storm of arrows like a scared-e-cat never to be seen again.

We never got into trouble, probably because he deserved what happened.

It was a wonderful feeling to do something that was both naughty and pleasurable without committing a sin.

4
The mysteries of religion and sport

Even before Dima Egoroff arrived at our convent things were not going particularly well. The first major problem I ran into started in arithmetic when we got to the figure 2. Every time I tried to draw a 2 it came out back-the-front.

The figure 3 was my next stumbling block. I could draw a 3 alright, that was easy: but I couldn't say it. It kept coming out "tree".

The only thing I was considered to be any good at was reading aloud from the School Reader. But then Sister Damian woke up to what I was doing. This particular morning, when it was my turn to read the next sentence, I stood up and read: "The big grey cow walked over to the fence", and there was an audible gasp from all the girls who turned from every desk to look at me like the plaster clowns that swallowed the ping-pong balls at the Exhibition. "Read that again Hughie Lunn," asked Sister Damian with a suspicious look on her face. They knew, they all knew now, that I couldn't read all these words. I must have made a mistake with a word, but which one? "The big grey cow ..." I said, and Sister Damian had me. The book, she told me, clearly said "brown" cow and a "b" sounded nothing like a "g". "You have been memorising every line," she said. And once again I had to write out the alphabet.

This wasn't easy because I couldn't seem to make the transition from slate pencil to pen and ink. It wasn't that I didn't have all the right equipment. Mum had got me a double-decker wood pencil case and, once the lid was pulled backwards a bit, the top part swung to the side to reveal the pens beneath. Plus I had a new propelling pencil with lots of smooth little lead pieces in a tiny glass holder to reload it with, and several nibs to stick in the end of my ink pens. But almost every day I got into trouble for untidy work, particularly when writing in my copy book. This was our most important book now that we were learning to write running writing. Across the top of the page were words already written in perfect girl's hand-writing, while, across the bottom, lots of lines were drawn to help us copy these words exactly. I found this difficult and the nuns used to claim that my copy book "looked as though the chooks had walked across it".

The trouble with using a pen and ink was that the ink marked wherever it touched and you couldn't just rub out mistakes like you could with the slates. One end of the rubber was supposed to rub ink out but all I could do when I used it was to rub a hole in the page. Also, unlike with a slate pencil, extra ink had to be added to the pen all the time—which increased the chances of an accident.

The letters we had to draw in the copy book were all at least an inch high and you could never get completely through a letter of the alphabet without having to stop to dip your nib into the inkwell, which was in a hole at the top right-hand corner of the desk. Then, after applying blotting paper to soak up the ink on the page, you had to try to start again at exactly the same spot as you stopped. If you got too much ink on your nib, a big blue blot would appear from nowhere and if you weren't paying enough attention it was easy to smudge it across the other letters you had just neatly finished. For some reason I could never understand, the ends of nibs were always split into two up the middle, which meant they wouldn't work properly if you picked up the pen the wrong way and tried to write with the side. Even if you got the nib the right way around, if you pressed too hard one side would break and flick ink all over the page.

Because ink was a liquid it was incredibly easy to drop some off the nib on the journey from the top right-hand corner of the desk to the spaces at the bottom of the copy book. As if that wasn't bad enough, someone was rolling up little bits of blotting paper between their fingers and dropping them in my inkwell because just about every time I dipped my pen in for more ink it came out with a blob of soft gunk on the end which made the nib slide uncontrollably across the paper like new leather shoes on a polished floor. The only way to remove this blue mass was to hold the nib firmly between thumb and forefinger and pull.

And then you had ink all over your writing hand.

Being a Catholic made being neat even harder. Our writing pads were called "exercise" books and they contained lots of shiny new white pages ruled with various lines to help us do our school work. Most had plain blue lines for writing on but some had narrow red and blue lines to help new writers learn where to begin and end letters. Another one was covered in hundreds of little squares made by horizontal and vertical blue lines for arithmetic.

These exercise books looked good, but even before I started on a new pad the pages would be inky because we were expected to write "A.M.D.G." in big capital letters on the top of each page before we wrote on it. This, we were told, meant "all my work is done for God". Of course no-one said you had to do it, but because it was for the greater glory of God no-one was game not to. Including me, even though it meant getting ink all over the pages after I drew the required ink line beneath the A.M.D.G. because the side of my ruler would end up coated with ink which would automatically make new ink lines wherever it touched.

The girls used to go to an incredible amount of trouble with these exercise books. They would cover them with brown paper, even though it meant covering up the times tables printed on the back, and then paste a Holy Picture—preferably one with carved gold edges—in the centre of the cover and colour around it with crayons to get a few extra marks when our pads were handed in for correction.

The girls covered all their text books as well and I could never work out how they got the time to put brown paper around them all, let alone to paste dozens of Holy Pictures and pictures of flowers from the *Women's Weekly* all over the front.

The only thing worse than my copy book was my drawing

book which had thick green pages, each divided by white tissue paper which was supposed to stop our pastels spreading all over our work. But the tissue paper was too thin and it would either get wet or accidentally folded or torn and the colours of the pastels would gradually spread all over the pages until it was very hard for the nuns to see what I had drawn. That was how I came to be accused of drawing Mary Mary Quite Contrary with three legs.

I hadn't, of course.

The third leg, I knew, was her hoe: but I didn't say that because it might have sounded worse.

Olive must have known what a deadhead I was because somehow I got the names of the nuns wrong when I told her about them: convincing her for a while that my teachers were Sister a'James and Sister a'Damian. But still she insisted I do my homework so that when I was thirteen I would stand a chance of passing the dreaded State Scholarship public examination like Jackie and Gay certainly would, and thus join the educated people by attending secondary school.

Mum didn't have to worry about Gay.

Gay got top marks at piano exams and was so good at ballet they made her an acrobat on stage and she was already earning a pile of silver money, aged five, appearing as a mouse and a fairy with a silver wand with a star on it in a play at the Theatre Royal in town.

Even I had to admit she was pretty, with her very blonde hair and dimples, but it really became embarrassing when Mum would tell people Gay could climb higher in the mango tree than I could, even though she was two years younger.

What else did she expect?

The nearest I got to acrobatics was having to hold a belt around Gay's waist while she practised bending over backwards to pick a handkerchief up off the ground with her mouth. And so what if she did better in piano exams? I didn't like playing the piano, and she loved it. She even rocked on the piano seat with contentment as she practised, while I had to be led to the keys by Olive and only played while guarded.

Another thing that made school difficult was the way everyone was allowed to show off their knowledge in the class. Instead of the nuns asking one of us a question, they would pose it to the whole room—after the usual "pencils down" shout to show that something public was about to happen. "Hands up all of those who know the answer," they would say. Which made it pretty awful for those left sitting in the class surrounded by a sea of wiggling hands.

If you happened to be the person who didn't know the answer, you would become more and more obvious as the others started flicking their hand or clicking their fingers and calling out "Sister, Sister". And it would go on and on until they were standing, yelling, and flicking all at once as if they were all busting to go to the lavatory.

But would the nun answer their call? No, she would ask someone whose hand was down. "Hughie Lunn, what have you got to say?" And, as punishment for not knowing, I would be made to sit with the girls.

Sister James was the exception.

She might have been old and ugly but Sister James was more like a mother than a nun. When she heard I couldn't draw a 2 she took me aside during Big Lunch and tried to show me how, but as soon as she left I lost the trick. It wasn't until a couple of days later, when I was drawing with a stick in the dirt under the house, that I suddenly got it right and I covered the whole of under the house in 2s of all sizes.

It was the same with telling the time and reaching the light switch: suddenly you could do it and you wondered why it was ever a problem.

Sister James also taught me how to say "three".

She took me to an empty classroom and got me to hold my right forefinger an inch in front of my mouth. Then, as I started to say "three", I had to touch my finger with my tongue.

It worked like magic.

After Sister James, the lessons and the nuns got tougher—particularly Sister Rosary in grade three who had a cane like a bamboo arrow and used it: especially if you didn't know all your times tables off by heart. Though she wasn't as frightening as Jackie's Sister. He said she had a bamboo pole so long she could land it on the desk of any kid in the class who was not paying attention. It was taller than the roof.

We were now big enough to start reading our Queensland School Readers which contained lots of proper stories and some poems.

There was a Reader for each grade, and each year they got more difficult, with longer stories and bigger words. And they always contained some colour pictures from the stories—which I found the most interesting thing. The first of these colour pictures I came across was of a wolf in pyjamas in bed talking to a little blonde girl who was so stupid she thought it was her grandma. And there were some frightening black and white drawings too, like the one of the Piper that went with the story of the town taken over by rats that "fought the dogs and killed the cats". This drawing showed little children being dragged along the ground by their mothers who were running away from the rats. And there was one with the little boy who got into lots of trouble because he called out "wolf" all the time.

They were pretty scary books, but they taught us what to watch out for and what happened to little boys who did what they shouldn't do, or went where they shouldn't go.

In grade four the School Reader had a drawing of a boy called Jack who climbed a beanstalk. He was hiding in a saucepan while a giant, armed with a huge sword, sat at a table chewing on a large bone. And there was a full-page drawing of a horse and sleigh being chased by wolves: the father didn't want to take the little boy with him but the little boy had insisted on going, and now wished he hadn't. And there was the Little Match Girl who froze to death in the snow when she used up all the matches she was supposed to be selling, trying to keep herself warm. In the colour picture next to the story she didn't even have any shoes on and her match lit up a Christmas tree.

At the back of these Readers were lists of "difficult words" we had to learn to spell, and another list of new words with their meanings.

Now that we were old enough, we got an inspector: a very important old man in a suit from in town who came to check up on us to see if we were really learning all this stuff. No sooner was he in the classroom than he started giving us spelling and adding-up tests. It was such an important occasion that I just had to try to cheat, but everyone was covering up their work with their left hand because they were too mean to give anyone else a chance.

The girls acted as though it was a mortal sin to let someone else see their answers. But I knew it wasn't because our Catechism told us that a mortal sin was only when you knowingly and willingly consented to something which you believed to be a mortal sin.

I could never see that finding out answers was a sin. That was the whole idea of going to school.

Then I had my first break in five years at school. The inspector got us to exchange books with the person next to us to correct each other's answers. I was pretty friendly with the boy next to me and each time he passed my work back, although I saw I only had one or two right out of ten, I put my hand up when the inspector asked for those who had got six right: I was too smart to draw attention to myself by claiming any more than that. And I got away with it until the inspector left. Then this goody-goody boy next to me said he was going out to tell Sister—and, as he walked out and spoke to her, I ran out of the classroom (although they both called for me to come back) and ran all the way home.

I worried all that night about what would happen to me the next day. Yet the amazing thing was that instead of giving me the cane Sister was really nice to me and didn't say anything about how I had cheated the inspector. Which showed that you just could never tell how the nuns would react.

Once I got into trouble over an accident that could have happened to any boy.

I was in the playground during Big Lunch and there wasn't much to do. None of the boys were playing tiggy or brandy and I wasn't old enough yet to play football down on the big boys playground, and we didn't have any swings or see-saws or anything like that. Along with everyone else in the class I had walked up towards the front gate to drink my compulsory daily bottle of free milk, even though the sun had made it warm and sour, and I was walking past a tree when I saw a thick piece of branch on the ground shaped a bit like a boomerang. I wasn't too far from the big brick incinerator and I thought I would see if I could hoick this stick so it would land in the hole in the top and get burnt with all the rubbish.

I checked to see if the coast was clear and noted that Valerie Parker was leading a group of girls playing fairies between me and the incinerator: they were running in a curving line with tiny steps, waving their arms up and down and pinching up their faces. But I wasn't worried, because I reckoned I could clear them. But, as luck would have it, the boomerang lost height rapidly and Valerie Parker fluttered right into it head-first, as if on purpose.

You should have heard her. You'd think she'd never been hit in the head before.

I expected her to cry, but not to scream.

I wasn't too worried until I saw a big patch of wet red on her brown hair. She was bleeding, and I was sent up a long flight of stairs that took me above classrooms and above the concert hall to a nun I only knew by reputation, Sister Bertrand, the Head Nun. I was trembling as I walked into the classroom where the kids in the dreaded State Scholarship year sat, and Sister Bertrand gazed down at me like a statue on a pillar. She didn't even want to hear that this accident had only occurred because I was cleaning up the playground, or that Valerie Parker was too busy playing fairies to notice what was going on. And I got the cuts across both hands in front of all the Scholarship kids who waited in vain for me to cry as the cane stung my fingers.

About the only success I seemed to be having was in collecting pennies for the black babies—children even worse off than us. I really enjoyed making the pin prick in each square of the card we were given to record each penny we got: and I liked the little green cardboard moneybox—with a drawing of a black baby on the front—where we kept the pennies. When it was full, you got to name a black baby and I named one after my cousin Gem.

But I made a mistake and called my little black baby girl "Jim".

I was also learning about God and the Holy Catholic Church—something we spent at least an hour on every day in class. That was why we were so unlucky to be born Catholics: not only did we go to Hell if we were bad, while those who weren't Catholics only ended up in Limbo, but we didn't finish school until 3.30 whereas the State School kids finished at three.

We started earlier too because, I suppose, we had to make up for all the time spent on prayers and learning about God.

But we learned about lots of things the State School kids would never know about. Like Holy Days of Obligation and apparitions and the Sign of the Cross and the Stations of the Cross and indulgences, fasts and dispensations from the Pope, and about saints and their Feast days and novenas and absolution and abstinence days and the Angelus and vestments and litanies and benediction and consecration and extreme unction.

I learned to recognise statues like the Sacred Heart of Jesus and the brown statue of Saint Anthony, who became my favourite saint, and the picture of Our Lady of Perpetual Succour—a special one for those, like me, in need of constant help. It wasn't the sort of information that helped with the inspector when he came, or with Scholarship. But that didn't worry the nuns who obviously believed the Catholic Catechism was much more important than the Queensland School Reader.

I learned about what the nuns called "the mysteries of religion"—things that even they admitted you weren't supposed to be able to understand: though despite this we were told to think about them—they called it "meditating upon the mysteries"—when saying the rosary on our rosary beads which you could buy in all sorts of beautiful colours.

Mine were Irish Horn in my favourite colour green.

There were joyful mysteries like The Annunciation and The Visitation; sorrowful mysteries like The Scourging and The Agony in the Garden; and the glorious mysteries like The Assumption of Our Lady into Heaven and The Ascension of Jesus forty days after his Resurrection—which was itself another mystery. In fact, the whole thing was a bit of a mystery.

I didn't understand why God was everywhere but you couldn't see him, and why, if he was so nice and kind like they said, he made life so tough on us with Confession and Hell and Purgatory and inspectors and State School kids.

And I didn't like the sound of some phrases which were never explained, like Sins of the Flesh, and I couldn't understand others like Immaculate Conception and The Miracle of the Incarnation.

It got worse once I was old enough to start wearing medals and scapulars.

The most popular medal was the Miraculous Medal which showed Our Lady and some foreign writing which meant "O Mary conceived without sin pray for us who have recourse to thee". Though I couldn't understand this either, this was the prayer you were supposed to say every day when you wore the medal to put you under the protection of the Immaculate Virgin. The trouble was grown-ups in the shop seemed to enjoy asking what the medal was for—and how could you tell them, if they didn't know, that it commemorated apparitions of Our Lady at Lourdes?

It was like trying to explain why I wore the brown cloth scapular. And I had a green scapular too at one stage though I lost it.

These scapulars were like large cloth stamps. They had something to do with relics of the church, and indulgences were gained by wearing them. Of course what you couldn't say to outsiders was that, with polio everywhere, you wore all you could get around your neck to protect you. In fact Mum didn't think medals were enough, and when polio was really bad—even crippling one girl in our class—Mum made us wear a block of camphor on a string around our necks to ward it off.

Indulgences were one of the hardest things to explain, even though they were such a great idea.

The idea was that various prayers or acts gained points which could be used if you went to Purgatory—ranging from a few days off your sentence to getting out of the whole ordeal with what was called a Plenary Indulgence. But this was very difficult to get.

Indulgences could also be gained for the holy souls already in Purgatory to help them get out sooner and up into Heaven. Mum used to tell a joke about the priest who called on the congregation at Sunday Mass to pray for a parishioner who had died, but not until the following Friday, saying: "We'll let him sizzle till then."

It was because the church was all so complicated that I got to like Saint Anthony whose special ability was simple: finding lost things.

Saint Anthony was, the nuns said, the leading miracle worker of all the saints. And I could vouch for it after the day I lost a fortune—six shillings—on my first time on the big boys playground.

Sister let me out to look for it after Big Lunch and I searched for a long time in the dirt and the stones of the huge grassless football field before I had the bright idea to say a prayer to Saint Anthony. So I walked over to a rock and sat on it and said a prayer to him and, just as I finished, I was amazed to look up and see all three two-bob bits on the ground in front of me. It was what they called a miracle.

As I got older I learned that there were convents similar to ours all over Brisbane, and we started to travel to them for sports days. It was good to find out that we Catholics were not alone—as I'd thought—at our convent in Brisbane. For a long time I had found the world so dangerous that, despite having a Guardian Angel, I used to sleep crossways across the bottom of the bed so that anyone who tried to stab me during the night would miss. Particularly after religious lessons about that favourite of the nuns, Maria Goretti, who was stabbed either thirteen or fourteen times when she was eleven, because she would rather die than commit sin with her attacker.

We were supposed to admire the way she died, and soon afterwards she became a saint.

Once a year all of these convent kids and their grown-ups would go to a big ceremony of about 100,000 people called Corpus Christi that filled the Brisbane Exhibition Ground. I don't know what it was for, but when I was old enough to take part we marched around the middle of the oval with thousands of other kids singing hymns and saying prayers aloud in front of grandstands full of Catholics who were also singing and praying.

Some of the songs made me feel uneasy about being a Catholic, like the hymn we sang called "Faith of our Fathers".

This song said our faith was a holy faith and over and over we sang lines like "we will be true to thee to death". The song also told of "Our fathers chained in prisons dark" and said that they had not denied their faith "in spite of dungeon, fire, and sword". The implication, as we marched around singing this, seemed to be that we were saying we also were prepared to meet dungeon, fire and sword: but where the threat was coming from I couldn't work out. I guessed it must have been from Commos like Egoroff or the State School kids.

Another song we sang was called simply "Tramp, Tramp, Tramp": "Tramp, tramp, tramp, the boys are marching, cheer up comrades they will come, and beneath the starry skies we shall breathe free air again, we are Irish sons and daughters of Australia."

I wasn't sure what "free air" meant, though it was a sign that all the garages had out front to get you to buy petrol for your car. But all the spectacle and atmosphere of march day, with its huge show of Catholic force, didn't make me feel more secure. Rather, it made me start trying to sleep under the bed—with a port between me and the outside so nobody even knew I was there. But the lino was just too uncomfortable.

We also sang Irish songs at our Saint Patrick's Day concert every year in the school hall: the day we dressed in white shirts and wore a piece of green from any old bit of material you could find. That was why the words of one song seemed strange, and not just because a swear word was allowed: "For there's a bloody law agin the wearing of the green". But anyway I never did get to sing. As they had with Jackie, the nuns discovered my voice was flat. They did this by walking around in front of the choir while we were singing songs like "I've Always Been a Rover" until they stopped in front of me and I was told: "At the concert only open your mouth but don't utter a sound."

It never crossed my mind that God was unfair to make some people who could sing and some who couldn't, but it did when it came to running. While I could beat the slow boys, I had no hope against the fast ones even though Jackie—who was very quick—told me his secret of saying to himself as he ran "feet go faster, feet go faster".

As we got older the boys who could run the fastest seemed to be looked up to by the others. Every day in the playground—and at sports days—it was obvious that people like Ray Halloran and Linton Shaw were too fast for people like Egoroff and me. So they could always catch you at tiggy, they could escape being hit by the ball at brandy, they could run away from anyone who was angry with them, and they made perfect players for the boys' captain ball and tunnel ball teams which the nuns wanted us to play. So it was impossible for me to get into our school team.

By now Dima was in my good books because, to my surprise, he had given me by far the best present at my birthday party—Olive allowed each of us one birthday party while at the convent. Dima's present was a moneybox shaped like a big brown penny. It was so well sealed that there was no way of opening it to get your money out—unless you knew the secret which Jim took me aside and showed me. I was amazed when he put the penny—which was as big as two meat pies—up to his lips and blew into the coin slot and it popped open. This was even better than the rubber Dunlopillo Olive had given me a few years before to cushion my burnt ear. Not that she was worried about the ear—she said I was lucky my skin was pink because, had it been dark, the scar would have been livid. As it was, it just made me look tough—like I was "a bit of a pug".

To try to overcome our lack of speed, Dima and me and big Sam Aherne formed a tunnel ball team of the fastest of the slower boys and, with better technique and more practice, we beat the fast team all the time until the trials for the inter-convent sports when Sister Rosary stopped us from winning.

To win, everyone in our team had to stand as close as possible together so the round ball did not have so far to travel through the tunnel made by our legs. But Sister Rosary kept making our team spread out so the ball had to travel much greater distances. Every time we crept close up behind one another she would say: "Spread out, spread out, that's when the trouble starts."

What trouble she never said, but, with our advantage gone, we lost to the faster boys.

We also had one proper football team which played Corinda Convent every year, and here I had success because—despite my lack of strength and speed—Jackie had taught me how to tackle in the back yard. He said that the only way to really stop someone was to tackle low around the legs, and we used to yell out "tackle low" as we ran at each other in the yard.

Now that I was in grade five I could play on the big boys playground with the boys in grade six and Scholarship. There wasn't a blade of grass on the field—but lots of stones— and we would sometimes divide up into two huge teams of all the older boys to decide who would play Corinda. There would have been about twenty boys in each team, so it was hard to stand out. Except of course for a boy in Scholarship called Lawson who was really tough and captained our school team. I had heard that he was unstoppable, and he ran through our team of twenty kids until, as he drew level with me, I yelled out "tackle low".

I had never tackled anyone so big running so fast, and the collision was so great that I was in shock, and he skidded for yards across the ground, gravel-rashing his knees before he hit a tree. Covered in dust, and with stones sticking to his skin, he got to his feet and said, ominously quietly: "Who did that?" Worried, I admitted it was me. "You're in the team," said Lawson, and he walked away to wash his elbows and knees at a tap.

I was so proud.

From nobody to somebody overnight.

I could buy a pair of football boots—we didn't have any special jerseys—and tell Jackie, who wasn't allowed to play football, and Mum. This would show Gay. And Halloran and Shaw and all the others in my class who didn't make it.

The only trouble was that one other boy from our grade also made it: Egoroff. Dima knew none of the rules and had never seen the game played in his life. He even asked me why the ball was out of shape!

When we played Corinda, Egoroff turned up for the game wearing a Russian version of rugby league headgear: a seal-skin Cossack cap which covered his black hair, his ears, the back of his thick neck and his narrow forehead. It was tied under his big round chin, making the pale scar down the middle of his nose the centrepiece of what was left of his face. The poor Corinda kids got the shock of their lives when they saw this determined foreigner, dressed like a wild Russian tribesman from the movies, who obviously thought rugby league was war.

Our opponents looked incredibly big and tough to me but, although they were a couple of years older, Dima proved able to run with two or three of them latched onto him, and his method of tackling was to first pick them up and then throw them to the ground.

This seemed so effective that I began to doubt Jackie's theory about tackling low, because when Dima threw them down they always lost the ball. The only trouble was that their priest, who was refereeing the match in a big park, didn't like it and continually penalised Egoroff for this and other offences: Dima kept tackling people who didn't have the ball and stood offside to take the ball.

At half-time Lawson tried to tell him the rules but Dima said he only tackled people who were, as he put it, "trying to get the ball". And, typically, he accused the rest of us of hanging back and allowing them to pass and run.

We won despite Dima and his head-high tackles and forward passes, but our Cossack Commo—for all his wilful ignorance of the rules—was hero of the match.

5
Was Dad a foreigner?

I really couldn't see the sense in school. Dad didn't go to school much at all and he had a shop with a till full of money and a house and a green Hillman car, and he didn't even have a mother. His mother died when he was a tiny boy and he and his little brother Bill were placed in a Salvation Army home because his father worked in mines and couldn't look after them.

Dad's name was Fred and he had a strange way of describing himself as "one of those little fellows who came along quickly", and I used to wonder what he meant by that because he never said much as he was always working in the shop.

And when Fred did talk he liked to talk in riddles.

As he put his white apron on for work every day he would call the apron his "badge of servitude" and instead of saying Jesus or God he would say "whatchamacallem". Sometimes he would refer to the women who served in the shop as "the adders", and when he wanted to attract attention to himself at the dinner table, when everyone else had been talking a lot, he would say "my uncle ..."—yet that would be the end of the story.

Fred spent most of his time working in the kitchen in the shop. He rarely got angry or upset, but when he did he sang hymns that we never sang at the convent, like "La da da dee Hope and Glory, God Save the King". These were the hymns they sang at the orphanage in Western Australia. It must have been pretty bad because Fred not only said we should never go to a boarding school but he said if it wasn't for the Missus he wouldn't send us to the convent because the nuns used the cane. Unlike Mum, Dad was against forcing kids to learn, or even punishing them. So whenever Mum wasn't around we were allowed to do what we liked.

One night, when Kenny Fletcher was playing with us in the dark around the shop, his father arrived with a stick in his hand because Kenny wasn't allowed out after dark. Kenny hid behind the flour bags while I watched as Mr Fletcher walked up to the counter and asked Fred—who was putting soft drinks into the refrigerator—if Kenny was around. Dad started to say he was there but, as he stood up from the fridge door, I saw him look at the stick Mr Fletcher was flicking against his leg and he said: "No, he's not here."

Dad said that he was so frightened of the people who ran the orphanage that if they yelled at him he peed his pants. But his biggest complaint about the orphanage was the food. He said that while the children got only bread and jam the people in charge sat up at the head table eating much better food in front of them.

This worked to our disadvantage because if we wouldn't eat tripe or cauliflower or something, Fred would always say: "The trouble with you is you're too well fed." And when we went to the pictures on a Saturday he would say that the only way he ever got into the flicks when he was young was to diddle the owners by holding on to the long dress of some unsuspecting woman as she walked into the theatre.

It was hard to work Dad out because we never met his mother or father and he wasn't a Queenslander. I wasn't even sure if he was a Catholic because, although he married Mum and went to some Catholic things, sometimes he worked in the shop on Sunday instead of going to Mass, a mortal sin.

And he didn't mind eating one of his pies on a Friday, another mortal sin.

Fred's father's name was Hugh too and he worked in the mines in Mount Isa. I knew this because when I was born— and before a name had been picked—he sent a telegram of congratulation (which he didn't do for any of the other children) saying "Hurrah for Young Hugh", and with it came a pound, which I never got.

I gathered Grandpa Hugh was not to be looked up to with the great respect shown to Mum's Pa, though Mum always insisted that Fred should not keep referring to him as "my old man". Grandpa Hugh didn't help his reputation by predicting in a letter that I would become a famous Communist. Mum's relations couldn't believe he would say such a thing, and Fred hinted that his father was a bit of a Commo himself and had been in big trouble for speaking about things he shouldn't: like telling everyone that if workers refused to work then their bosses couldn't make any money.

This was probably why the only advice Fred ever gave Jackie and me was to always keep all our thoughts to ourselves and not to speak out, or else risk getting arrested by police. That was why he would never tell anyone how he voted. Not even Mum. And not even as a family secret.

In some ways though, Fred's father interested me even more than Mum's Pa.

His religion was "the Cosman faith" and we had drawings on the shelf above the hot-water system of something he had invented which was supposed to be the first helicopter, but to me it looked like three parachutes holding up a plane. There was also a photo of him outside a shed, and on the back was written "the first house in Mt Isa", and Dad used to write to him at his address "care of the cattle yards, Mt Isa".

This grandfather had been married three times: I knew this because his third wife came to visit us once from Melbourne and she had terrible skin on her hands and constantly kept covering them with a special cream.

When he died he left Fred only one thing: a brace and bit with a flat red handle which we kept under the house, the only tool Fred had. A woman friend of Hugh's brought it down to Brisbane after he died and she met Olive in town to hand it over. Still, Fred must have liked him a lot because the day Hugh died Fred really belted the pastry hard and ignored everyone in the shop.

Actually, Grandpa Hugh thought he was going to die a decade earlier because Fred had a paper called *Man! A Journal of the Anarchist Ideal and Movement* from New York which he kept hidden, folded up in a biscuit tin. It contained an article on the Spanish Civil War on which was written in pencil: "Hughie Lunn's Last Will and Testament sent just B4 he died 4.7.38 to his son Fred. To be read Sunday mornings. Retained by you till you are fifty and reread every 10 years and then to live this life."

After he left the orphanage, Dad followed his father from mine to mine, and Fred said his father was always lecturing him. At night Hugh would open a bottle of whisky and start drinking and say: "Now I'm going to tell you what is in this bottle." And it was during one of these lectures that he told Fred he shouldn't wear an apron because it was "a badge of servitude".

He could not have been completely against work because he also taught Dad to say "procrastination is the thief of time", and he used to urge Fred to get a job on his mine site at Yallourn in Victoria, but would give no help in getting it.

Once he was out of the orphanage, Fred just wanted to enjoy himself and so instead of seeking work he would go and fish and come back at the end of the day and tell his father he couldn't find any work. Until one day a foreman saw Dad fishing and asked him if he wanted some work, saying: "I need two good men or twelve footballers." This appealed to Fred because he knew that lots of men got employment purely because they could play football and therefore didn't have to work very hard.

Also Fred disliked football because he said it was like war. And he hadn't fought in the war.

This made me wonder about him.

Mum liked football. Jackie, naturally, liked football. Even Gay and Sheryl played football in the back yard, though they were too small and Sheryl fractured her arm when I tackled her and stopped her from scoring a try near the tank stand.

I couldn't help noticing that Dad had dark hair and brown

eyes that went black the few times I saw him really angry, yet all of us kids and Mum had blue eyes and fair hair. And he was short and wide with big forearms, whereas all of us kids had narrow shoulders and thin arms.

Then one morning at the convent all my worst fears were realised.

I had left my jumper at home and Dad made his only visit ever to the school, though he sometimes (when told to by Mum) took cakes and pies that were left over to the convent on the weekend as a present for the nuns.

I couldn't believe it when Fred appeared in the doorway of our class with my jumper in his hand. Everyone turned to look at him and somehow I knew what was coming. As the bell rang, Kathleen Vingo came up and said in a loud voice: "Is your Dad a foreigner?" I never said anything to anyone, but now I suspected it was true: that perhaps he wasn't our Dad at all.

He was certainly married to Olive, though they only met by accident, and they nearly didn't get to meet each other at all.

Fred had always wanted to see New York and, as he always said, it was Mum who stopped him because, when he met her, he already had his tax clearance to go.

No wonder he wanted to get away after being brought up in the orphanage during World War I. He got put in the ophanage when he was about six, after his mother died at Boulder City near Kalgoorlie in Western Australia. She died with her baby, and Dad wasn't allowed to go to the funeral, though he saw it go past. But he must have liked the place because he always talked about Boulder City as if it were New York.

He nearly got away from the orphanage once when a woman agreed to take him and his younger brother Bill. But then she found she could only afford to look after one, and poor Fred had to go back in by himself. The only way he eventually got out was to take a job they got him on a dairy farm. But it turned out it wasn't like a normal job at all. He said he worked seven days a week and was treated as a servant and didn't even get to eat with the family. So, as soon as he was old enough and could afford a bike and a rifle, Fred set off around the countryside, glad to be free of compulsory hymn singing and "masters", as he called bosses. He was going to live off the land by hunting, but found that it was easier to get a feed from work gangs along the way who fired his rifle in exchange.

Eventually he befriended a couple of young Englishmen who wanted to go rabbit hunting to make some money.

Fred sold his rifle and, with the Englishmen, bought a horse and cart and some rabbit traps. They headed for rabbit country and, when they stopped, they unhitched the horse in the bush to let it have a rest and graze while they set the rabbit traps. But when they decided to catch the horse again they couldn't: and they had to pull the cart themselves into the next town. That was when Fred decided to go east and join up with his father, and eventually they ended up working at the new silver, lead and zinc mine of Mt Isa in far northwestern Queensland.

Because he had cooked on the farm, Fred got a job in the miners' kitchen where he was amazed at how good the food for the workers was and how the miners were allowed to eat as much as they liked. And it was here he learned to be a good cook—because if the miners didn't like the dinner they would come into the kitchen and tell the cook what they thought of his food.

Fred said they were such a big rough lot that he used to hide the knives as soon as the meals were prepared.

Dad lived in a boarding house where he had various roommates and had a great time playing snooker every night after work because he wasn't married, even though he was getting close to thirty years old. He didn't have much money though, because he said that whenever he lent his mates some money they didn't pay it back. Once I heard him say that until he met Mum he hadn't even had a girlfriend: he had only ever known a group of girls he called "useful women".

He also said he was a peaceful sort of person. If someone came up and twisted his nose, he would wait to see if they did it again "to see if they really meant it". But that didn't mean he couldn't be nasty. When he was little, he said, some boys next door used to kick a football all the time and he used to watch over the fence hoping they would invite him to have a go—but they never did. Occasionally, the football would come over the fence and Fred would get his long-awaited chance to kick it back. But before he did, he always gave it a scratch with a piece of glass he had hidden in his hand, because he was envious that they had a football.

Even though Olive was older than Fred (another family secret), she too was still single when they met. Her younger sister, Vera, had gone to Duchess, a tiny town near Mt Isa with my Uncle Bill, a policeman, and Vera wasn't very well. So Mum caught the train up to Townsville and west to Mt Isa—a journey that must have been nearly two thousand miles—to make sure everything was alright.

Because of her experience working at the boys boarding school, she got a job serving in the Mt Isa miners' canteen. One day Fred saw her making a cup of tea and he asked her to bring him one too: but Olive said that wasn't her job and told him to get one himself. You would think that would have made them enemies but Fred liked the fact that she didn't do what one of her bosses asked. "You're a cheeky one," he said and smiled nicely at her and got his own tea. The very next day, Mum made him a cup of tea without being asked.

Not long afterwards Fred bought Mum what he called "a bit of glass", but she said it was a very expensive engagement ring. He planned to marry Olive against the strong advice of his father Hugh. Dad's father didn't like the Catholic church and always claimed he had been "caught" by Fred's Catholic mother.

Before they were married, Fred had to go with Mum to Nerang where Pa and Cyril and Les showed him how to run a bullock team and split logs in the bush, while Mum spent a month preparing for the wedding. Fred didn't mind where he lived or what they did, but Olive had very definite ideas: she wanted to start her own business in Brisbane, just half a day's travel from Nerang, and to have a large family of Catholics.

The only problem was that they hardly had any money.

They found two possible shops to rent and Fred said he wasn't sure which one to take. But Olive said "Take the one with the worn step." This shop was owned by a rich man called Mr Matthews and was right at a tram stop at a small shopping centre several stops past the Gabba Cricket Ground on the southern outskirts of Brisbane, on the way to Ipswich. The centre was a busy place, with everything that was needed: a hotel, a picture theatre, a paper shop, a drapery, a bike shop, a barber, a chemist and a grocery shop, all on the main road.

This was Annerley Junction.

And they decided that Fred's experience as a cook in Mt Isa—particularly as he ended up making all the sweets for the miners—meant they should open a cake shop, even though there was already a cake shop at the other end of the shopping centre. It was run by the Ganis family, a group of foreigners we never met or spoke to. They had children our age but they were State School kids.

Our shop was perfect because it also had a flat out the back to live in.

The only trouble was that, by the time they stocked the cake shop with some flour, sugar, margarine and other ingredients to cook with, they didn't have any money at all to put in the till for change. And that was when they had their first argument.

As soon as they sold some pies and cakes Mum spent the money buying some boxes of chewing gum from a travelling salesman. Fred thought this was a crazy thing to do, but Olive said it was no use having a shop if you didn't have things to sell. And the more you had to sell, the more people would come into the shop.

Of course it was easy to be optimistic then.

It was just before the War started, before the Japs looked like getting us, and well before the big bomb saved us and the Commos started taking over the world.

By the time Jackie turned one on October 29, 1939, the War had started—though you wouldn't have guessed it because they were still mucking around holding baby competitions. And, of all people, Jackie won the "bonniest baby in Brisbane" competition—and received a certificate to prove it. In 1941, the year I came along, the Japs attacked and there were no more baby competitions to win, and by the time the Japs had given in I was nearly five.

My birth caused another argument because when Fred arrived at the hospital he called me "Jasper", and for some reason this made Olive cry.

Although the Japs didn't get us, they still made things tough in Brisbane. Mum told us how she had to argue with the government at a hearing like a court case in the city for the right to get sugar to make our pies and cakes—and how the government planned to give Brisbane and the rest of Queensland to the Japanese if they landed, in order to protect the rest of the country. The government also made Dad leave the shop and go and make fruit cakes for the troops at Websters' Bakery, so Mum had to run the shop alone.

I suppose this sort of made up for Fred not going to the war, but it didn't prove he wasn't scared of the Japs. Not that I blamed him. I was secretly very scared of them myself, even after the war was over. So I was happy Fred didn't have to fight them, though I would like him to have walked around Annerley in a uniform with stripes on the sleeve like his brother Bill did when he came over from Perth to stay with us.

It was a bit embarrassing when the boys at school asked what your Dad did in the war and you had to say he made fruit cake. But I had proof that he actually tried to join the army because Fred complained that, like everybody else in Australia, the first question they asked was, as he put it: "What are ya?" Fred didn't like anyone discussing his religion, which was understandable in his case.

Fred used to either ride a bike or run to Websters from his shop, cutting all the corners along winding Annerley Road. He had to do this because, before he went, he had to cook for the shop so Olive had cakes to ice and sell, and pies to heat for lunch.

By the end of the war Mum had three kids—Sheryl came

58

along later—and went looking for the house she had always wanted. She had to do this because Fred always reckoned a house wasn't necessary. "All you need is a tent, some camp pie and some kerosene boxes to sit on," he used to say.

She found it three blocks from the shop, and being Queensland it was a timber house (brick houses were made of dirt and were unhealthy, she said). It had verandahs on two sides, and sat up on wooden stumps. There was a big garden behind a white paling fence at the front, and up the side ran a brown flat-topped fence. Mum arranged for us to pay off the house at a pound a week.

The shop was doing so well Fred bought a 1936 Hillman with a crank handle at the front to use if it wouldn't start. The car wasn't for drives, but mainly so we could get to Nerang to see Pa and Ma. It sounded like a great idea, but the road was so rough after we turned right off the Pacific Highway on the Coombabah Road that I hated the trip. This road was no more than a dirt track which wandered left and right through the bush as though designed to miss all the trees, and some of the washed out gullies were much deeper than the car and filled with stones as big as soft drink boxes.

But when we got there it was worth it.

Nerang was only a tiny town but it had a proper cricket ground with its own timber grandstand. This was where Pa had scored his ninety-six with the broken finger, and I used to like to sit in the big grandstand by myself and in my mind I could see him out there slogging with the bat. It was under this grandstand that they held the Nerang show, with jam and chooks and sewing everywhere.

There were only about a dozen houses that I ever saw— and so far apart that you could only see two at a time — and a river which Mum said she used to swim across, but I didn't believe her because it was so wide. There was a hotel and a provisions store which Pa once walked me to and I was surprised to see a large hessian bag of Queensland nuts out the front. I thought these sort of people would grow their own nuts like we did in our yard at Annerley.

Pa's house was strange.

Instead of glass windows, it had solid wooden windows which were opened by pushing them outwards and upwards until a special stick could be inserted to hold them out from the wall. Kookaburras used to come and sit at these windows and eat the witchetty grubs we got out of the huge pile of red sawdust in the yard. The bedroom area was separated from the kitchen by a room that was as wide as the house and looked a bit like an internal verandah. In one corner of the timber floor there was a neatly cut hole so that the water from the tank tap could drip straight through to the ground about six feet below, and on one wall was a mounted pair of giant polished bull horns. The kitchen had an iron stove which Pa filled with pieces of wood and paper every morning at dawn and lit—a process he called "barla-yakka", which he told us was Aboriginal for "light the fire". Pa's father spoke Aboriginal and danced at corroborees, and he and Mum liked the blackfellas. Olive always used words like "mundoeys" instead of "feet".

After he lit the fire, Pa would take Jackie and me outside where he had a couple of bowls and some soap, and he showed us how to wash our faces in a tiny amount of water at the bottom of the bowl.

Pa had a white horse called Dawn which he helped us ride and Jackie liked it so much that when he got home he made a horse by nailing a board between two stumps of the tank stand and covering it with cloth so we could jump up and ride it.

Down at the bottom of Pa's huge yard where Dawn lived was a waterhole where I almost caught a black yabbie three times, but every time I got him above the water he let go of the meat on my string and fell back in. But one day Pa saw a red-bellied black snake down there and we were banned from the waterhole. Jackie still went down but—seeing as Mum said that if it bit you you swelled up until you exploded—I stayed well away.

Pa had lots of brothers in the area and it was almost frightening when Bob and Hughie (it was never Hughie and Bob) arrived, on a Sunday. Bob and Hughie were both huge men who wore three-piece suits on a Sunday and broad hats, and when they rode up on top of giant brown horses, with saddles that creaked and jangled, it was like coming face to face with some of the giants from Grimms' fairytales.

Bob and Hughie were bachelors who lived on a rise somewhere not far away in a small house where the kitchen was completely separated from the house by a long narrow covered walkway. Under the trees outside were the remains of a big old buggy Jackie and I used to climb up into, and out the back was bush so dense that Mum said they used to win money by betting people they could not penetrate more than ten yards into the bush unaided. Yet these two men went into this same bush every day to fell timber and make a living.

Another of Pa's brothers, Tom, always wore a hat because it was said that he had two holes in the top of his head from an accident. They said that you could see his brain beating. I wanted to see this for myself, so one day at Nerang when he took his hat off to sit down in the house I went and stood behind him to have a look. And I can say without fear of telling a lie that there really were two holes in the top of his head, one bigger than the other, but both big enough to put a finger in. There were hairs growing inside the holes and I swear I saw his brain move.

But he told us his injury was nothing compared to what happened to Pa in the bush when a steel wedge sprang out of a log they were splitting and smashed his knee. Uncle Tom said Pa insisted they lay him up against a tree and finish the day's work because they needed the money.

Pa was such an influence on his kids that all three (Mum, Vera and Cyril), who had children of their own, called their first-born sons "John" after him.

In the middle of the day, Pa would sit in the shade and cut a piece of wood with his pen-knife, and while he did this he would tell stories about Australian cricketers we had never heard of, or about snakes.

He used to say that the death adder was the snake he most feared even though it was deaf: thus for a long time I thought it was the "deaf adder". Pa said that there were some marks on its stomach which blackfellas said meant:

"If I could hear as well as I can see, neither man nor beast would pass by me."

He took us yabbie fishing in the local creeks, emphasising the need to first organise all the rods and string and meat. He explained the importance of this with a story: "Once I saw this New Australian in the hills near here desperately trying to chop down a huge cedar tree. He was sweating and puffing and getting nowhere because the wood was so hard. I watched him for a while from in the bushes and when he finally took a breather I walked out and tried to help him. 'The reason you're having so much trouble,' I said, 'is your axe is blunt.' But instead of taking notice he just said he needed to make some money in a hurry: 'I just don't have time to sharpen it,' he said. So let that be a lesson to you."

Another of his lessons was never to put anything off. He said he hated the word "tomorrow": "Tomorrow never comes," he would tell us, but I could never understand what it meant.

6
Serving the shop

The one big advantage I had over all the other kids in Annerley was that Fred owned a shop.

Not just any shop, but a shop full of gigantic glass bottles of lollies, shelves of red Nestles and blue Cadburys chocolates, cardboard cartons full of Hoadleys Violet Crumble Bars, a glass-fronted stainless-steel fridge full of soft drinks of every colour, shop windows filled with cakes, and milkshakes in every flavour from vanilla to lime. And he let us have anything we wanted.

My favourite milkshake was one scoop of every flavour and a big scoop of ice-cream from the long round cans packed with ice-cream in six flavours beneath the stainless-steel flip-top doover on the fridge. We were supposed to use the small ice-cream scoop for milk-shakes but, seeing as they were both kept in the same jar of water to make them easy to use, no-one could tell if you were being a greedy guts and pulled the big one out of the milky water: so long as you didn't draw attention to yourself by putting so much into the silver steel can that it would overflow when it was being mixed on the milkshake-making machine.

There were so many different cakes to eat that it was hard to make a choice: butterfly cakes, lamingtons, rock cakes, Napoleons, custard slices, jam tarts, sweet mince tarts. But ahead of everything else I favoured a big slice of rainbow cake because it came in three colourful thick layers of sponge cake—chocolate, strawberry and vanilla—with whipped cream in between each layer. It was such a good cake, Fred always said you could tell a Queenslander because he would have a pound of rainbow cake with him.

The choice of soft drinks was even greater than the cakes but my clear favourite was Cottee's Passiona followed by their Lime Coola and Tristrams sarsaparilla. Most of the soft drinks seemed to be named after fruits, but they tasted much better.

There were no fruit juices to drink at all, but there were Mynor cordials.

For lunch or dinner there were pies or pasties straight out of Dad's huge oven: and, as everyone who came into the shop said, Fred's pies were even better than the famous "Yatala" pies at the place near Beenleigh where everyone stopped for lunch halfway to the Gold Coast.

For dessert, the butter melted on contact with the inside of the steaming hot buns or scones as you tore them off the hot black steel trays Fred pulled out of his oven.

The shop had people coming in and out all day telling stories, lots of drunks stumbling past from the Annerley Hotel at night, nice women serving behind our counter, lots of other shops around us, and a back yard with two giant green camphor laurel trees. In fact, every shop in the street had a big back yard and most of them never used it—except as a place to put their rubbish. This gave us a huge area to play in and explore with Kenny Fletcher, who lived in a small white house next to the shops, and the children of other shopkeepers: particularly the three daughters of one of the local barbers, Mr Heath, two doors away ... Karen, Esland and Vivien.

Our favourite game was played after dark: Beware of the Bear. One of the kids would go off and hide, and the others would then go looking for the bear after shouting "coming ready or not, no back answers". Whoever got caught by the bear became the bear next time.

This game meant going into places that would normally be avoided. Like under Mr Mewing's grocery shop next door where he stored his old packing cases, bags and boxes behind timber battens in an area full of cobwebs that was even dark in the daytime. Or getting into Penneys' dump—a big hessian bag, taller than me and overflowing with old bits of cardboard and packing paper. Or the old outhouse lavatory that was like a tiny old house which hadn't been used for years.

But there were unexpected rewards.

One night in Penneys' dump I found a toy tank that must have been thrown in with the rubbish by mistake. It was the best toy I had ever had and it fired sparks as it travelled across the ground under its own power, something we had never seen a toy do before.

Another time, when hiding from the bear right up under the front of the drapery shop, I found heaps of coins—including threepenny bits, zacs and two bobs. It was right below where people waited to catch the Tarragindi bus. The coins were half-buried in the dirt, having fallen through a tiny gap between the shop and the footpath.

During the day we tended to get off the ground and spend our time in the trees, mainly up in the two big camphor laurel trees, well away from adults.

There were a surprising number of things to do up there. For one thing, you could say what you liked and no-one would hear you. And we could watch what adults and other kids were up to behind all the shops because the branches of the trees were so long they stuck out over fences. We could hide ill-gotten bottles of soft drink up there and throw bottle tops at people in the street and they couldn't work out what was going on. We could even watch the woman next door hang her red wig up on a wire and brush it, and she didn't know.

And we had special games you could only play in a tree.

Jackie found that we could get from one camphor laurel tree to the other by creeping out to near the end of a long branch and leaping across to catch hold of a thin branch of the other tree, at the only spot where the two trees almost touched. The thin branch would go right down with our weight and then spring back up, so that if you stuck your legs out at the right time you could just get your feet onto a main branch of the other tree.

This made the green bark of the branch we were grabbing more and more slippery until, after a hundred goes, Jackie lost his grip as the branch lifted him upwards.

For a moment he was suspended in mid-air but then he turned and fell head-first towards the ground, way below on the other side of the high fence. I froze in the tree. I dared not go and look because I knew what I would see: Jackie's head split open.

To my great surprise his face appeared back above the fence and I realised he was standing in Penneys' hessian bag. He had landed in their dump. He didn't say anything. He just picked up a wooden box of ours and put it on his head, so it hung down over his back, and got on his bike and cycled home. There he went straight to bed. But Mum knew something was wrong, and I broke down under cross-examination and told her what had happened. Once again Jackie ended up back in the Mater Hospital, this time with concussion.

If we were on the ground at the shop in the daytime we played "hit the tin". For this game you had to get an old tin and a box and everyone had to get a stick. The tin was placed on top of the box, and one person was put in charge of the tin. He had to go looking for the others but, if someone knocked the tin off with their stick while he was out searching, he had to go back and replace the tin before again beginning his search. Whoever he caught got put in charge of the sacred tin.

If there were no kids around, there were always lots of kittens under the shops to play with—mainly the babies of our grey and white cat who Mum had named Waistcoat because of the beautiful fur on her belly. But even here it could be dangerous to play alone. Once when I was playing with the kittens a big boy from one of the shops showed me his rifle and how it was loaded by pulling downwards on a curved piece of steel behind the trigger. I asked him what happened if the rifle was fired with this piece of steel left down instead of back in position behind the trigger. He smiled and offered to let me fire the gun with it down.

When I pulled the trigger this steel handle snapped back up into place, right across my three fingers curled under the rifle behind the trigger guard, and just about chopped them all off. The people from that shop weren't very nice, but they were better than the New Australian who replaced them: he used to sit behind his shop on a box and strangle fully-grown chooks with his bare hands. When he let them go the chooks ran all over the place with their heads hanging down by their sides until they finally dropped into heaving bundles of twitching feathers.

Even when it rained there was plenty to do at the shop.

Ipswich Road was so wide, because of the tram tracks in the middle, that it caught lots of water and the gutter outside our shop flowed fast with raging water every time there was a storm. The wide footpath was dry because each shop had an awning out to the gutter to protect shoppers from the weather and to display their shop name. This meant that we could throw paper boats and sticks into the gutter and watch them race along from beneath the comfort of the awnings. Under these awnings each shop hung another name sign, and we used to run the length of the street seeing how many of these we could leap into the air and touch.

Though most of the shops were shut at night—when ours was still open—there was just enough light from windows and street light to bounce a ball against a wall or, if Gay had her way, to tie a rope to an awning post and skip. I didn't like this game because, no matter how fast I swung that rope, Gay could keep skipping until she was doing what she called "pepper"—something even Jackie never tried.

There were so many shop entrances along Ipswich Road that it was a great place to play hide-and-seek or "What's the time, Mr Wolf?" at night. On Friday and Saturday nights there were always lots of drunks around to talk to. This always appealed to me because, although I never saw it happen, it was said that if you stood on their toe and asked for five pounds they would give it to you. I was never game enough to try, but one of them used to ask a group of us kids questions and give a shilling for the right answer. Another, Biddy, used to come and sit at one of the tables in the shop and eat a pie and talk to us. He dribbled and had big warts on his face but he was great fun to talk to because you could say anything to a drunk and they couldn't think properly to answer you back. It was like meeting a really dumb kid, and they weren't serious like other adults. Though not all the drunks were nice.

One we stayed away from was called Mr Bess.

Mr Bess was a big man who shouted insults at people and the world in general all the way down the road past the shops from the Annerley Junction Hotel, the place from which all of our drunks originated. Once he picked up a loaf of bread and threw it at Mum and it hit her in the chest and Fred had to fight him then and there on the footpath outside the shop. Mr Bess was much bigger than Fred, and Mum said everyone in Annerley was so scared of this drunk that when a policeman arrived and saw who it was, he went to the Gabba for reinforcements instead of helping Fred, who was fighting with a brand new clean white apron on.

It was this story told by Mum that gave me new respect for Fred, who seemed so gentle and cautious compared to Jackie and Uncle Cyril. When Dad drove Uncle Cyril home one night Cyril ordered him around and Fred didn't answer back. He just did as he was told. Fred's headlights were weak and Uncle Cyril pointed to the car in front and said "stick on that fella's arse". Fred never said a word and just followed this car through South Brisbane. But when this car turned north—away from Uncle Cyril's—Fred, who knew the way as well as anything, followed the car. Uncle Cyril really went crook then, but Fred didn't even attempt to make an excuse. He just said "you told me to stick on his arse".

Jackie, on the other hand, was so tough that when Mum punished us by making us eat a teaspoonful of castor oil he would just swallow the stuff and say he liked it, even though everyone knew he hated it, as we all did. Whereas, if Mum was trying to get Fred up early on a cold morning to go to the shop, he would call out: "Help, police, murder!" Then he would go and climb over the back landing onto the old tank stand, which was just about rotted through, and raise his two white arms to the sun and, bowing, call out "Allah, Allah be praised!"

While most men wore suits and smoked cigarettes, Fred was always in his white apron, which looked like a dress because it went from under his chin down to his shins. Fred didn't smoke, even though he kept a packet of cigarettes on the lowboy in his bedroom: he said these were his "temptation packet"—in case he ever decided to take it up. Though it was more of a temptation to us kids who longed to try one instead of smoking dry grass in pipes made from hollowed-out guavas.

Fred even spoke differently from everyone else. He called Mum "Duck" and "the Missus" and, if he had an upset stomach, he would say he had a stomach on him "like a poisoned pup". When he had a sleep it was always "forty winks", and everything was as bad as "a two bob watch". He never asked us if we had our lunch for school, he called it our "crib". And if something was going to happen soon he would say it would happen "directly".

He loved to scratch his back by standing against a corner and rubbing with his back—or by using a curved wooden hand on a long handle he bought at a Chinese shop. And whenever he ventured out with us, which was rare, he wore a white pith helmet to keep the sun off, even though he knew everyone would laugh at it.

Fred didn't like to bathe and sometimes when Olive manhandled him into the bathroom he would call out "help police" as a bit of a family joke. But he was serious about not washing too much, saying people "washed themselves away". He didn't even like people mowing the lawn and called it "killing grass". He was also against punishing us. Once, when Mum demanded I be belted, he took me into the bathroom and told me to yell out while he hit the bath: until Mum called out through the locked door, urging him to stop.

Not much could upset Fred: only the soft drinks exploding in the fridge because they got too cold and froze, or if he got behind in his cooking at the shop, which seemed to happen all the time. It wasn't that Fred was worried about being behind, he just didn't like people harping on it. As far as he was concerned, customers should wait for his pies and buns to come out of the oven, because then they would be fresh and hot and good to eat. But the people serving the shop would keep coming into the kitchen asking when things would be cooked.

When this happened, Fred would sing his orphanage hymns or "Moonlight and Roses" or "If I had the wings of an angel over these bloody walls I would fly", and he would put the emphasis on the "bloody". If the sausage rolls were late coming out of the oven and people were waiting for them, Fred would say to anyone who dared ask how long they would be: "Three inches." This was what he called "getting snakey". And if he perceived that someone in the shop was upset, but not saying anything, he would say there was "undercurrent".

There were just too many things that could go wrong in a shop. Particularly a cake shop. If the weather turned suddenly cold too many people wanted pies. If it turned hot they wanted apple pies. If the scones were left in the oven just one minute too long they burned, and if the buns were left too long before being put in the oven they got too big and soft. And, with many orders to fill, someone was always bound to forget an order for a specially iced sponge birthday cake.

But no matter what went wrong in the shop—even if no-one warned him we were running low on Coca Cola or meat pies—he wouldn't actually tell any of the women staff off. He didn't like bossing people, and said he would rather do things himself, quoting his father's saying: "Some were born with silver spoons, others with spurs to ride them."

The best way to make the shop run smoothly was to have Mum there, and thus she spent most of her time behind the counter making sure there would be enough of everything, including people to serve the shop. And, if there were not, she would yell out "shop" and any family member or family friend in sight knew it was their duty to get behind the counter and try to stem the tide of customers. She also made sure there were few wasted left-overs. Someone wanting half-a-dozen buns would find themselves buying a tea cake if Olive served them, and a bachelor who came in for half a loaf of brown bread could easily leave with a date roll and half-a-dozen buns instead.

Mum was always at the shop helping, except in the mornings when she got us ready for school and listened to her fifteen-minute wireless serials while she did the house-work. These serials, and the movies on Saturday night, were her entertainment. She listened to the serials so much that I knew the introductions off by heart. They were always spoken by a man with a soft voice: "When a Girl Marries .... for all those who are in love, and all those who can remember". And "Portia Faces Life ... the story of the only woman who ever dared to love (pause) completely". After they were over, she would grab her big green basket and walk the three blocks to the shop.

Sometimes on the way home after dark she would break off a piece of foliage from Dr Winterbottom's garden to plant in her own and would always say "The phantom strikes again". She always referred to this doctor as "Summerbum".

At times we didn't know if Olive would be at the shop or at home, so we could often be seen travelling the three blocks there or back looking for her. None of us used to walk. Gay would skip, Jackie would run, although he wasn't supposed to, and I used to ride my pretend horses like they did in the flicks and the comics and I said the things the cowboys said as I took off for the house as fast as I could go: "scratch gravel, Whitewing" or "git-e-up Bayard".

Halfway to the shop there was a frangipani tree which each summer was covered in pink flowers with a golden centre and a lovely smell. The leaves were large and thick and, though the tree was said to be poisonous, I used to pick several flowers and stick their hard stems through the leaf so it looked like one big red and gold flower and give it to Mum.

Sometimes we would deliver bottles of milk to houses on our way home by putting the bottle through the railings onto the front verandah, but this stopped after Jackie tripped when they concreted the footpath and landed with his hand on the breaking milk bottle. When he got up I couldn't see his hand for blood and the hospital spent hours stitching it up.

After the shop, being at home was pretty quiet.

For years toys were hard to buy because of the War so my favourite game was to make armies by lining up hundreds of soft drink bottle-tops I carried home from the shop—the Pepsi army, the Coke army, the Helidon army—and seeing which ones could wipe the others out by pushing them across the floor into each other and removing any that tipped over.

In the back yard I used to mainly play with my collection of old tyres. I had about ten different ones: big fat ones and tall thin ones and short ones, and I used to race them around the yard or down the hill while hitting them with a stick to make them go faster. Or I could build a high pile of them and hide in it.

After learning about crocodiles and sharks at school, I liked to imagine two of them fighting and I used to try to work out which would win—maybe because we had read a story at school in our Reader about a bull that went down to the creek for a drink, and the crocodile grabbed him by the snout and dragged him in. For fun, I would knock nail holes in the lid of a peanut-paste jar and creep up on spiders and butterflies and green stink bugs and grasshoppers and ladybirds and big moths and the black bugs in roses, and I'd trap them in the same jar to see what would happen when they fought. But, although I watched for hours, they would all ignore each other and wouldn't fight. It was more fun watching my silkworms munch their way through mulberry leaves. You could almost see these many-legged creatures growing, until they wove golden cocoons and a moth emerged and laid eggs all over the inside of the box.

Trying to catch birds was fun.

I used to get a soft drink box and put some breadcrumbs under it, and tie string to a stick which held one end of the box up until a sparrow walked under it and I pulled the string. The government paid you money if you sent them sparrow heads, but I couldn't bring myself to kill them at close quarters, though I shot some in the trees with our air gun.

We could pick our yellow loquats and eat them or break our Queensland nuts on the concrete and eat them or even dig up sweet potatoes growing wild in the garden. We could even eat the monstera fruit when it was ripe, but you had to be careful of the hot black bits in among the white flesh.

But our favourite thing was to sit in the mango tree in summer and pick the biggest mangoes and eat them up there on a branch so the yellow sticky juice fell harmlessly down to the ground below.

At night, the only thing to do at home was to read Mandrake or the other comic in the *Women's Weekly* about the three pups. Or, if we were lucky enough to have swapped some comics, to read Donald Duck, the Phantom, or my favourite Captain Marvel whose word SHAZAM made him unbeatable.

By the 1950s, some toys had become available but there was little choice: just things like complicated Mechano sets, cap guns which quickly broke, and tinny toy cars. But plastic arrived soon after, and you could buy little hard yellow plastic Sabre jets and MIG15s, and the Korean War could be fought under the house.

The biggest thrill of the night always came when we heard Dad's car come around the corner from the shop. Even though the shop was so close, Fred always drove, and we all slept much better after his car braked as it came down the steep Ekibin Road hill and turned the corner to drive up under the house. When we were little, sometimes he would bring home Freddo chocolate frogs and, if it was early enough, he would tell us a story about Tom Mix and the three bears. I could never understand how Tom Mix could have been such a famous cowboy because he always needed the three bears to save him. If other kids were staying, Fred would frighten us all by pulling his ugly octopus face.

Fred brought the drawer of the till home with him in case the shop was broken into overnight and, to save time, he always balanced it on the front mudguard of the Hillman. One night, as he came around the corner, it fell off and we all had to go out and try to find all the threepences and sixpences on the road under the street light. Olive told him she had warned him a hundred times it would happen, but Fred said he had wanted to see if she was right.

By the time I was nine and the 1950 pennies were out, I could add up and subtract money well enough to serve the shop by myself: though Jackie first did it when he was seven.

Mum taught me how you served the shop: always to walk up behind the counter and look at the customer and say "Yes please". I thought this was a strange thing to say instead of "what do you want?" but that was the way it was done at our shop. You never put into the till the money they gave you until they had accepted the change, so they couldn't rook you by saying a red ten-shilling note had been a green pound note—because it would still be sitting on top of the till.

It was a complicated business, with different prices for everything and a special way of giving the change back. For example, if they had spent three and fourpence halfpenny, and they gave you a ten-bob note, you didn't just plonk all of the change in their hand. You got the change and said the amount to them and then counted the money into their hand like this: "Three and fourpence halfpenny—(put a halfpenny in their hand) three and five—(put a penny in their hand) three and six—(put a sixpence) four shillings— (put a two bob) six shillings—(another two bob) eight shillings—(and another two bob) ten shillings, thank you." I learnt all of that, but the one thing I couldn't understand was why Mum insisted the customer was always right, even if they were wrong.

At night you had to count the money in the till and put it in a white rag money bag with Commonwealth Bank stamped on it which pulled shut at the top like a marble bag. Coins going to the bank had to be stacked tightly together and rolled in brown paper so they were like a little round weight which fitted neatly in the hand.

You also had to know which paper bags—brown or white— to use for which cakes, and how many buns would fit in which brown paper bags and what to wrap in grease-proof paper (which was expensive) and what to wrap in tissue paper. Most difficult of all was how to cut a pound of sultana or Genoa cake from a large piece, and work out the cost from the scale on the weighing machine. And if there was more than one customer you tried to serve two at once.

At first it was fun but I soon got sick of people not saying exactly what they wanted. They would say they wanted some bread and I would have to ask if they wanted half a loaf or a whole. And if they said a whole I had to ask if they wanted Vienna or Promax or ordinary and they would just say "Yes" and I would have to ask again.

It was also pretty boring when no customers came in. But if Fred was there doing his homework I could talk to him. Every day he had to write down how many buns and scones and butterfly cakes and everything he had made so that he could pay sales tax on them. And he always added them all up and wrote down "ten dozen and two scones, twelve dozen and one buns, three dozen and eight lamingtons". I asked him why he bothered with the ones and twos, since they hardly made any difference. "Ah ha," he said. "If you knock them off soon you start knocking off the eight and then instead of twelve dozen you make it ten and then the government comes and takes you away." After that I always hoped he got it right, and made a special effort when asked to count the scones on a tray coming out of the oven. Dad said he had to pay sales tax because the government considered his cakes a luxury. And they were, because of the way he made them.

Fred had cases and cases of eggs which he used to make the cakes. He said most shops didn't use fresh eggs because it took so long to break them. But Fred didn't take long at all. He used to pick up an egg in each hand, crack them both and empty them—one from the left hand and one from the right—with the same motion, and he just kept repeating the process over and over. If he wanted to separate the yolk from the white he would crack an egg in half and toss the yolk from one half of the shell to the other half, while letting the white part fall into a jar.

He could spin a pie tin on the end of the sharp knife he used to trim the pastry hanging over the edge of each pie before he put it in the oven. He could even spin a rectangular cake tin on the end of his finger like a man in the circus. And he could write really well on the top of cakes. He would roll up a piece of grease-proof paper, cut a hole in the end, drop a tin nozzle through and fill the paper with coloured cake icing. With his left hand guiding the nozzle, he would squeeze the icing through the nozzle with his right hand and write "Merry Christmas" or "Happy Birthday" in different colours, or make roses around the top edge.

Olive used to say he could write much better with one of those than with a pen.

We loved the shop so much more than the house, so it was just too good to last. But it wasn't the government that took it away, or the rich man who owned it. A big store named Woolworths—which didn't even make pies or cakes and wasn't even from Brisbane—wanted our position at the tram stop and so we had to move out. Fred lost his big fridge, because he couldn't take it with him, and Mum had no shop to go to anymore. But we kids got a lot of chocolates that were left over when we finally shut down.

But nothing made up for losing the shop and all the fun down the back and underneath and out the front, and before we moved I took the tomahawk and cut some letters in the hard dirt of the yard so they would see it when they came: "I HATE WOOLWORTHS".

7
How we stopped Demon Dillwell

Even though the nuns said we Australians were banning the Communists, it seemed to me Russians were practically taking over Annerley. Not only had Sister Veronica forced me to be friends with Egoroff at school, but blow me down if another Russian didn't buy the house next door off Mrs Merrill and move in.

This time it was a Russian claiming to be called Dave, a name he couldn't even say properly himself: we used to say he liked to go "diving" because that was how he said his name. He didn't seem afraid of being found out because he always talked Russian to his wife and two daughters—Zoya and Vera—and even when he was going crook on us over the fence. But we had the answer: we would just yell out "Chickery Chick, Cha-la Cha-la Check-a-la Romey In a Bananika Bollika Wollika can't you see Chickery Chick is me" from the hit song on the wireless, and they didn't know what we were talking about. We didn't know what the words meant either, but we knew how to say them because Mum bought the sheet music for our piano and we sang the words at sing-songs.

If there was one dead giveaway for someone who was not truly Australian, Pa said, it was that he didn't understand cricket. Pa knew so much about cricket that he could listen to the wireless from England and move little men he had made on a toy cricket field into their correct positions. He even made cricket bats for us out of a lump of wood with his pen knife and, when those bats got too small, our Uncle Arnold, when he was up from Melbourne, bought us a proper cricket set, wickets and all, to use in the back yard.

Davey the Russian didn't understand cricket at all. He didn't seem to realise what a six was, and used to get very upset when one of us hit one over the fence into his yard. He was frightened of the ball because he reckoned it was too hard and might hurt one of his children. And he told Mum he wanted us to use a tennis ball! Image that! Only sissies played with tennis balls in Annerley. Only sissies played tennis we used to tell Kenny Fletcher. The whole idea of cricket was that the ball was so hard that girls were scared of it and couldn't play. Whereas men weren't scared of it at all, even if it hit them. At least that was how Jackie explained it to me when he bowled a bumper which hit me in the jaw.

We always listened to cricket on the wireless and it was our favourite game in the back yard and, now that we were bigger and had a proper cricket set, we needed a longer pitch. But the persimmon tree was in the road. Jackie thought we should chop it down: I wasn't so sure. But Jackie was really the boss in the back yard and—with Mum, myself and the girls protesting from the breakfast room windows— he got the axe and chopped it down. I was glad really, but I couldn't believe he had the guts to do it until I saw the axe bite deep into the trunk with an awful sickly sound and the living, fleshy centre of the tree opened and dropped out.

There were lots of reasons not to like the persimmon tree: unless the fruit was eaten on exactly the right day it made the mouth shrivel up where it touched. And when the big round over-ripe orange fruit plopped on the ground, it made mowing under the tree a wet, squishy, dirty job.

As Jackie finally chopped through the small trunk and the tree fell over, I could see it made room for a perfect cricket pitch but for the first time I had seen something I was close to disappear forever: no amount of wishing could now bring back the dead persimmon tree. It was a nice small tree to climb and to swing upside down in because it was close to the ground, unlike the big mango tree.

But I knew it had to go.

On the old short pitch the batsman only had to snick the

ball as it rose and there was a very slight danger that it could go straight through the glass in the large bathroom window above. In fact that is what had accidentally happened the previous week.

It gave our new boarder Jimmy Stewart—who, being a foreigner from America, had no idea about cricket—a hell of a fright because he was standing next to the window at the mirror shaving at the time. He was really upset and shaking, with his face covered in soap. He was a bit of a boofhead and reckoned the ball could have killed him, which was ridiculous—whoever heard of people getting killed by cricket balls? He obviously didn't know there was always the danger of a snick in cricket—that was why they had fieldsmen in slips.

It transpired, in fact, that he had never even heard of Don Bradman. And he couldn't understand why it was necessary for us to hang a ball in a stocking from the clothes line and practise hitting it back and forth to get our eye in.

Mr Stewart was a small bald man with a tiny nose and thick black-rimmed glasses. He'd been born in Ireland and had lived in America where they didn't play cricket at all. He came into our shop one night and stayed talking until closing time, and Mum offered him a bed in the corner on the front verandah which Uncle Cyril had enclosed with glass louvres and fibro, getting rid of the old-fashioned railings and lattice, and making more places to sleep.

Mr Stewart had been a merchant seaman and now had a job painting railway coaches. We had to call him Mr Stewart, but he liked Gay so much she could get away with calling him "Stew". He smoked big cigars or a special strong tobacco called Erinmore in a pipe and took no interest in sport as he said he was never able to play any because he was unable to walk until he was six years old.

He did follow wrestling and he used to go into town on a Friday night to see Chief Little Wolf and Lucky Samonavitch fight, and he said he used to yell out "Come on Chief, pull out his arm and hit 'Son-of-a-bitch' with the wet end." He said he liked big men and that was why he didn't like the Australian Aborigines. This always caused arguments with Olive, who praised them up as great hunters and fighters.

But Mr Stewart said they were all so weak and thin "you could read a newspaper through them".

Mr Stewart stayed with us for a long time and always insisted the tea leaves be thrown down the sink because he said it improved the smell of the kitchen. He was often our babysitter while Mum and Dad worked at the shop. He painted the lounge room for Mum all shiny full-gloss: lime green walls, pink above the yellow picture rail, and another, worse colour on the ceiling, and then bought two paintings of snow-capped mountains for the room.

The only thing I liked about him was that he bought us a bobs set, and he used to play bobs with us on the breakfast room table. He fancied himself with a cue and he used to beat us regularly, knocking the little wooden balls through the scoring holes nearly every time. But he used to get very snaky because Fred, who hardly ever played, could easily win on account of his snooker-playing days.

But Dad was lucky he didn't play draughts. He would have stood no chance against Mr Stewart who was a champion. He taught Jackie and me how to play draughts to win, by setting up two-for-one or three-for-one moves several moves ahead. And he taught us not to man-off as soon as you got one up and thus ruin the game. He also showed us how to play chess, and he bought us a chess set in a varnished wood box with "J & H Lunn" in gold letters on the lid which slid out like the lid of a pencil case.

Eventually, Davey the Russian took the cricket balls that we hit over his fence up to the police station and reported us, but what he didn't know was that the policemen there used to come into the shop and give the balls back and say: "That bloody Com next to your place still thinks he's living in a police state."

We put chicken wire behind our new pitch—made of dry dirt dug up from under the house—to try to stop the balls going into the Russian's. We aimed to drive the ball in the other direction—scoring six if you managed to knock a paling off the brown fence, because that was where the fieldsman always stood. That way, even if the ball went over the fence, it landed harmlessly out in Lothian Street since we lived on a corner.

The only problem now was that, for a left-handed batsman, a snick over slips was the kitchen wall of old Mr Reeves' house on the other side of our yard. And not only was Jackie a left-hander but, because he taught me how to bat, I was a left-handed batsman too—even though I was right-handed. Therefore the pill sometimes hit Mr Reeves' side wall with a big bang and Mr Reeves, who lived by himself, would lean out of his high window and threaten us. But at least we never hit his window.

Not like the time we were playing cricket at the Kidstons' house behind the shop when Jackie announced "I'll show you the shot Neil Harvey makes his money with", and lifted the ball straight through the glass window into their grandmother's room. After that, whenever we played at our place, we opened all the breakfast room windows so that if a ball was accidentally skied in that direction over mid-on it would go harmlessly into the house, missing the wall-to-wall expanse of patterned and coloured glass.

That was the theory—but one day it went wrong.

Jackie bowled a ball on a good length on the new pitch and I accidentally lofted it towards the windows and, to my relief, saw it sail harmlessly through into the room. But still I heard glass breaking. Mystified, I went up the back stairs and there was the red ball sitting on the silky-oak sideboard as if it had been gently placed there. Then I noticed a lot of little diamond pieces of glass all around the room and I realised what had happened. The best wedding present Mum and Dad got was a crystal bowl with a crystal fork and spoon, and this took pride of place in the breakfast room. The ball had landed on the full, right in the middle of the bowl, smashing the lot. You couldn't get much worse luck than that.

One Christmas we got a proper six-springer bat and leather ball and we used to take a waterbag down to the soccer oval and pick two teams of local kids by Jackie's method of each captain alternately picking a player. I didn't like this system because it was awful if Jackie didn't pick me first. But I liked being on Jackie's team because once we passed the total of the other team he used to say: "Come on. Every run now is sheer profit."

Kenny used to play sometimes, if he wasn't playing tennis, but he always had to leave early to get home. And he wasn't used to cricket where you had to accept you were out even if you weren't. Once, he angrily knocked all the wickets out of the ground with our six-springer and protested so much that Jackie broke all the rules and let him stay in.

That was one good thing about Mum: she never worried about us at all, so long as we came home by tea time. She even let Jackie and me go off on holidays once with some strange people who came into the shop, before we lost it to Woolworths. They drove a big Ford truck—from the olden days—and the father had a long beard and the mother was very fat. They had a couple of sons and lived way out in the bush somewhere and the woman said it might be an idea to take us with them for a week. Jackie said they were hillbillies and I didn't want to go, but Olive said it was a great idea to go bush.

They lived in an old farmhouse and dinner was always a big feed of corn-on-the-cob that they grew themselves. We shot a goanna and drank billy tea in the bush, but my biggest thrill was when I saw a mile post saying it was forty-something miles to Brisbane and I wondered if I could walk home and how long it would take. These people had no phone—or even a wireless—and seemed to have no contact with anyone else at all except when they went to town on a Saturday morning. And we didn't know what they were like or even if they were Catholics—though I was sure they weren't, because I never saw any Holy Pictures on the walls in their house. And every Catholic house had at least a picture of the Sacred Heart of Jesus. They all seemed a bit mad to me, and the only things Jackie and I had to protect us were our Phantom skullrings we'd bought through the post from the back of a Phantom comic.

One day the father took us through the bush to show us the railway line to Sydney. We walked because they didn't own horses or anything sophisticated like that. When we got there he made us a cup of tea out of a stagnant muddy waterhole and, though I was thirsty, I couldn't drink it. So I went and stood on the bridge over the railway line to see the interstate express pass directly beneath me. As the engine went under, the driver blew a whistle and the hot steam and coal smoke hit me in a blast from below. The heat seared the inside of my nostrils and burned my face and made breathing difficult. It nearly knocked me over and the old hillbilly, instead of helping, just laughed at me. And so did his two boys.

I guess Mum felt there was nothing to worry about because Jackie was pretty grown up now. Not only had he mastered the kidney punch, the rabbit killer, the escape from the Full Nelson by throwing the arms in the air and dropping to the ground, and the two movements for stopping a knife thrust from above or below, but he had a gun: a Daisy Air Rifle No. 1. This was pretty important because we were now spending a lot of the holidays down at Ekibin Creek at the bottom of the hill.

Much of this country was completely unexplored, and the undergrowth was so thick in parts that the only way we got through it was for Jack to put his back up against it and for Kenny and me to push him as hard as we could. The exploration was worth it because we found a place where the narrow muddy Ekibin Creek was nice and wide for the canoes we were building out of old roofing iron, with the help of a friend, Neville Walters.

We first had to knock the corrugations out of the iron and then fold it up so it was sharp at the front and wide at the back where it was nailed around a board. The first canoe we made was too narrow and unstable but the next one was wider and hardly leaked at all. The trouble was that it was impossible to keep your balance and they kept tipping over until we learned how to do it. It was a bit like learning to ride a bike—you had to be confident you could do it and be prepared to get back in after you tipped yourself out. Our main game was to try to sink the person in the other canoe—and it wasn't much fun being sunk all the time because the water was murky and the bottom was muddy and the undergrowth grew right down into the creek.

On the other side of Ekibin Creek was a high cliff face which could be seen from all over Annerley Junction and, once we had mastered the creek, we pushed on and discovered that the cliff was actually a giant quarry. Eventually we learned how to get to the top by walking up washed-out red dirt gullies at the back. At the top Jackie used to stand right at the edge and look over but I didn't because I was frightened the land would give way and we would fall down. It was so far down to the stones and gravel below that the trucks looked like toys.

Beside the quarry was a dirt track that led away from the creek, and it was lucky Jackie had the gun with him the first time we went exploring along there because we came around a corner and ran smack into a group of tall untidy State School kids we somehow found out were called the McGraths. They had the biggest shanghais I had ever seen—inch-wide rubber bands hanging down more than a foot from the giant forks, with a leather piece as big as a sausage roll to hold the stone. When they saw us the McGraths immediately opened fire and for the first time I knew what it was like to face certain death and found myself involuntarily saying the Hail Mary.

All we had between the four of us—Kenny, Neville Walters, Jackie and myself—was a one-shot Daisy Air Rifle which could only be reloaded by screwing out the top of the barrel, dropping a lead slug down, blowing it to the bottom, and then screwing it into the barrel again.

But this did not deter Jackie.

"Drop your shanghais or I'll shoot," he said, levelling the Daisy at the half-dozen McGraths. Perhaps they had been to too many matinees, because to my surprise they did as they were told. Then Jackie said we had to go home but he would fire one warning shot so that they knew he meant business. He fired into the air as we backed around the corner of the track, and then we raced away back to the quarry where we made nulla-nullas from pieces of wood dipped in thick black tar they kept there—and stuck bits of broken glass in the tar in case they came after us.

Often we would become separated on these excusions into the unknown, but Jackie had taught me his whistle which was so loud that anyone within twenty yards was forced to cover their ears. He did it by curling his tongue upwards and blowing air beneath his top front teeth but I could only do it with the left side of my mouth. By whistling we could keep contact over long distances even when we couldn't see each other.

It was after this shanghai incident that Jackie decided we needed to be better armed. So the following Saturday morning we went to town to a gun store in Albert Street near the Saint James picture theatre and, with our savings, each bought a big knife with a bone handle for thirty shillings—much bigger than the ones the Scouts wore. I had always wanted to join the Scouts to get a knife but Olive said they were all non-Catholics, so the nearest we got was a Scout belt each for Christmas. They were very handy belts because the buckle could be used as a bottle opener.

Jackie said he had read that the most effective use for a knife in a fight was to throw it: it penetrated the body much better than with a stab—and you could keep your distance from your opponent.

The trunk of our mango tree was about the size of a man and it had a swelling at heart level, and for weeks and weeks we did little else but practise throwing our knives into this spot on the tree from about six paces away. After a while we were disappointed if we couldn't do it ten times out of ten.

The trouble with flicking the knife from the shoulder was that it conveyed a warning to your opponent that you were about to throw, so we also practised throwing underarm, upwards from the knee, but this was much more difficult. Four out of ten was a good result, and penetration was much less. With the overarm throw the knife went in so far it was very difficult to pull out of the tree. To try to get over the problem of telegraphing a throw, we tried to attach our knife pouches behind the right shoulder after seeing it done in a cowboy movie, but it didn't work.

We learned a lot by going to the pictures every Saturday afternoon. We had the choice of three theatres within easy walking distance—the Annerley, the Odeon or the Boomerang—but mostly we went to the Annerley because it was nearer and, anyway, you had to return to the same theatre to see the other fourteen parts of the serial. The serials always came on for ten minutes after the two movies.

It was the pictures that inspired us in the back yard: after Robin Hood we made swords and cardboard armour; and after the Durango Kid we made wood guns and wore handkerchief masks around our necks. But the biggest impact on me was made by the Batman serial where Batman and Robin battled to get the atomic ray gun from the Japanese— and mindless Zombies captured "the Batman", as the crooks always called him. A Japanese man with an evil moustache and a horrible slimy accent hid in a cave behind the Zombies and urged a pack of crooks to "get zee Batman and stop 'im getting zee ray gun". This serial was so scary and so real that no one ever played it as a game or said they were Batman or Robin. At the end of each serial we had to wait to next week to see how they would escape.

It was incredibly noisy at these Saturday afternoon shows because the theatre was full of hundreds of us and everyone screamed for Batman's sake. We used to like to sit up the back in the canvas seats and yell out "mush, mush" if the actors kissed, and the local blacksmith, Mr Bowers, patrolled the aisles to keep order and to make sure there were no impure actions in the dark. Once Kenny and me got Jackie into trouble when we dared him to sit with a girl called Helen and kiss her. Mr Bowers—who knew Mum and Dad— shone his torch on them and told them to cut it out. Then Kenny and I decided to trick him and we pretended to be hugging and kissing. When he shone his torch on us he got a big surprise because we'd fooled him.

We always agreed that our favourite flick was called *Objective Burma*, starring Errol Flynn. We liked it, not because he wiped out all the Japs, which was good, but because there were no women in it at all. But secretly I liked the pictures about the blue coats versus the grey coats in America and I always wanted the grey coats to win, but they never did.

At interval and afterwards we would collect any old soft drink bottles from under the seats and sell them to the shops for tuppence each and buy some ice-cream buckets.

Because Gay sometimes appeared in plays at the Theatre Royal, occasionally we missed the pictures to go in to watch her matinee performance. Just like the pictures, the theatre was always full of hundreds of screaming kids. In one play there was this real baddie called "Demon Dillwell" who wore a red costume and cape, and had horns like the Devil and big evil black eyes.

Demon Dillwell was always creeping up behind this nice girl in the play, and we all shouted and screamed when he was behind her to warn her: but she always took ages to wake up to what was going on. And, when she finally saw him, she would say "Ah ha, Demon Dillwell."

At the end of the play Demon Dillwell ran down into the audience, daring anyone to stop him. He ran up one aisle and back down the other, with screaming kids running and hiding. He was a big strong man and he wasn't even slowed down although dozens of boys stuck out their hands to try to stop him. Suddenly Jackie grabbed me and headed for the next aisle saying "tackle low", and as Demon Dillwell came charging down the aisle of the Theatre Royal, threatening and growling, Jackie and me went straight in around the knees and the Demon crashed in the aisle like the Lord of Luna in "Horatius Defends the Bridge".

I froze with terror as his big black eyes looked at me from just a few inches away as we lay on the carpet, and I leapt backwards as he struggled in obvious pain to get to his feet and dust the dirt off his red cape.

It was the perfect opportunity for all of the kids to leap on him and capture him once and for all, but a big space cleared around Demon Dillwell as everyone, and especially me, expected that Jackie had got us all into big trouble. Maybe you weren't supposed to stop Demon Dillwell, I suddenly thought.

Demon Dillwell stood looking down on an ever-widening

circle of eyes and lifted his red cape in the air and yelled and ran off back up onto the stage.

Although we only got to go to the pictures once a week we had plenty of entertainment after school listening to the serials on our wireless in the lounge room. It was a brown cabinet wireless, standing on the floor, and it had a long thin white marker that swept around to choose your station, and Jackie somehow knew all the times and stations for serials off by heart. Late in the afternoon we could listen to "Search for the Golden Boomerang" and "Biggles" and "Jeffrey Blackburn's Adventures". And at night, if we weren't at the shop, there was "Pick-a-Box" with Bob Dyer. The white marker was on a square glass dial that gave off a nice green glow, and if you sat and looked at this as you listened you could see Bertie firing his gun as he helped Ginger escape with Biggles. The sound of the gunshots always sounded exactly like Queensland nuts dropping into a tall tin like the frozen liquid whole egg tins Fred kept under the shop. When we were older, Jackie and me listened to the boxing from the Stadium on Friday nights and, though we never saw Mickey Hill or Stumpy Butwell, or even knew what they looked like, they were our heroes.

Jackie was not allowed to mow the lawn because he had had the fever—it was a tough job trying to push the mower through the grass, so tough that Mum used to walk in front of me cutting it with her carving knife unless Uncle Les had come over with his big scythe and shortened it. Thus, Jackie seemed to have a lot of energy left over and was always leading us off on some expedition or other. We travelled to many unknown places miles away from Annerley—even to the river to swim in a big mud-hole which some said was a submarine harbour.

Once we travelled into the bush out past Yeronga because Jackie had heard of a cave there.

The cave was just a hole in a hillside but, once past the entrance, it felt like you were in a deep cave although, even with Jackie's candle, we couldn't see very much. I could feel the damp dirt walls and we hadn't gone very far in when I began to feel very, very cold. I suggested we turn back in case of ghosts—and I was sorry I spoke because my words kept going around in my head as if said by someone else. But Jackie wouldn't stop until, suddenly, he was on the ground and the candle was out.

I could still see the exit—as a round hole of bright white light in the distance, and we headed straight for that. When we got outside Jackie was holding the back of his head and blood was coming out between his fingers. For a minute I thought someone had got him, but he said he slipped backwards on some slime and fell on a rock. We had to head straight home where Mum applied a poultice. No wonder she always seemed so worried about Jackie, when I thought she should really have been worrying about me.

I think it all started the day Mum got one of those new machines that washed the clothes. It had a pair of rollers and when the clothes were washed, Olive had to lift them up and stick them between these two white rollers which squeezed the water out as the clothes went through, emerging as flat as pancakes on the other side.

While Mum was upstairs Jackie had a go at the washing machine and, without any warning at all, his left hand got caught between the rollers which started crushing it and dragging it further in. I couldn't do anything except yell because I could just imagine his whole arm emerging on the other side of the rollers as flat as a pie top.

Olive arrived on the scene from nowhere like Batman. She had just washed her hair and, instead of being in plaits, it was flowing behind her like a dark cape. She lifted her right hand in a fist above her head and smashed it into the top of the machine and the two rollers fell apart, broken by the incredible force of her impact.

Jackie was saved, but only briefly.

When cracker night came round we watched the sky waiting for someone to send up the first skyrocket. Then all hell would break loose with skyrockets flying all over Brisbane. We always saved up for months, storing crackers away all the time, and had plenty of double-bungers and strings of tom thumbs and throw-downs and roman candles. But Jackie also liked to break bungers in half and light the gunpowder to show how the flames would shoot out from his hand, until one exploded backwards and he had black burnholes the size of matchheads on his fingers. This was going to be yet another setback to his piano exams: the only thing besides her religion and the shop that Mum held sacred. She was so proud of her Broadwood piano that she used to tell everyone it was "the Rolls Royce of pianos", and you had to wash your hands before you were allowed to play it.

So we had to tell her a lie: that a boy lit a bunger and handed it to Jackie just as it went off.

The reason we could visit places on our own was that Fred had, out of the blue, bought us a three-quarter sized red Massey bike. Fred was standing in the front door of his shop, just before Woolworths kicked us out, when Jackie said he wanted a bike. With brass knobs on, I thought. But Fred, while I watched in disbelief, opened his wallet and gave Jackie the money and we walked up to our favourite shop in the whole of Annerley—Lloyds Bike Shop—and bought the Massey. We only needed one bike because Jackie could double me if I sat sideways on the bar.

The bike had a foot brake, but no hand brakes, which made it very difficult to stop if the chain got loose and came off. Then we usually had to crash it to stop.

It was at about this time that a new boy, a High School boy, moved in next door because his parents were poor and were going to rent part of Mr Reeves' house. Luckily for us he was a nice bloke who was interested in doing all the things we liked and, being even older than Jackie, he knew lot of things.

His name was Neil and he showed us where to oil our bike and helped us build and paint another bike out of old parts. This Neil also showed us how to blow up cans with bungers so that the cans flew high in the sky, and how to make little bombs with matchheads which went off on the tram line when the tram passed over them. And he walked with us across to Logan Road to count how many Holdens we could see, Australia's own car.

Neil was quite big and a good cricket player and he helped

us build our new cricket pitch as well as a tin-roofed cubby house in the mango tree, with its own secret place for keeping soft drinks, and a separate lookout post. We quickly became such close friends that we used a saw to cut a shortcut through the old fence which was practically falling over. This upset Mr Reeves, though he never went down in the yard anyway.

We never looked on Neil as a State School kid. But then he never said anything against us or our religion: he just helped us, even with homework, because he was near the top of his class and had scored almost ninety per cent in the dreaded State Scholarship examination, which made him a genius.

He also showed us some new wireless serials to listen to and every Friday night for months Jackie and me went over next door to listen with Neil to "Journey into Space"—a frightening story about "a journey to the Red planet Mars". Neil could even show us Mars in the sky. I think Neil was even smarter than Jackie, though he wore thick glasses all the time and wasn't as tough. Jackie remained the one who decided what we did: though what none of the State School kids knew was that Jack had to wear glasses in school to read.

Jackie fought the toughest bloke at Junction Park State School—Johnny Dunn—when they caught us cutting through their school. Johnny was by far the toughest boy I had seen. He could not be stopped by mere straight lefts, but Jackie held him off so well with his boxing, and for so long, that both sides decided to toss a coin and if it came down heads to call it a draw.

With the arrival of Neil, the new bikes, and with State Scholarship still a few years off, things could not have been much more fun around Annerley in those early days of the '50s.

Then suddenly two terrible things happened to ruin everything.

One night I woke up because I could hear Jackie crying: something I had never heard before. He was holding on to his knee and sobbing with the pain and I knew we were in big trouble this time. I immediately started to pray to Our Lady and every saint I knew to ask them not to let this happen to me.

Dr Holmes was away and another doctor put Jack back in the Mater Hospital, this time with osteomyelitis, saying something was wrong with his leg bone.

A few weeks later Dr Holmes dropped into the shop for a pie and asked how we were, and Mum told him about Jack and I can still remember his reply: "That's not osteo—that boy's got rheumatic fever again." And he left his pie sitting on the counter and went and jumped into his Austin and drove straight to the Mater Hospital and had Jackie removed to a different ward and given different treatment.

And Dr Holmes was right.

Jackie had the same fever again and was back in hospital for months and months.

As if that was not bad enough, some people told us Neil's family were Communists and should be avoided. It sounded impossible. Not only were his mother and father very old, but they did not have foreign accents and the whole family were very white skinned. Neil's father sharpened saws under the house to make some money, so it was unlikely he was being paid by a foreign government, and his silver-haired mother was very nice.

But still it made me wary of his parents.

His sister's husband did say some things that would have worried Fred: like when we were listening to a rugby league Test match one Saturday and Australia led the weak touring French team by thirteen points, with ten minutes to go. He said Australia would lose so that there would be a big crowd for the next Test.

I told him he was mad.

But ten minutes later Australia had lost.

8
The secret sound

We spent a lot more time at 40 Ekibin Road now that Dad was what he called a wage slave. And, with no shop to go to, Fred was home on weekends and we got to go to the beach sometimes.

Fred didn't like his job, but I thought it was great because he helped mow the grass on Sundays—even though he didn't agree with it. And, because he was so strong pushing the mower, we finally got the grass really short for cricket.

It also meant that he had time to take Jackie and me to the Brisbane Exhibition. Mum was tight with money but Fred, when he was by himself, splashed it around. And, to our surprise, he gave us more than a pound each to spend once we got in. This meant we could each have a go with the bows and arrows, shooting at balloons on targets, and we saw Slim Dusty sing in sideshow alley and watched a woman beheaded in another tent, and we dropped ping-pong balls down the mouth of the clowns and won some statues, and we went on the octopus ride and bought lots of fairy floss and we each got a Jaffa bag with a cardboard gun in it which shot bits of cardboard with a rubber band.

I never saw where Fred worked, but it was at some sort of factory that made pies and pasties by the thousands for sale at school tuckshops. He never talked about it much, and we didn't ask him, because it wasn't very interesting. The only thing I knew was that Fred wouldn't eat the pies himself and said they worked him so hard at the factory that after he joined they put two men off.

Like everyone else in the family, and especially Mum, he was happiest when he talked about one day opening another shop at Annerley: and it was always pointed out by someone at the tea table in the kitchen that he still had his mirror-backed glass cake display case and his big four-tray oven under the house.

When he had the shop, Fred never drank beer and never swore. I even saw his brown eyes go black one day when a man told a dirty joke in the kitchen, and Fred didn't look up from rolling the pastry on his wide timber table—he just said loudly that he didn't want that sort of talk in his kitchen and told the man to go elsewhere and tell his jokes. Since Fred was wielding one of his thickest rollers—and not one of the wooden ones, a steel one—the bloke shot through immediately.

Fred used these rollers like nulla-nullas to belt the pastry on the table from a thick pile of margarine, flour and water into something low enough to roll out—so that he could fold it over into three layers and belt it out again, and then do it again and again to create the layers in the pastry. No wonder he had such broad shoulders. He delivered these blows from high above his head and each time he folded the pastry over he poked it with the end of the roller to mark how many times he had done it.

Fred always told me he didn't drink beer because he didn't have time—and he was right.

Now that he had to "saddle up", as he called working for someone else, he started drinking beer. Only a little bit, but instead of having two mangoes in the fridge for every summer evening, he would sometimes have two beers. Then came the inevitable night when small sins led to a big one, as Sister said they did, and Fred came home stumbling around and talking rubbish like an Annerley drunk.

It was hard to believe it was him. He was picking me up in his big arms for the first time ever: slurring his words, and saying how bloody happy he was. This man who pitied all the poor old drunks in the Junction, and hated grandfather Hugh's drinking, had suddenly become a drunk himself. Olive wouldn't let him touch her, and I was convinced that our family life was at an end.

Mum had been waiting for Fred to come home from work

to take her for the nightly visit to Jackie at the Mater, and Fred became serious when she said Jackie would be sitting there in his hospital bed, sick and wondering where his parents were.

And what was she to tell him: that his father was drunk?

So, somehow, he managed to drive her to the hospital— and it never happened again.

While Jackie was in hospital I had the additional responsibility of looking after the animals in the yard. Fred had bought some ducks and chooks to feed up for Christmas, but when the time came to kill them he couldn't do it— and, surprisingly, nor would Jackie. So we had at least a dozen fully-grown ducks, including a huge drake called "Big Fella", plus a rooster who used to be a better watchdog than Nigger—he would drop his left wing to the ground and chase visiting kids around the yard.

At one stage we had so many baby ducks that they were like a small yellow cloud as they trooped around the garden together—but some died after getting wet in storms and four were killed by the rats when I locked them in the toilet overnight to keep them out of the rain, though Nigger got one of the rats later near the room under the house.

I found the little yellow birds splattered with their own blood on the concrete floor of the lavatory, and I thanked God that Jack had not succeeded in getting Mum to buy a Shetland pony after he had read about them in the *Women's Weekly*, because I would have had to look after the pony as well. What would have happened if something happened to that? Horses were such difficult things to look after. Occasionally wild horses would wander lost into our yard and one night one galloped down Ekibin Road, I heard it go past, and it ran straight into a car and was killed—and nearly killed a woman inside.

The ducks who survived made huge nests of eggs all around the yard under old fences and in bushes, and I didn't know what to do with them. I happened to mention this at school and Dima said he knew about ducks from his China days, and I was very relieved when he came to inspect.

Egoroff—after fixing the air rifle for me—carefully counted

the eggs in each nest—some had eighteen or nineteen—and he made nests of torn-up magazine paper in boxes and neatly put the eggs in these. But something went wrong and none of the eggs ever hatched.

I also had to look after my pet budgerigar which I called "Dewdrops" after the little spots of colour under his beak. I had always wanted one ever since Mum took us into the Botanical Gardens in the city and we saw a huge aviary as big as twenty houses filled with yellow and green budgies near the monkey cage. Dewdrops used to sit on my shoulder as I walked around Annerley Junction and, for the first time in my life, people took notice of me instead of Gay, Jackie, or Sheryl.

Everyone was starting to notice Sheryl because she had suddenly grown hundreds of red curls and even Gay was getting jealous. Gay cut some of the curls off Sheryl's head and tried to stick them on to her own hair. Mum took the hairbrush to Gay's bottom when she saw what Gay had done, but all Gay said was: "I should have destroyed the evidence."

Pa called her "little Gay", but under that fair hair and skin she was as tough as a nun.

Once when Mum bought her a new dress she didn't like she cut it up with a pair of scissors so she couldn't be made to wear it. Yet I had to wear all Jack's old hand-me-downs.

Gay nearly went too far one Sunday when Fred took us in his Hillman down to the oval swimming pool next to the ocean at Wynnum. This pool was as big as a back yard, with a slippery slide in the middle, and we had a picnic and swam for hours. When it was time to go home, Gay just flatly refused to get into the car. To teach her a lesson we drove off without her, leaving her standing on a corner by herself sulking. But sulking didn't work with Mum. She just used to say: "We've got the sulky, now all we need is the horse."

Mum had lots of sayings for various situations: like "do what you're told when you're told" and "that went out with straw hats". Gay had a lot to say about how things should be done, so Olive called her "know-all not". If we asked what something was, and Mum thought we shouldn't know, she would say "It's a wing-wong for a goose's bridle". If someone did something she didn't like, she would say they had "more hide than a highwayman's horse". If you couldn't keep a secret she called you "a Balsam seed" after a small plant with a pretty flower which grew wild in the garden. As Olive said, if you touched this plant the seed fell out in your hand.

Mum never walked to the shop she went on shanks's pony, and when we lost anything she would invariably say: "You'd lose your head if it wasn't screwed on."

If we left without saying goodbye she would say we left "like Billy the blackfella"; if I was unhappy and had a sour puss she would ask—"lend me your face to fight a bulldog"; and if you didn't take her side in an argument she would say you were a black snake: "The black snake bites the hand that feeds it." She always described her job in the shop as the "wooden water joey"—meaning she did everything, "waiting on people hand and foot". She skited about her mother's father who, she claimed, owned a big estate in Scotland and was a knight, Sir Charles Halcett-Hay, but if she thought a woman was putting on airs she would refer to her as Madam Muck.

That time Gay got the sulks at Wynnum, we drove slowly around the block, but when we came back Gay wasn't crying in the gutter as I hoped. She just said: "I knew you'd be back." The liar.

Gay also had a lot of awful sayings, like "yummy yummy chookie's bummy", and came out with ridiculous statements on purpose to gain attention. Like the time I wanted to know the name of a "domestic animal" for my homework and she said "a rat", and I got into trouble at school for my answer.

Sheryl was a nice little girl but she had a ferocious temper which would often embarrass Mum: so Olive always said she was like "the girl with the curl down the middle of her forehead—when she was good she was very, very good; but when she was bad, she was horrid". Once Sheryl got so angry that, although she was only wearing coloured beads and a pair of tap shoes, she raced out of the house and up Ekibin Road in the nude, screaming at the top of her voice.

A policeman brought her home.

She was the same when we tried to help her climb the mango tree.

We nailed a wooden sultana box—with the side knocked out—onto a thick branch and dragged Sheryl up and tied her to the box so she couldn't fall out. Instead of liking it she screamed so loudly that Uncle Les came and took her down. Then he went crook at Mum, even though she had nothing to do with it.

That wasn't the only time Sheryl got Olive into trouble.

They used to have a competition on the wireless every morning in Brisbane in which people rang up to try to guess a "secret sound". No-one could possibly guess the sound, so the prizemoney went up another shilling each day until it was hundreds of pounds.

One night when Mum's relatives were over, sitting in the breakfast room with all the windows open to try to get cool, one of us kids got up to use the tall frozen liquid whole egg tin we kept in the hallway for peeing in at night to save having to go downstairs, because Olive said she had "a Woolworths' bladder".

Being a tall tin, it made a lot of noise, and Sheryl leapt out of bed and raced into the breakfast room and yelled in front of everyone: "Mum, it's the secret sound!"

Although Jackie was still in hospital, he had recovered pretty quickly from the fever this time, and whenever I went to see him in hospital—since he was over twelve he was in the adult ward and could have children to visit—he would list all the men who had died in his ward, and their time of death. And he seemed to know who would go next.

He had befriended another boy, who kept running away every time they were due to operate on his head, and he and Jackie used to sneak around the ward looking behind screens to see who had died. Jackie claimed the nurses put pennies over the eyes of the dead to keep them shut.

God certainly did work in mysterious ways, as the nuns always said he did, because the very next day after Fred came home drunk the hospital announced that Jackie was coming home. And when Jackie got home, Fred said he had

had enough of the pie factory and he was going to look at another shop just near where our old one had been.

To celebrate, Olive—who now made Jackie drink barley water for his constitution—said we should have one of her sing-songs and invite her relatives around .... people like Aunty Vera, Aunty Rosey, Aunty May, Aunty Merle, and Aunty Joan.

Not that they were all real aunties.

For example, Aunty Rosey, the singer, was Mum's aunty whereas Aunty May was from Nerang and was called aunty because she had once taught Mum the piano, though it musn't have been for very long because Olive couldn't play much at all: unlike her sister Aunty Vera who was very good at it.

Aunty May was a big woman like Mum, but with a deep rich old-fashioned Australian voice like in the newsreels at the pictures. She used to amaze everyone because she drove the family car. Her husband Ernie, who was a house painter, couldn't drive. One of their sons, Don, was famous because he had flown over England in the Battle of Britain, and Mum and Dad kept the letters he sent them from the War.

Once Aunty May turned up in a brand new beautiful car called an Austin of England and she gave us a fright when she took us for a drive. We travelled to the end of Lothian Street when suddenly we heard a man's voice in the car. We couldn't work out where it was coming from until we discovered it was from a built-in wireless which worked as you drove along. The wireless had taken a street to warm up, as Aunty May knew it would, and she laughed when it caught us out.

Aunty Joan was a young woman who had been adopted by Pa when she was abandoned as a girl, but Mum said they lost Aunty Joan in a big court case with Aunty Joan's real parents when she was old enough to go to work. But she remained good friends with the Duncans, and particularly Mum.

Olive spent all her spare money buying sheet music, at two bob a time, for the latest songs printed on two pages of thick paper that folded together, with a drawing or photo on the front illustrating the song. A part of another song was always printed on the back to get you interested in buying that one too.

Most of the songs were about how men loved girls and wanted them so badly that they would die if they didn't get them—like "Lavender Blue (dilly dilly)" which was a big hit about how a grandfather fell in love with a grandmother, or "Sioux City Sue", a song I liked because it was about a cowboy who loved his girlfriend so much that he said he would swap his horse AND his dog for her. This song was printed with a green cover and a photo of the singer of the song—Bing Crosby—on the front. But we liked the drawing of the girl on horseback with a whip, watching a cowboy chase and lasso a calf.

Most of the love affairs ended in disaster in these popular songs—sometimes even for the girls: like in one of our favourite singing songs "Let him go, Let him tarry" where the girl sings "let him sink or let him swim, he can go and get another that I hope he will enjoy, for I'm going to marry a far nicer boy". Or that favourite of everyone who came to sing at our place: "If I were a Blackbird", a sad song about a girl whose sailorman has left her and she wants to be a blackbird to whistle and sing "and follow the ship that my true love sails in". "And in the top rigging I'd there build my nest, and I'd pillow my head on his lily white breast". The sheet music here actually had "his or her" depending on whether the singer was a boy or a girl—which was a bit stupid because we knew there were no women sailors.

But they covered this with a special "4th verse for male version". These were the things you got to know if you had the original sheet music instead of just hearing the song on the wireless.

From all these songs—and others like "Some Sunday Morning" which had a pink cover with Errol Flynn dressed as a cowboy with his holster in an unusual cross-draw position on his left hip (we wore our guns down near our knees for the quickest draw)—I knew that one day I would fall hopelessly in love with a girl. And I could see why, because already some of them made me feel good to be near.

I knew girls were pure and innocent but I couldn't work out what that meant exactly, except that in some way they were untouchable. I gathered this was to do with their different pogeys—which I had once seen—and the noi nois they grew on the chest. But what these differences meant I couldn't work out, except that one night I dreamt I had my arm caught between the legs of a girl in my class at the convent—not one of the ones I liked, but an ugly one with glasses.

It was a very complicated side of life because no-one ever talked about these parts of the body, unless you were ill.

When I had the mumps Mum said if I didn't stay in bed it could go to my balls and they could become as big as footballs—and she joked that she had heard of a man who had to wheel them around in a wheelbarrow in front of him after an attack of the mumps. So I did what she said and stayed in bed.

Some boys at the convent were starting to get visibly swollen and sore nipples—and we were all not supposed to notice. And the girls were swelling up even more under their dresses. And why did we have little noi nois if we weren't girls?

The songs kept us curious even if they didn't give us any answers. And we had plenty of songs because relatives gave Olive sheet music as presents. Uncle Les gave us "Wild Goose, Brother Goose" because he liked to hear it sung and played. Gay and Jackie were so good on the piano that they had song books too. Even Aunty Vera's daughters Mel and Gem could play—and Aunty Rosey sang in the city centre for the Salvation Army, and her high clear notes could be heard a street away.

Although none of us was Irish we seemed to sing mostly Irish songs, as if we came from the land of shamrocks instead of hot old Australia.

Olive had the music for songs like "Christmas in Killarney" and "If You're Irish Come Into the Parlour" and "That's an Irish Lullaby". They always had green covers.

Another Bing Crosby hit we used to sing was "Galway Bay", but I was never sure whether this was about Ireland or about the blackfellas. Anyway, whenever it was sung at our place there seemed to be a lot of significance put on the words: "For the strangers came and tried to teach us their way. They scorned us just for being what we are. But they might as well go chasing after moonbeams, or light a penny candle from a star".

Jackie and me liked the songs with a bit of action like "Clancy Lowered the Boom" about a bloke called Clancy who was pretty tough. It went: "Now Clancy was a peaceful man if you know what I mean—the cops picked up the pieces after Clancy left the scene." We also liked him because "he never looked for trouble, that's a fact you can assume—but nevertheless, when trouble would press, Clancy lowered the boom, boom, boom, boom."

At some stage of the night the kids would have to play some classical piece they had learned for a piano exam, and it was important to Mum that we be superior to her relatives' children: like Uncle Cyril's only child, Johnny, who was so good on the piano accordion that even Uncle Cyril used to skite about him playing on the wireless.

Jackie could always belt out Chopin's Military Polonaise or Waltz in A-flat Minor or his favourite Barcarole, and Gay had no trouble with Dvorak's Humoreske or Beethoven's "*Fur Elise*" or Minuet in G, but I mucked up the "British Grenadiers" and the next day Olive made me play it a hundred times while she sat and supervised.

Sometimes at these parties we had to recite poetry, and Mum would lead off with one about a woman who is going to give her sister a grand piano for her birthday and then slowly convinces herself she can give her something less, and less, and less expensive ..... until she ends up sending her "best regards".

Jackie used to recite a poem about a doctor who wouldn't give medicines that "taste like tar and smell like ink"—so that his patients would all be cheerful when he came—and Jackie said he wanted to be both a boxer and a doctor so he could treat his opponents after he knocked them out. Gay did one about "a little elfin man" who lived down behind the rose bush. And mine was about a brave warrior called

"Hopkins" who was made of special tin and kept his war paint bright—"he does his best to live at peace, he doesn't want to fight".

Which always made everyone laugh.

While the grown-ups stopped for tea and cakes we played games which involved not being able to see.

There was Blind Man's Bluff where one kid was blind-folded and turned around and around and then had to try to catch someone; Pin the Tail on the Donkey; and our favourite game, Dark Room, where all the kids hid in a room with the light off and curtains drawn and looked for each other. The only way to find someone was to touch them, so it was an exciting game to play with girls.

To cap off the party everyone sat in a circle around the lounge room and played "Billy Johnson's black pig with the dirty snout"..... which was what you had to say no matter what question anyone in the room chose to ask you.

If you laughed, you were out.

They could never get Jackie no matter what they asked him, but they always got me by asking: "Hughie, who are you in love with?"

9
Lunns for buns

I suppose it was because we hadn't had a shop for nearly two years, but everyone in the family thought the new shop—at 496 Ipswich Road—was even better than the first one.

It was only four shops, a laneway, and across Dudley Street from the last shop and, though it didn't have the tram stop outside, this time it had the bus stop: which Olive said was very important.

Fred liked it because it was a bigger shop and brand spanking new—the old broken-down shop that was there before had been shifted down into the back yard. Fred rented this new shop from the paint shop, which occupied the other half. The old shop out the back was used by the blacksmith, who removed the glass from the display windows and could be seen standing there in goggles, heating steel over charcoal fires and twisting it into things like horseshoes and branding irons. He must have made a lot of money doing this because he bought himself a big new black Ford car called a Customline. Like everyone, he was more interested in cars than horses and he used his skills to specially strengthen a car that the local policeman planned to drive in the Redex around-Australia reliability trial.

It was an exciting time as we got the glass display case out from under the house and cleaned it, while Fred washed the big black trays he cooked buns, scones and cakes on.

Olive said everything had to be done properly so that people knew the Lunns were back at Annerley Junction, and so a signwriter was hired to get up on a ladder and write on the front of the shop awning in big letters "Lunns for Buns".

Uncle Cyril, of course, was brought in to put up shelves

for the chocolates and to make three alcoves for customers who wanted sit-down meals in the shop. And Mum bought some nice new teapots for these tables very cheaply because they had been made for the royal visit. The teapots had a drawing of King George and Queen Elizabeth on one side and on the other they said "To commemorate the visit of the King and Queen to Australia 1952". But they didn't ever come because the King got sick and died. Mum was delighted with these teapots and loved to show them off with their mistake and say: "It would never have done for the Duke."

The funny thing is that no customers ever seemed to notice that the teapots they used commemorated a royal visit that never took place.

This new shop was even more fun because, now that I was nearly twelve, I could talk more to the adults in the shop. And, for the first time, when I went up to George Bellbooth's to get a haircut he didn't put a special leather-covered board across the arms of the barber's chair for me to sit up on to save him bending over when he cut my hair. And I started to get some of the jokes he told to the dozen men who seemed to have nothing else to do but sit along the bench that ran the length of the shop and listen to George and Stan talk all day while they cut hair. George was a fat happy man but I didn't like it when he said: "I see old Fred's back putting jam in tarts' holes again Hughie"—and all the men laughed.

Because we had the three alcoves, which were stained a dark tan, lots of lonely bachelors came into the shop for a pie and peas on a plate. But once Mum got to know them they usually got whatever she was cooking for us, unless it was tripe or chokos in white sauce, or a Friday when we kids had to have fish.

There were only a few types of vegetables in those days so we had carrots and beans, or pumpkin and peas to go with our potatoes. Sometimes Mum skited she cooked dinner for nineteen or twenty-one people, or whatever it was for the night, and occasionally we had a feast because Olive traded all the unsold pies and cakes with the pig man in return for a suckling pig.

She would put an apple in the pig's mouth and put it on a tray in the oven and everyone who knew us well got to eat some. The only trouble with these big dinner nights was that we kids usually had to do the washing or wiping up. Though I usually got out of it because I often landed the worst job of all: sorting the soft drink bottles.

All the soft drink manufacturers in Brisbane had their own wooden boxes with their name branded on the side, and they delivered glass bottles of all sizes in these—up to two dozen in each box, depending on the size of the bottle. Each morning Fred would take some of each soft drink out of the high piles of boxes against a wall near the entrance to the shop, and pack them in the fridge. As the bottles were drunk, or returned, they were just thrown in the nearest empty soft drink box and taken down and piled up underneath the shop—which was enclosed by battens a few inches apart. Then, each week, the "traveller"—as they called anyone who delivered goods regularly to the shop—would call to deliver new drinks and collect the boxes of old bottles so they could be washed and refilled at the factory. So somebody had to go under the shop and take all the bottles out of their mixed-up cases, sort all the empty boxes into various piles— Tristrams, Owen Gardiner, Cosgroves, Helidon, Cottees, Coke, Pepsi—and then go through and sort all the bottles into the right boxes.

Both bottles and boxes always said they "remained the property of" whichever soft drink company owned them.

It might sound simple, but it was only about three feet high under the shop and there was no light—and giant spiders loved to hide in among the bottles and would run up your arm when you picked up the empties. And you had to know, among other things, that Kirks bottles went into Owen Gardiner boxes.

It was a dark, dirty, dangerous and unrewarding job where no-one saw how hard you worked: not like Gay's job of making the butterfly cakes, where you just cut a piece off the top of a patty cake, put cream in, cut the top in two, whacked the two parts in the cream, and tipped icing sugar over the top and everyone said "Oh, aren't they beautiful Gay!"

To make it worse, many people left some soft drink in the bottom of their bottles, so every second time I tipped one upside down I got drenched with week-old Passiona or Creaming Soda that had lured a giant cocky to his death down the neck of the bottle.

This spilled drink, mixed with the dirt, made the ground muddy, so one day I decided to build a dam in the dirt and make a navy of paper boats to fight each other. It took dozens of buckets of water to do it—and it was hard to keep the water in—but it worked: except that the Tristrams traveller stomped all over the dam—and then complained to Fred who said the landlord had gone crook about the mess and so Fred had had to stop cooking and go and clean it up.

But at least Fred got to know what it was like being stuck under the shop in the dark while everyone else was upstairs smelling the hot buns and selling chocolates and listening to stories.

No-one was ever lonely at our shop.

Fred was teaching a tall Englishman called Maurice to be his assistant cook, and a woman he had worked with at the pie factory, Gladys—a glamorous blonde—came to serve the shop. Another lady who served the shop, Grace, was so nice that once she took Jackie and me over to spend the night at her house at Paddington.

Then there was Mary—a migrant from Lancashire, who constantly said "give over" in a musical voice—and, for a little while, her dainty married sister Elsie, who had some strange effect on me: I liked to watch her, talk to her, listen to her, stand near her behind the counter. She seemed to make me feel like I had never felt before: like I was floating around. It was such a nice feeling I knew it was bad, so I never told anyone.

I didn't think it was a sin, but I knew it wasn't far off.

A lot of army men came into the shop for a bite to eat because there was a Northern Command depot down the road, and we kids became friendly with a young fair-haired man called Sergeant-Major Bewly who marched around in a perfectly ironed army uniform and the most polished shoes I had ever seen. He took me and Jackie down to the depot and showed us some bullets and guns and even let us pretend to fire one.

We also got to know Mr Hunter, a nice man who lived alone in a small one-room shed behind a nearby shop. He had lost the bottom part of one leg in the War, and walked on a round piece of heavy iron to keep him level. And there was an Irish bachelor, George John Sloane Clark, who came in for a pie one night and stayed until after midnight—and then spent the night at our place.

He was a tall man with a big hooked nose and droopy eyes and an accent that was so soft it put me to sleep. He was another New Australian, who said he had come here to escape the Cold War in Europe.

Although he always said he was against war, Mr Clark told us lots of stories about the fighting in World War II and the many run-ins he had with the Germans while fighting for the British army, and he showed us the scars of two bullet holes in the side of his back—each the size of a halfpenny. He got hit trying to run across a clearing under fire from the Germans. This was one of his best stories—and he always drew diagrams on paper as he told it. But my favourite was about the cook who made him some sausage sandwiches for a trip on a motorbike, and it turned out they were fingers off a dead German.

Not all his stories were funny. He said that before they went to fight the Germans in Europe, the British soldiers were told the Germans only had wooden tanks. He insisted this was what they were told: but how could the government tell such big lies?

Another great mystery to me was that, although they had shot him, Mr Clark seemed to like the Germans. He had been stationed there after the War, and liked to go to the German Club in Brisbane and speak German. He was more worried about the Russians than the Germans and I used to hate it when he said no-one could beat the Russians in a war.

"But what if you had America, England and Australia and Germany," I would say, thinking of my bottletop armies lined up in order, while we sat in the alcoves late at night waiting for Fred to shut the shop. But no matter how many countries I put up against the Russians he would say, "No, Hughie, not enough."

Mr Clark said he had seen the Russians soldiers in action in Berlin and they were too tough and vicious for anyone else.

Like everyone else, Clarkie, as Mum called him, was worried because the Communists had done so well in Korea. One Australian soldier who had been there, and was now driving a Yellow taxi, told us over a pie one night that the Americans, of all people, ran from the Communists when he was in Korea. "It took us a week to take the hill and we handed it over to the Americans—and they beat us back to base camp," the taxi driver said. And he and Clarkie agreed that the Commos were slowly taking over the whole world.

Mr Clark, who—like everyone who worked in our shop or who came to stay at home—didn't drink, came into the shop for years and often stayed at our place for weeks at a time when he wasn't required by the air force, where he was an education officer. Unlike Mr Dyer and Mr Stewart, he seemed to favour me over the other kids. He bought me a special book of Grimms' scary fairytales which he would read out in his soft lilting Irish accent while we sat in the shop's back alcove, against the partition which hid the piles of flour bags and sugar bags. Often I wanted him to stop because the stories were so awful, but I didn't want to interrupt him because he seemed to be enjoying them so much himself, making the scary parts even more frightening by the way he read them.

When I couldn't do my arithmetic homework, Mr Clark would try to help but he seemed to make it much more complicated, though I was really impressed by the way he became so upset when I cried because I couldn't do it. That was the sort of bloke he was: always worried for the sake of us kids. "Mind the motors" was his favourite saying whenever we left the house or the shop.

And he put me in front of everyone else in the class by teaching me how to "take 45 from 45 and have 45 left". I even tricked the nuns with that one. This was done by writing down 9,8,7,6,5,4,3,2,1—which added up to 45. Then you wrote the same numbers in reverse order underneath. And when you subtracted them you got the same numbers again: which added up to 45.

Poor Fred never got to sit in the alcoves and talk to anyone. He was always in the kitchen cooking. Maybe that was why he didn't have any views on politics—and if a customer ever mentioned Liberal or Labor, Fred would say "What's that, I can't hear you" and hold his hand cupped to his left ear. But I knew he could hear them: he just wanted to stay out of trouble.

Mum always complained that he wouldn't even tell her how he voted at elections or even at the big "yes"—"no" votes like the one they had on banning the Communists, and every footpath and wall on the way to the convent had a YES or a NO painted on it by someone.

But I wouldn't mind betting Fred voted for the Commos because everyone was against them. Fred didn't mind telling lies though. People were always coming into the shop to ask the time because they couldn't afford watches and didn't know when the next bus to Tarragindi or Wellers Hill or Moorooka was due outside our shop. I knew they couldn't afford watches because in the Christmas school holidays I got a job cleaning the windows of Mr Quinn's jewellery shop across the laneway for seven shillings and six a week, and he got me to mind the shop sometimes when he had to go out. Even the cheapest watches cost over seven pounds—which was a week's wages for most men—and so hardly anyone ever came into the jewellery shop. Anyway, Fred was so sick of people asking the time that he told everyone it was "half past"—no matter what the time really was. And they always seemed to believe him. Fred said it was never far from half past anyway.

In other ways, though, Fred always put the customer first.

Olive struggled all the time to get him to agree to put prices up: particularly the pies because she said we were losing money selling them at threepence each. But he always argued against it. Once Fred cut a piece of rainbow cake for a customer to have with a cup of tea, and Olive—shocked to see how big it was—rushed over and grabbed it from off the table before the customer could take a bite and weighed it and found that the piece weighed half a pound.

So it was lucky that Fred hardly ever served customers— unless there was no-one else around. Then he would pick up the bottom right hand corner of his apron and fold it across into the waist string on the left-hand side, in order to present a clean front to the customer.

Keeping the cake shop clean was always one of Fred and Olive's major tasks, apart from doing the books. The way Fred mixed the flour, milk, eggs and sugar by hand on the big wooden bench meant that sticky bits of flour inevitably found their way onto his apron—and from there onto the floor, where they stuck like glue. Particularly when other liquids also got spilt. Like the yellow milky mixture we dipped the pie tops into before fitting them over the meat. This mixture helped stick the pies together and made the top go shiny and hard and brown when cooked. And there was the sticky honey mixture Fred painted the top of the buns with, when they came out of the oven, to make them shiny, not to mention the big daubs of cream that fell off the side of the buns when the tops were slit, and cream and icing sugar applied to make them into cream buns.

Thus, each night someone had the job of scraping these flat round blobs of dirty dough off the floor. And not just in the kitchen, because they were invariably walked out past the flour bags and the sink into the shop itself.

To do this, Fred had a special scraper like a flat hoe on the end of a wooden handle.

I suppose, because it was a little bit like lawn mowing, this job increasingly fell to me, particularly after Fred bought a machine to roll the pastry. It had a handle and two rollers like the top of a washing machine. This meant the pastry for the pie bottoms and pie tops—each was a different mixture—could be rolled without wielding a big metal roller, and so Jackie got the job of making the pastry, while Gay helped Mum take the cakes out of the two shopfront windows.

Now that I was nearly a teenager, I was learning more and more about working in a cake shop, and even helping

Jackie make the pastry, though I avoided serving the shop whenever possible.

Making pies was easy, so easy that Kenny Fletcher used to beg his father to let him come down and help us cut the bottoms and tops out of the big sheets of pastry rolled out by Fred to the right thicknesses. Fred used to be really puffing by the time he did this, because the pastry was hard since it was kept in the fridge after it was made. So he would let us get his big silver steel chopper and hit it into the pastry and cut out the bottoms or tops.

The worst job was cleaning the little round pie trays before the bottoms were placed in. Because he bought proper mince from the local butcher for his pies, and didn't thicken them with things like cornflour as other shops did, Fred's pies always overflowed with meat when they were cooked, and this stuck to the silver trays and had to be removed before re-use.

To scrape this burnt meat away, Fred had a small knife whose blade had almost been sharpened away. This knife was also used, after the pie top was applied, to cut the overlapping pastry edges off by holding the knife hard against the edge of the pie tin and turning the pie around against it. Then two holes were poked in the pie top to allow hot meat out when it was being cooked.

The pie meat was cooked in a huge saucepan on a gas ring and it bubbled and popped until Fred said we could start scooping it with a large spoon onto the pie bottoms. But you had to beware of trays just out of the oven. Sometimes Fred had to take out all four trays at once and he would spread them around the kitchen. One day I backed into one and got a big burn across the back of my leg. Olive put butter on it and gave me a Bex. She was a great believer in Bex, and they certainly fixed the headaches I used to get at the pictures on a Saturday afternoon.

Making buns at the "Lunns for Buns" shop was the hardest job to learn.

After Fred had made the thick white bubble of mixture, which was to be cut up and made into buns, he covered it with a flour bag to keep it warm so the yeast would make it grow into a doughy mass double its original size. Then we would cut off large hunks and weigh them to make sure they were eight ounces each.

These hunks would be divided into four, and each of these would be hand-rolled into a bun.

It looked simple enough: one piece of the soft white stuff was placed in the palm of each hand, the wooden table was sprinkled with flour, and the mixture was rolled into two round balls between the fingers and the table, and they were placed neatly in rows on a big black oven tray. Fred could churn these perfect little white balls out as fast as I could cut the eight-ounce pieces off—but every time I tried it I ended up with my hands stuck to the table by a mess of glue which oozed up through the tops of my fingers.

But I had to learn.

Buns were one of our biggest items, and one day each year—Holy Thursday—we used to make and sell more than 450 dozen buns in our shop: hot cross buns.

Jackie and me always got this day off school because the shop needed every bun-roller it could find. And, eventually, I learned that the mixture could only be touched very lightly when being rolled, and that the palm had to be rubbed rapidly across the bun in a circular motion many times before it would form.

Mum said that after hot cross bun day, Fred would roll buns in his sleep for the next few nights.

It was on one of these hot cross bun days that I began to see how the world of business really worked: and I didn't like it. At school we were taught that everything was supposed to be fair, but it wasn't very fair in the shops.

After the buns were rolled they were compact and quite small, about the size of a scone. But they contained yeast and, if put in a warm possie, like on top of the oven, they would slowly grow bigger over a couple of hours. Meanwhile, Fred made up a special mixture in grease-proof paper and put crosses on all the buns before putting them in the oven. Thus, on hot cross bun day, we had to get to the shop by 3 a.m. and start opening the big hessian bags of flour and sugar, and the cube-shaped plywood boxes of margarine, if we were to have plenty of buns ready for when the shop opened at eight. Jackie and I could carry the sugar bags, which weighed 70 pounds, but had to leave the 110-pound flour bags to Fred.

The trouble was that, soon after we opened this shop, a new type of shop opened up the road. A type of shop people said had been successful in America—one where customers went and took everything off the shelves themselves and paid on the way out.

It was a giant shop, halfway between our shop and Kenny Fletcher's house, and was called "the BCC"—which stood for "Brisbane Cash and Carry". And one hot cross bun day they suddenly started selling hot cross buns, and much more cheaply than ours.

Our buns were three shillings and sixpence a dozen and they started selling them for three shillings: but still we couldn't keep up with the customers waiting for our buns to come out of the oven, four trays at a time—each black tray carrying probably eight dozen buns. So at least thirty customers could be supplied by each oven-full.

But, by the afternoon, demand fell off—and for the first time in history we had trays of buns everywhere: so many, in fact, that the shop was invaded by scores of bees heading for the honey mixture painted on the bun tops to make them shine. And everyone who bought a dozen buns got at least one bee.

I went up to the BCC and bought a dozen of theirs, and I found that they were now selling them for one and sixpence a dozen, and lots of our customers were now buying from there. Dad ripped off four buns and weighed them and I was amazed to see that together they weighed only six ounces. Yet they were as big as ours. Fred, as he usually did with food he hadn't made himself, ripped one open and stuck his nose in it. "They made them yesterday and let them proof for hours so that they rose like bigger buns," he said.

So I had an idea.

I got a Pepsi blackboard we had for writing signs on, and got some chalk and made a sign I put at the entrance to the shop: "Two-ounce buns; not one-and-a-half-ounce ones".

Then Jim Egoroff turned up to help us. Fred called him "egg rock", but he didn't seem to mind. Jim had a great idea which we wrote on another Pepsi blackboard: "Lunn's buns give you the runs .... to our shop". The customers loved it because I saw them all laughing outside, but Olive was furious when she read the sign that night.

Except for hot cross bun day, Friday night was always the busiest time preparing cakes, because everyone went shopping Saturday morning in Annerley Junction and you couldn't move for people.

One of the jobs we kids had on Friday night was to make the lamingtons. Mum prepared a large round dish of liquid chocolate while we filled a square dish of equal size with desiccated coconut. Fred would cook large trays of flat sponge and these were cut into scores of little squares. Some of these were dropped into the chocolate and then lifted out with a wire scoop onto a wire drainer and, when they were no longer dripping chocolate, were rolled in the coconut while more squares were being soaked.

We kids made particularly good lamingtons because we left them so long in the chocolate that it soaked right through the sponge. By the time everything was ready for the Saturday morning rush it was always midnight, and Gay would be asleep in her blue school uniform on top of the flour bags.

On Saturday morning customers were three deep in our shop until midday. Outside on the footpath, under the awnings, were large raffle wheels and lucky tickets, with men standing next to a table covered in goodies, calling out to the passing crowds "one-shilling-a-ticket-a-pick-of-the-table". At Christmas, there'd be lucky dips outside the newsagency in a big bottomless box.

We kids were lucky that we couldn't work in the shop on most Saturday mornings because we had to go to our dancing lessons in the RSL Hall next to the Annerley Theatre. But learning tap-dancing was only slightly preferable to sorting bottles or serving the shop. I always had trouble keeping time, even with the teachers Dawn or Robyn screaming into my ear as we practised for our concerts: "One and two and, one and two and, throw-away, throw-away, stamp, shuffle, hop, side, back, shuffle, reverse...."

There was a lot more to tap-dancing than meets the eye.

The whole idea was to learn a complicated series of little steps, to make the aluminium taps on the bottom of your shoes hit the floor in different ways, and then to string them all together in a set order to a tune, so that it looked like you were dancing to the music.

About eight boys and sixty girls learned ballet and tap-dancing, and they overflowed in the RSL Hall—with sequins and tu tus, slippers and tap shoes all over the place, and everyone struggling for a space to dance on the polished floor, with a dozen girls staggering around looking ridiculous trying to walk on their toes in special shoes.

Each year Dawn and Robyn prepared everyone for a massive concert at the Rialto or the Cremorne which was always a sell-out—and everyone had to get a part. For six months the mothers made exotic costumes of lace and net and satin and sequins for the girls, and white or black satin top-hats and tails for the boys. Dawn and Robyn devised the dances and tried to teach us how to do them. I always rehearsed in a mass dance of boys but could never keep time, and ended up having to dance by myself so that there was no-one to get out of time with.

This was a bit of a lucky break because, while all the other boys had to dance together, I got to dance on my own. Dances like the Sailor's Hornpipe and then—the highlight of my career—"The Hit and Two Misses" where, in white top-hats and tails, I danced with Cheryl Ackworth on one arm and Gloria Juxson on the other. The dance was to the tune of "Honey Hush" and was cleverly re-devised by Dawn so that I hardly danced with them at all: they would dance off without me and stop and bend over and lean on their knees and look back at me—and I would come tapping and shuffling and throwing-away after them, only to see them move off again. But, by the end of the dance, they were in my arms.

That was when I first fell in love. Cheryl lived at Greenslopes and was a beautiful wavy-haired brunette. For the first time in my life, I looked forward to going to dancing just to see her. But I only saw her once a week and, after the concert, she never came back to dancing lessons.

But there were plenty of girls around Annerley, and Fletch and I started to befriend some of them. At first they were our sworn enemies, and we rode into battle against them like the grey coats against the blue coats. We called ourselves "bottletop Lunn and bottletop Fletcher", and we carried hundreds of bottletops from Fred's shop and exchanged fire with the local girls, pinging bottletops at them whenever we found them. Mum used to call Kenny the Scarlet Pimpernel because she said no sooner had she shoved him out one door than he would re-appear through another.

Kenny was becoming a very confident boy because he was such a good tennis player that grown men used to come to his court to play him. Whenever Kenny won a championship his father would come down to the shop with a milk bottle, place it on the fridge, wait until the shop was full, and say: "How are the boys, Mrs Lunn?" And Mum would have to ask "How is Ken?" .... and Mr Fletcher would then skite about Ken's win. One day he told us of a married man who arrived to play a championship final and asked where his opponent was, and Mr Fletcher had to tell him: "That's him down playing on the swing." But no matter how good Kenny was at tennis, he used to complain that Jackie won all his marbles from him when they played in the dirt of the tennis court.

Kenny had made up a poem which showed how tough he had become: "There was a young fella named Fletcher, who said to a boxer I betcha, I can knock off your nose, in one or two goes, and the boxer went off on a stretcher." But although he must have been good at tennis, Kenny was hopeless at remembering the words of songs. The biggest hit tune was "Davy Crockett" and it was on the wireless so much that we all knew the words. But Kenny had to keep asking me to tell him the words after the first part: "Born on a mountaintop in Tennessee, greenest place in the Land of the Free" .... which we sang as "Born on a tabletop in Joe's cafe, filthiest place in the USA". In our version Davy "shot his father with a .303, and blew up his mother with TNT".

Then one day my attitude to the girls we fought with bottletops changed.

It was the day Mum bought me a new pair of trousers that had just come out called jeans, and I wore them with my scout belt and buckle to the shop and, as I was passing the honeysuckle-covered fence behind the barber's shop residence, Esland Heath whistled me.

That week we all started to play together in the late afternoon on the lawn behind the newsagency. We were joined by a blonde girl called Helen who lived in a small flat with her mother on top of the newsagency. We all played until after dark, but not this girl: as soon as the sun went down, her mother stood at the high window and blew a whistle, and it was time for Helen to go home.

We started out playing "no time for standing" where anyone standing up was pulled off their feet onto the lawn and, eventually, we started playing spin-the-bottle after dark.

It was such a big thrill to be allowed to kiss these girls that I never really enjoyed it because I was afraid of being caught, or that they wouldn't like it, or of committing a sin. Particularly when they agreed to Kenny's idea of going around behind the blacksmith's shop for the kiss. It all smacked of the Devil offering us pleasure in the dark. And, although no grown-ups could see me, I knew God and the saints and the angels could see everything: and holding girls close to me, between the fence and the old shop, led to strange sensations which were no doubt impure, and I began to understand why the church put so much emphasis on "the flesh" when talking of impure actions.

This was obviously the sort of infinite pleasure saints died to avoid.

So I avoided spin-the-bottle and instead invented a new game, of which I was very proud. A game I called "CAK"— which stood for "catch and kiss". In this game you chased the girls and if you caught them you could give them a kiss.

It was more like a game, and so much like tiggy or brandy that the kisses were brief, and exhausted, and public.

The threat of soft girls in the dark had been removed, and I was much happier for it.

10
Dima and the
three-legged giant

Sitting next to Egoroff at our twin desk with lift-up lids
proved to be not such a bad idea after all.

There were, of course, lots of disadvantages. He often
smelled of garlic, particularly in summer when the classroom
was so hot that I was in danger of dying of thirst at the
desk and the sweat from my writing arm mixed with the
ink on my pad. And Dima was so aggressive that, sooner
or later, everyone had to fight him: including even me.

He had an iron grip, and I knew that once he got hold
of me I was a goner so, as we wrestled at our desk while
Sister Veronica was out of the room, I reached out and picked
up my pencil and thrust it into his leg. To my surprise it
went straight in like a straw into a sponge cake and he let
go immediately.

Sister Veronica rushed in as if Dima had just been run
over by a car and started treating his leg and she warned
me gravely that he might die of lead poisoning. I spent that
night terrified that I might have committed the sin of murder.
But the next day my prayers were answered when he turned
up for school the same as ever. He didn't even say anything
about the pencil incident. From then on it didn't seem to
matter that he was a Russian Commo. At least Jim wasn't
a goody goody like most of the other boys who were too
frightened to do a bit of cheating in class. Egoroff was more
than willing to help you get a reasonable score in a test.

The system adopted by the nuns was that all class tests
were corrected by the person sitting next to you. And Jim
was having as much trouble with the English language as
I was. We both needed some help.

At first, after exchanging exercise books for correction, we tried to write in the correct answer for each other as the nun read out the answers: while appearing to be making a tick. But this was difficult to do quickly and it was too obvious that someone had been tampering with the answers: especially as Jim's handwriting was much neater than mine. So Jim suggested that we leave a space when we didn't know the answer. He would tick my spaces, and I'd tick his, and, when we got our own exercise books back, we could quickly write the answers in ourselves.

Of course we never did it with all the answers. We weren't cheating to finish ahead of others in the class or for any personal gain. That would have been a sin. We would never cheat in a big, proper examination like State Scholarship where it really mattered. We just wanted to get enough answers right to survive at school without too much trouble.

Four or five out of ten was plenty for us. It was better than getting one or none. Anyway, any more than six and the nuns would have become suspicious.

Jim and I also teamed up in the playground.

Like me, he was not a fast runner, though neither of us was slow. In fact we ran at a similar speed. So we decided to try to win the boys' three-legged race at the school sports. It was not an event that boys were good at and Jim told me he thought we could win if we practised. I said I would run with him, but only if he promised not to eat garlic on the days we were running. He agreed.

Using a hanky to tie one of his ankles to one of mine we practised up and down the big boys playground.

At first I started on the right, probably because I sat on his right in class. But with his powerful right leg tied to my weak left leg it didn't work. Every time we got even slightly out of step we ended up in the dirt, and crashing to the hard dry ground with Jim was like falling down with a house stump tied to your leg.

It was smoother with Jim on my right.

After weeks of experiment we found that the hanky had to be tied really tightly, and that the closer we could get to each other the less likely we were to crash. So we each had to bind an arm tightly around the other's shoulder, push off hard with our free leg so that our mutual leg took the first step, and then rely totally on an ability to run at the same speed as we careered across the grassless playground.

It was no use counting or saying "left right, left right" or any other system. There just wasn't time. If we were to travel at top speed then we had to act, run, and think as one.

The other boys thought we were crazy.

The good runners believed that they would beat us anyway with their superior speed. And the non-athletes like big Sam Aherne or studious Terry Callaghan wondered why we bothered with such an obscure event.

Well weren't they all surprised at the sports when Jim and I swooped across the ground right from the word go.

I couldn't believe myself how fast we were travelling. I felt a confidence and strength I had not known before as we hurtled like a mythical three-legged giant towards the finish. I was sure I had never run so fast in my life. The faster Jim went, the faster I had to go. And the more power he found, the more I had to find.

We won easily.

It is hard to explain how great I felt. It was the first time I had ever won anything. It seemed like a miracle to be able to beat all those fast runners like Kevin Hailey and Ray Halloran. I thanked God, Saint Anthony, and Our Lady and again prayed to them to intercede and help me pass State Scholarship.

Passing was the name of the game at the convent. It was the only thing the nuns ever talked about, besides religion. It was so important to pass piano exams that Sister Leonora made me practise before exams, sitting next to me with a ruler in her hand as a warning to keep my wrists up: you lost marks, it was said, if you let them droop. She wouldn't let me do a music theory exam until I had scored 100 per cent in a past paper, which meant I had to do six or seven exams in a row up on the nuns' house verandah, next to the two piano rooms. The exams were all about crochets and quavers and demi-semi-quavers, and it was just like learning lists of feast days and saints and indulgences.

But much more important than music exams, or even religion exams, was preparing for the biggest exam of them all: "State Scholarship", an exam unique in Australia. Everyone in Queensland under the age of fourteen—even the State School kids—did Scholarship to see who could go on to secondary school.

It was an exam everyone called "the stumbling block".

Personally, I didn't mind if I didn't even do the exam at all. Secondary school meant nothing to me and there was no way I was staying at school one week longer than I had to. Everyone had to stay at school until State Scholarship: then all those who failed could leave school forever.

That meant—out to work, where I would buy one of those big square two-bob Nestle's chocolates every day. No more embarrassing dreams of turning up in our class at the convent in my pyjamas.

I saw in the paper that men were earning seven pounds a week, which would buy seventy two-bob chocolates. Not that you would ever want that many, but it just showed you what you could do. And I saw advertisements in the paper with drawings of men in suits going off to work, and when I day-dreamed in class—as I did a lot of the time by just letting one eye drift slightly to the side so everything was out of focus—that was how I saw myself.

Sorry Mum, but I just didn't have the brains to stay on. So it was out to work for me, straight after Scholarship.

Anyway, I wasn't going to have much choice.

Scholarship was famous for being incredibly hard, with 40 per cent of kids failing.

Mr Clark, the Irishman, was disgusted to see how difficult it was and—after I showed him the past papers—he reckoned it was an exam set to stop Queensland children from going on to secondary school so the government didn't have to build more high schools.

The exam had been going for eighty years—since 1874 when the kids were asked: "Give the meaning of the Latin roots *ira*, *plus*, *spondeo*, and give three English derivatives from each of them. And name the auxiliary verbs, and exemplify by the verb 'seek', the use of the auxiliaries of voice, mood and tense."

The fact was that most of the things you had to do were things I was just no good at.

I couldn't remember too much history, and Sister Vincent showed us a 1913 question which said: "Tell the story of the following: the Capture of Quebec, the Relief of Lucknow, and the boyhood of King George V."

My sums weren't the best either, and the two-hour Scholarship arithmetic paper was always full of sums that Mum and Dad would have had no hope of doing. "A sheep station has an area of 30,000 acres of which 3% is not available for grazing. The carrying capacity of the remaining area is 1 sheep to 4 acres. If the average fleece weighs 8lbs, the average price of wool is 79.4d. per lb, and shearing costs 9 pounds per 100 sheep, what will be left of the gross return for the wool clip after the cost of shearing is deducted?"

What did I know about sheep, except that they ate grass?

"Social Studies" was a new exam—a combination of the old history and geography exams—and was mostly learning off the dates of famous English war victories.

The English exam was full of questions asking you to analyse sentences by "classifying clauses"—whether they were "nominative" or "possessive" case or something else; and parsing words, which meant saying if they were a preposition, a participle, an adverb, an adjective, or a dozen other things.

If it hadn't been for Dima I would have never scored anything for Latin roots or suffixes or prefixes in class. But he couldn't help me in State Scholarship: the nuns said we would be put in a big room to do the exams at seats by ourselves, and people would be paid to walk around and watch the whole time to see that we didn't cheat.

Prayer was becoming less and less of a possibility.

"Ask and you shall receive; seek and you shall find; knock and it shall be opened to you" was quoted by every priest and nun who ever gave us a talk. But I wasn't exactly in a good position to start asking favours of God or the saints. Or even of Our Lady, whom I now knew by perhaps fifty different titles: virgin most faithful, mirror of justice, seat of wisdom, spiritual vessel, mystical rose, tower of ivory, ark of the covenant, gate of heaven, refuge of sinners, help of Christians, Queen of angels, lamb of God, among many others. She would have been the person to help me: by praying to the picture of Our Lady of Perpetual Succour.

The nuns had taught us that this was one of the best ways to get help for something you wanted, and there were even special prayers you could say to her like: "Remember Oh most loving Virgin Mary that never was it known in any age that anyone who fled to your protection, implored your aid, or sought your intercession was left unaided.... do not, Oh Mother of the Word Incarnate, despise our prayers, but graciously hear and grant them, Amen."

But I couldn't really go to the Blessed Virgin for help. While everyone else was going around being pure, my whole life seemed to revolve around impure thoughts. It was not that I wanted them, they just seemed to keep cropping up: as if the Devil had specially chosen me as an easy target. A weak person.

We had to study a book called *Sea Change* and I found this book under the house called *Sea Chase* which was very different from our set book. It described a man cuddling up to a woman in a very sinful manner, touching her, and enjoying it. Behind the shop I stumbled across a picture of a partly nude woman looking into a mirror, and when the priests warned against "sins of the flesh" I thought of her, or a woman one of the foreign legionnaires had a wrestle with in a paperback book Jackie had bought.

When the nuns talked of purity I thought of Elsie behind the shop counter, but, instead of feeling holy, I felt intense pleasure and excitement which grew and grew with every thought.

So much so that, had I been bad, I might have indulged in impure actions. I was so bad I even felt good looking at the nail-polish advertisements in the *Women's Weekly* and, though they were just black and white drawings of a woman's hand with long painted nails, I cut them out. But at least I was smart: I told everyone I was against women wearing nail polish.

Sin was a complex business.

You could, we were taught, sin by "thought, word, deed, or even omission". A prayer book at school contained "short tables of sins" to remind us. "Have you doubted in matters of faith? .... believed in fortune tellers? .... taken the name thy God in vain? .... spoken irreverently of holy things? .... been wilfully distracted in time of Mass? .... have you ignored your parents, superiors, masters according to your just duty? .... borne hatred? .... have you been guilty of lascivious dressing, lewd company, unchaste songs, discourses, words, looks or actions by yourself or with others? Have you wilfully entertained impure thoughts or desires?"

Even "looks" were listed as sins. It was almost as if we were expected to sin. Yet I couldn't imagine girls sinning. At least not all the goody goodies in our class. And I couldn't imagine Fred or Olive sinning, or Pa and grandma. Yet all Catholics had to go to confession at least once a year, under the commandments of the church.

I could not be the only sinner because prayer books contained lots of prayers especially written for sinners to accuse themselves: "O Lord my God, thou unfathomable abyss of compassion, my sins are greater in number than the sands upon the seashore, and I am not worthy to lift my eyes towards thee. My soul is a loathsome sink of iniquities. Within me reigns unchecked pride, vain-glory and all kinds of evil. What shall I do, wretch that I am?"

Before confession was a time to "examine your conscience" as you waited in queue to confess your sins and receive your penance.

One prayer we learnt by heart called on Our Lord: "Blot out all my iniquities. Wash me yet more from my iniquities and cleanse me from my sins. I am resolved by Thy grace never more to turn to my sins. Oh rather let me die than offend Thee wilfully any more. I am resolved to avoid all evil company and dangerous occasions."

"Dangerous occasions" were often mentioned in religion periods, but never explained, though it was obvious they were not talking about watching the motors on Ipswich Road. The girl in the mirror in the book behind the shop was a dangerous occasion, I guessed.

"Evil company" I used to think involved people like Dima Egoroff or Johnny Dunn, but now that I had made it into Scholarship I began to understand that it had to do with girls. In fact almost all sins seemed to involve boys looking at, touching, or just thinking about girls.

Even babies were sinners, because we Catholics were all "conceived with original sin". "Original Sin" had to do with a girl called Eve tempting Adam to sin with an apple. It was something that was very hard to understand but which I began to realise had something to do with being born wanting to touch Eve's apple. Only baptism restored sanctifying grace and meant we could have a chance to go to Heaven.

I didn't mind being a sinner—it was sort of similiar to failing tests at school. What I didn't like was someone else knowing about it. Not only did you have to tell the priest that you did something bad, but you had to tell him how many times. And, during a holy period I went through, I feared that my estimates were always way short of reality and thus I might not really be receiving Absolution and thus committing a Sacrilege: the biggest sin of all.

When I asked a priest about this in confession he got very upset and, instead of facing away from me with his hand partially over his face, he turned front-on through the small wire grate and said he would have to see my parents. But I don't think he did, because they never ever said anything.

No wonder they called our life on earth "this vale of tears" in prayers, and talked about "suffer the little children". But at least the church acknowledged that it was hard to be good: "It is hard to be good because of our fallen nature and the Devil" said an answer in the Catechism.

So how could I think of school work, with my fallen nature and the Devil putting all these evil thoughts in my head every time I examined my conscience?

The only way I was ever going to pass State Scholarship was by a miracle.

I started to enjoy thinking how wonderful it would be if suddenly I became so good that I could go into confession and say to the priest: "It is just a week since my last confession father ... and I have no sins to report." And what if at the same time I also became one of the smartest kids in the class?

I spent more and more of my time imagining that one night God or Saint Anthony had arranged for a thick black scum—which had been covering my brain, stopping me from learning and being good—to be lifted off like a pie top to expose the meat. Suddenly I would know all the answers: and everyone would admire me in class. Mum would be really happy and boast about me to the relatives. Not only would I be top of the class every year and score 100 per cent in every exam but I would help teach the dumb kids in the class to pass.

The removal of the black scum would also make me much more athletic—and suddenly I would be able to run faster than anyone else in the school. No more three-legged races for me. And, instead of being weak, I was suddenly tall, muscled, and fast.

I wouldn't bash people up. I wouldn't have to—no-one would ever be game to fight me because I would be so strong and intelligent.

Boy, wouldn't everyone be surprised. Particularly Jackie and Gay.

I wouldn't tell anyone at school. I would act dumb until State Scholarship where I would suddenly finish top of the state and win the Lilley Medal and save face for Dad's cake shop, since Perry Ganis up the road had won the medal the previous year. And when Egoroff grabbed me in his vice grip I would gently force his fingers apart with my left hand as if he were letting me do it.

On the way home from school I would confidently lecture the State School kids on their evil ways, knowing that I could handle any situation if they were silly enough to actually let it arise. Esland would admire me and want me to take her to the pictures.

But it wasn't going to happen.

Which was why my whole world always started to disintegrate every Sunday afternoon as it started to get dark. The only thing left then was tea, bed, and a week of school. And no homework done.

No wonder I was late for school every morning. And no wonder I used to try to talk Mum into letting me stay home sick. But she used to chase me out of the house, still hoping I would learn something. And I hadn't seen Esland for months.

The only good thing about being in Scholarship was that we finally got to learn about Horatius, which was one of the poems in the Scholarship Reader we had to study.

This was a hardcovered brown book of more than two hundred pages, published just before World War II and full of good stories and poems, but far too many for one person to read: more than sixty. My favourite poems were Horatius, and "The Saxon and the Gael" where the King of Scotland fought the Highland chieftain Roderick Dhu in a "dreadful close" and killed him. I got great pleasure out of looking at the colour picture of Horatius with his shield and sword and an anguished look on his face as he stared at "thrice thirty thousand foes" before him and the broad flood behind. And for some reason I couldn't understand, I savoured the caption under the photo which said merely: "keeping the bridge".

I liked these poems because I could understand them, unlike the poems "To a Skylark" and "Elegy Written in a Country Churchyard" and "Mark Antony's Oration". Our School Reader said that if these poems were all learned by heart they would be a joy forever and that the stories would "afford a compendium of beautiful thoughts". But the only one I could be bothered learning off by heart was "Horatius Defends the Bridge".

There were also some interesting stories, like the one about this foreign woman called Madame Curie who made a wonderful discovery which, our Reader said, could unlock the secret "of how to get all the power from the atoms to do man's work", which would lead to a whole new world. Her discovery was something called "radium" and the Reader said: "The great thing about radium, besides its tremendous power, is that every ounce that is added to what we already have is pure gain, for the metal will last almost for ever. It will continue to give off light and heat for sixteen hundred years, and, even then, it will still be half as powerful as at the start."

It sounded like something only God could invent; like a fire that never went out.

Or only half went out.

The funny thing was that, even though Scholarship was so important, we still spent nearly an hour every day learning more and more about the Holy Catholic church. Which seemed a waste of time to me because the nuns said that not only would there be no religion questions on any of the Scholarship papers, but not to use any of this information in our compositions.

I suppose I wasn't all that interested in religious lessons because we weren't a very religious family. We never prayed, even though the answer to the question "when should we pray?" in the Catechism was "Every morning and every night and frequently during the day". That was why you had to know the prayers off by heart. We didn't say prayers before bed or even grace before meals like most Catholics. We didn't even say the family rosary—which was said to be wonderful for the "destruction of sin" and was highly recommended on the basis that "the family that prays together stays together". But it took at least twenty minutes to say, going as fast as you could, and we were always at the shop until late. You couldn't say prayers in a shop.

While most Catholic families went to Mass on week mornings as well as Sunday, we (with the exception of Jackie when he was altar boy) only went on Sunday because it was a mortal sin if you didn't "keep holy the sabbath day".

So many people went to Mary Immaculate church on a Sunday that, while there was only one Mass on other days, there were four Masses on a Sunday morning—6 a.m., 7 a.m., 8.30, and 10 a.m. to fit all the people in. Going to the 10 a.m. Mass was considered a sign of laziness: but we were flat-out making that on time, which was why Mum always called us "the last minute Lunns".

Entering the church late was always embarrassing because usually the only vacant seats were right up the front, and the priests in their Sunday sermon from the pulpit often

129

criticised late-comers. But it was no use hanging around on the steps outside, as some late-comers did, because once I saw the priest run down the aisle from the pulpit shouting at them and telling them face-to-face to get inside. What he didn't know was that if you hung around outside you could leave early.

There were three parts of the Mass which you had to be there for to be deemed to have attended—and you could do this by arriving fifteen minutes late and leaving ten minutes early: thus cutting a fifty-minute Mass to twenty-five minutes.

But even then you didn't miss the two collections, when the holiest men stood up and passed the plate around. The first collection was for the church and the second for the priest—this plate always had much less money on, probably because the priest knew everyone's sins. Some people put ten-bob notes on, and when Fred came I couldn't believe it because he would always put a two-bob bit on the round wooden plate with its green velvet surface—a whole two-bob chocolate.

In the end we even stopped going to Mary Immaculate for Sunday Mass because Mum found out that St Stephen's Cathedral in town had a Mass at 6.30 p.m. on a Sunday, which suited us down to the ground now that Fred had bought a brand new 1954 Ford Zephyr to replace the old Hillman. There was plenty of room for all of us in the Zephyr and it had a wireless so that we could listen to the "top eight" hit parade which was on every Sunday night at six on the way into town and find out what was number one before we arrived. Great songs like Doris Day singing "Secret Love" and the Stargazers with "I See the Moon".

There were only really two cars to choose from—unless you wanted to buy an English Austin—and we bought a Zephyr Six even though everyone said we should have bought one of those new FJ Holdens. A relative told us the Holden was too light in the rear and was only good with a bag of sand in the boot. And Fred liked the better view he got of the road in the Zephyr and Jack and I liked the fact that it had a push-button starter and a silver aeroplane riding the bonnet at the front.

The whole family agreed on the Zephyr, including Gay, and we ordered a buff tan one with red upholstery, but couldn't get buff tan and had to make do with a cream colour. We decided to get a wireless put in it as part of the price Dad would have to pay off, because the man said if we didn't get one then, we would probably never be able to afford one. The rego number was Q 652 159.

Jackie and Neil from next door and I did a lot of research and when we used to walk over to Logan Road to watch the Redex cars go through, covered in dirt and rally numbers, we used to see how many Holdens or Zephyrs we could count. I was always disappointed that the Zephyrs didn't win.

Even though we weren't religious, I learnt that we had to go to the convent because, as well as God's Ten Commandments, there were seven other commandments: the "Commandments of the Church", and one of these was "to send Catholic children to Catholic schools". Which was why, the nuns said, the Archbishop was trying to build so many Catholic schools that no-one would be forced to go to a state school.

The idea was to have these Catholic schools within fifteen minutes walk of every house in Brisbane.

State schools, it turned out, were supplied free to all the non-Catholics, while we had to pay for our schools. Mum paid one shilling and sixpence a week for each of us, plus extra for music. Some people, the nuns said, argued that if Catholics wanted their own special schools then they should be happy to pay for them. But they told us the answer to that one, if we heard it, was to say: "If we closed all the Catholic schools tomorrow there wouldn't be enough schools to take all the children."

Anyway, the nuns said, the best way to ensure we passed Scholarship was for us to go to a Catholic school. They would make sure we passed, because they cared about our future. Plus they would teach us about our religion.

One of the things I had to learn in Scholarship was how to ring the Angelus at noon, a job I enjoyed. It meant you got out of class and it was really exciting to be able to grab the giant rope that hung from the brick bell-tower and pull it down as hard as you could to make a loud gong that could be heard over most of Annerley. Getting it right was the hard part. You had to ring it three times and pause, three times again, then three times again, and nine times in succession: and every Catholic who could hear it would have to stop and bow their head and think of Christ's birth.

It wasn't as good as being an altar boy and ringing secret little groups of bells and swinging burning incense in a thurible during the Eucharist, which filled the church with a heavy sickly smell I didn't like. Or putting out the rows of sloping candles with a long stick with a cup at the end, which gave me something interesting to watch because so often the altar boys had trouble putting the candles out.

Altar boys got to go places even the nuns couldn't go: like up on the altar during Mass. In many ways they were more important than nuns. They could go into the sacristy where the priest prepared his vestments—chasuble, alb, amice—for Mass: the colour used depending on the day, for example red on feast days for martyrs and purple during Lent and black for All Souls' Day. And the altar boys got out the sacred vessels—the chalice, the paten, the ciborium. And they got to see the piece of cloth called a "purifactor" up close and the wafers that were to become the body of Christ, and they couldn't help but glimpse inside the gold tabernacle, like a small toy yellow cathedral, in the middle of the altar where the blessed sacrament was kept locked up for communion.

Sitting in the audience I found Mass boring and hard on my knees. Transferring my weight from one knee to another, or leaning my bum heavily against the edge of the long wooden pew, I could stay awake. But once seated, the never-ending sameness of the Mass would soon bring on yawns, which I would try to stop until, like water running downhill, they would break out somewhere—usually with an embarrassing throat squeak in the silence of the church.

Everything being in Latin didn't help.

Although I understood some Latin, and my missal gave the English translation next to the Latin, I never once successfully followed a Mass right through—introit, collect, epistle, gradual, gospel, offertory, the consecration of the sacred host, the communion, and other prayers—although I had attended hundreds and hundreds. And, for as long as I could remember, we always had to say three extra Hail Marys at the end of each Mass "for the conversion of Russia", so they wouldn't want to fight us any more.

Even tougher than Mass—where everything was done for you by the priest—was learning the really difficult prayers we were expected to know by the time we were in Scholarship. The Nicene Creed—in which you said you believed in God, and where he came from, and what he stood for—was impossibly long. But I did learn the Confiteor which began: "I confess to Almighty God, to the blessed Mary ever Virgin, to Michael the Arch-angel, to John the Baptist, to the holy apostles Peter and Paul, to all the saints, that I have sinned exceedingly in thought, word, and deed, (striking the chest three times) through my fault, through my fault, through my most grievous fault, therefore I beseech ...."

But none of this was going to help me with the Scholarship exam at the end of the year.

Our teacher was the head nun, a fierce old woman with a little face made more lined by the white material that squeezed her face from all sides. No-one was game to take her on—not even big boys like Neil Fallon who had once warned Sister Rosary after getting the cuts that he would get his big brothers onto her. Sister Vincent always warned us that she didn't "come down in the last shower". But much more ominous was her warning that in all her decades of teaching she had never had a failure in State Scholarship, and that she wasn't going to start with us.

At first I thought this was good news, until she said that if we failed to measure up she would not nominate us for the exam and we would have to stay at school another year to prepare again.

Unlike Sister Veronica, whom we had had for the previous two years, Sister Vincent concentrated solely on the examination. If she had to leave the room, Sister Vincent handed out special white cards covered in sums for us to do until she came back. And, towards the end of the year, she made us come to school on Saturday morning for extra lessons.

133

After we got into Scholarship I missed the pretty young Sister Veronica, despite her weakness for Jim. She used to tell us stories and get us looking forward to the next school picnic and put on class plays or tell jokes. She got us to make up words to use instead of swear words and mine was "jumping jewfish".

Sister Veronica was also very easy on us. She forgave me for always being late, and allowed Jim time in class to frame Holy Pictures specially for the school fete. She always let the class stop to listen to the Melbourne Cup on the wireless, and asked who we thought would win and why. I had been very interested in the Melbourne Cup since I was nine when I had picked Comic Court and Jackie picked Chicquita and Dad Morse Code and my horse won with Jackie's second and Dad's third. Not only did it win, but it broke the record and everyone thought I was very smart.

Sister Veronica loved elocution and singing.

She had a special woman who came to school and taught us to say poems like "Hist! Hark!" and tongue twisters like "The hot-headed Highlander hit the hard-headed Hollander on the head with a heavy hammer" or "Your brother Bob owes my brother Bob a bob". This woman emphasised the use of the diaphragm—"a dome-shaped belt of muscle forming the base of the chest"—for reciting poems. And we learnt to sing songs like "Finiculi Finicula". Though I couldn't sing, Sister Veronica told the class it was a pleasure to hear me read aloud.

Sister Vincent was totally different. She was right into spelling bees and mental arithmetic and reading aloud and was always catching me out—like the time she asked "hands up those whose family buys the *Sunday Truth*". Mum always loved to read the *Truth* and so I put my hand up, expecting most people to do so. But I was the only one, and Sister Vincent told everyone how surprised she was that the Lunn family would buy such a bad newspaper. After that Francis Triggs used to tell me "you wouldn't know it was Sunday unless the *Truth* came out".

Sister Vincent seemed to be so much more old-fashioned than Sister Veronica, who didn't mind if you went out for a drink of water or had a drink from under your lift-top desk. When the men building a new classroom took their shirts off in the summer heat, Sister Vincent issued an edict that they were never to do it again, and they didn't. She was also very religious: when a circle of cloud started to form in the sky she got us all out of the room for a look and said it might be a rosary, but it turned out to be just the exhaust from a plane.

She did coach us at rugby because there was no priest to do it, but she had a funny way of picking the team. Instead of practice matches on the big boys playground, she lined everyone up in order of height and made all the tallest boys the forwards, and then had a mass footrace and made all the fastest boys the backs, no matter how scared they were of getting hurt. No wonder the team didn't do any good against Corinda Convent. And, although I had been in the team since grade five, I was now out.

And she did teach us dancing—the Pride of Erin and the Gypsy Tap and the Imperial Two-step—using the girls in our class as partners. She even allowed us to have a dance when we reached Scholarship, in the Hibernian Hall. The nuns didn't go and it wasn't much fun but, right at the end, Dima was walking around looking very stiff and not knowing what to do with his hands so, to loosen him up, I asked him and a couple of the girls if they had heard of this new dance called jive which I had heard about on the wireless and seen done by some of the dancers mucking around at Saturday morning dancing lessons.

Naturally, they hadn't. So, in the corner of the hall, I gave them a demonstration—though I didn't really know what you did, except that you had to leap about a lot. It only lasted half a minute, but one of the ladies looking after the dance saw me and on Monday I was called out by Sister Vincent who said she heard I had been dancing jive at the class dance. And she gave me the cuts with her cane.

Sister Veronica would never have done that. In fact, she didn't even give the cuts. If you got things wrong then she just tried to help you get them right. That was why she got on so well with Jim.

Sometimes she would talk to him for fifteen minutes, but when I asked Jim what it was about he would just say "she has some problems". They got on really well because his English was a complete disaster—he said things like "did you ever had"—and she wanted to help him. Once she sent Egoroff to Sister Vincent to ask when Benediction was on and he came back with a dictionary. He had asked her for "a better dictionary". When we all laughed, Sister Veronica told us how naughty we were.

But you just had to laugh because he had such an unusual way of looking at things. For example, one day the Websters Bakery cart tipped over outside the school and the horse broke its leg. We didn't see it but Sister Veronica told us that some men had been called to shoot the horse on the road outside and so we were not to worry when we heard gunfire.

Shortly afterwards, with the class in complete silence, there was a loud explosion from Ipswich Road and then another and another and another. I couldn't believe it took so many shots to kill a horse, unless of course they kept missing. Then silence.

Sister Veronica bowed her pretty face and suggested we all say a prayer for the horse, but one of the girls wanted to know where the horse's soul would go now that it was dead. There was general agreement on Limbo until Jim said: "He has most probably gone to horse's heaven."

I think it was Jim's lack of words which got him into so much trouble with the other boys. At first the only phrase he used, to react to something he didn't like, was "bastard boy", and otherwise he tended to react with his hands rather than his tongue. That was why he was always reaching out and grabbing boys who argued with him, holding them in various grips which hurt.

Marbles and cricket were the two most popular games in the school yard. But Jim didn't even carry a marble bag and didn't know what was meant by having a favourite tor or fudging or even the difference between a game of poison ring and big ring. Or what a blood alley was for. Whereas Jackie and me had half a sugar bag of marbles of all descriptions which we had won over many years of playing. In fact, Jackie was such a good marble player when playing for "keeps" that we had never bought any. He could win because he fired off his thumb knuckle instead of thumbnail—and the marble flew much harder and further. I stuck with my grip until I wore out my thumbnail and had to adopt his style.

Jim also hadn't a clue how to play cricket. In fact to let him loose with a cricket ball was a dangerous thing to do. He could throw it with tremendous power but had absolutely no idea where it was going. And he threw it with the same velocity no matter if he was on the boundary or returning the ball to the keeper from silly mid-on: a position he had certainly never heard of.

Strangely enough, he knew our swear words and got very upset when boys swore and, if they didn't stop, he belted them up. Perhaps, I thought, Sister Veronica had told him of these naughty words when she gave him extra help with English.

Dima just didn't seem to know all the things you were supposed to do to stay out of trouble in the playground. He got bashed up himself by a bully two years older when he told him to stop swearing, and he was once stupid enough to wear a funny hat to school called a fez. Which was like coming to school in a dress. The result was that he was picked on by other boys, though they tried to avoid his powerful hands.

Once, about ten of them got together and decided they were going to put Jim in the monkey hole down the drain at the bottom of the big boys playground. This was very difficult for me. It was obviously expected that I would help them. And, if I joined Jim, I risked becoming as unpopular as him.

At lunch-time we all met on the long grass out the back of the church where no-one ever went. Seeing Jim on his own, I just had to join him even though I knew I wouldn't be much help. But Johnny Summers, to my surprise, joined us and I grabbed this strong bloke called Gerard in a headlock. I knew he was much stronger than me—you could see the muscles in his arm—and I was so desperate not to let him go that I held him. And with Gerard held, and Summers helping, they were unable to capture Jim and carry him down to the monkey hole.

The nuns knew nothing of these fights. They were always busy with the girls preparing for fetes and organising raffle tickets and toffees for sale to make money. Or planning a school picnic on the SS *Koopa* down the river to Redcliffe or by bus to Shorncliffe pier.

As Scholarship drew near, Sister Vincent decided that myself and one of the girls could not pass—and she called the two of us out to her raised desk and told us she would not nominate us. But we could nominate ourselves if we wished. Mum said I would still be thirteen when school started the next year and she thought I should stay back and become more mature and do Scholarship the next year.

Then my many prayers were answered.

Old Sister James, who still taught the infants, stumbled across the field to the big school one day to speak to me. She said she thought I would do much better in tests if I had no distractions around me: and she arranged with Sister Vincent for me to do a Scholarship arithmetic paper sitting by myself on a concrete slab up behind her infant class under the big church between the classroom and the dirt.

Amazingly I got 110 out of 150, by far the best I had ever done, and Sister James told Sister Vincent she felt this proved I could pass the exam. Sister Vincent said she didn't think I could, but said I could have a go, provided I nominated myself.

The worst thing about the Scholarship was that it was held at state schools because it was a state exam, not a Catholic one. So we all had to gather at the convent and then walk the six or seven blocks to the home of our natural enemy, Junction Park state school.

Olive was very worried about this. So worried that she went to town and bought some "relaxing tonic" from Chemist Roush who had talked about it on the wireless in his show "The Radio Chemist Speaks". It was a pink-coloured liquid in a big bottle and, although I said I didn't want it, I was told to take a tablespoonful. It didn't make me feel any different, but Olive relaxed after I took her potion.

The nuns couldn't come with us, so Sister Vincent gathered everyone around for a last talk—while Sister James pulled me aside. The first thing Sister James did was to produce a big blue fountain pen which you could fill up with ink by operating a lever on the side. This way you didn't have to keep dipping your nib in ink. Like an indelible pencil, it just kept writing. "No-one who has ever used this pen has failed State Scholarship," Sister James said gravely. "So I want you to use it." Then she produced a medal with the face of a saint on it and pinned it to my shirt with a small safety pin. "This is the medal of St Jude," she said, "the patron saint of hopeless causes." He was a saint we had never heard much of, but she said he was the man Catholics around the world prayed to "in grave necessities". He was one of the twelve apostles and, Sister James said, he "secured the crown of martyrdom in Persia when his head was cleft with a broadaxe".

Was this really the saint I should be relying on? But I dared not question Sister James who said his martyrdom made him the perfect saint "to console those oppressed with heavy trials".

And that was me.

She gave me a copy of a short prayer I should say to him: "Glorious apostle, St Jude Thaddeus, true relative of Jesus and Mary, I greet you through the Sacred Heart of Jesus. Through this Heart I praise and thank God for all the graces he has bestowed upon you. Humbly prostrate before you, I implore you, through this heart, to look down upon me with compassion. Despise not my poor prayers; let not my trust be confounded! God has granted you the privilege of aiding mankind in the most desperate cases. Come to my aid that I may praise the mercy of God! All my life I will be grateful to you and will be your faithful devotee until I can thank you in Heaven." And the prayer was accompanied by a litany which said St Jude could "impose silence on demons and confound their oracles". Lastly, I had to say: "St Jude, help of the hopeless, aid me in my distress."

Jim and I walked together that hot morning—December 8, 1954—down to Junction Park, past Lindsay Graham's house where he had a fantastic new electric machine that played records so there was no need for sing-songs. I liked the record he played for me: "Change Partners", about a girl whose heart felt empty when her boy danced with someone else.

At Junction Park they had schoolrooms and desks just like ours, but in a big brick building instead of a timber one, and a Protestant man showed us where to sit for the first exam, English.

Instead of having to write an essay on a bushfire, this time it was "A Cyclone". And instead of the life of a penny there was "A Moonlight Night"—which all the girls would love. And I nearly despaired when I read the sentence we had to analyse: "In the morning as we strolled leisurely down to the cove where the boats were lying at anchor, he described as clearly as he could the events of the previous evening." It didn't even seem like English to me. But then nor did the sentence we had to rewrite: "In your report of the incident, state what you recommend." And another sentence on the paper sounded like one of Jim's: "That he had left the country." This was to be rewritten as a noun clause in apposition.

The toughest question of all for me was substituting words based on the Latin roots *tendo*, *cedo*, *monos*, *maneo*, *polis* and *vinco* in various sentences. We also had to correct four sentences and say why: including "In the auction rooms we noticed a broken ladies umbrella". But the worst news for me was that there was no question on Horatius, or on any of the other poems. Instead of picking a question on poems from the School Reader, they had picked questions on characters from six extracts from novels.

Despite the summer heat, that afternoon we had to return for the Social Studies paper, which was equally tough. We had to describe "the form of government used by our Anglo-Saxon forebears", and the paper was full of questions about English Kings, but nothing about the Popes.

There were no less than ten questions on the sugar

industry, plus questions on other things we had never learnt about: "By what name is the meeting of state ministers presided over by the Governor known?"

With the exception of Madame Curie, all of the questions were about men—famous or otherwise. "In what court would a man arrested on a charge of dangerous driving first be charged?" said one, and another asked: "The letters M.L.A. and M.H.R. are to be found after the names of certain public men. What do they stand for?"

When I got to the shop at four o'clock that afternoon Mum was really happy when I said I had done well, except for knocking a bottle of ink over during the exam which soaked poor Terry Callaghan's papers: and he was looking to get a very good mark.

The maths paper the next day was, of course, full of questions about horses, sheep, and butter, and there was even a messy one on jam: "A jam maker mixed 256lb. of fruit pulp at 1s. 1d. per lb. with 2 cwt. of sugar at 8 1/2d. per lb. The mixture was boiled and made into 3 1/2 cwt. of jam. For every pound of jam made, boiling, bottling, labelling etc., cost 6d. What profit was made by selling the jam at 3s. 9d. for a two pound jar?" I did that one, though I couldn't do the geometry question and I wasn't sure about the man who bought b apples at x pence each and c pears at y pence each. And even though the last question reminded us that pi equals 22 on 7, I couldn't get it out.

But I didn't care.

At last school was over, or so I thought.

11
Travelling south

With the new shop and the new Zephyr both going well, the family decided to at last take the holiday we had always talked about: to drive the 2,700 miles to Melbourne and back during the Christmas holidays to see Fred's cousin, Uncle Arnold, and his wife Aunty Alice. It meant that Fred had to shut his shop for three weeks, but it would sure be worth it. We would see Sydney Harbour and Melbourne and go down the coast highway and come back inland and get to know the rest of Australia, instead of just Annerley Junction.

Jackie was appointed official navigator, and he got a book of maps from the RACQ so we could find our way, and we planned to leave early on the Sunday morning.

The plan was to go to 6 a.m. Mass at Mary Immaculate, but everyone was tired from cleaning up the shop until late Saturday night, and we just made ten o'clock Mass by 10.15. Packing the car took much longer than expected because of all the things we had to take and because the steel roof rack we bought to carry the tent on top of the car took a long time to fit.

Jackie and Olive made the tent themselves by cutting up the small white tent Jackie and I had got one Christmas—with a cowboy painted on one side and a big Red Indian chief's head on the other—and sewing it to the edges of a large green tarpaulin. Ropes were attached to the tarpaulin so it could be tied to the Zephyr's roof rack. The tarpaulin would protect us from the rain, and the cowboy tent—along with the Zephyr—would make it private.

Jackie and I had also made a collapsible table from a timber cake tray—with four legs that fitted in the corners. But we didn't have any mattresses or stretchers, just some old canvas to lie on.

Mum practically filled the Zephyr's small boot with her cast-iron camp oven and billy-can and the loads of food which she said we had to take with us. So our cricket bat and wickets had to go up on the roof with the tent and everyone's clothes in school ports. Then Olive appeared from a bedroom dragging her soft kapok double mattress. In disbelief we men asked what she was doing with that.

"I'm taking it with me," said Mum. "I wouldn't go without it."

This white mattress was like a giant soft pillow, and it had to be tied across everything else on top of the roof rack with the canvas hammocks, which had lots of holes for ropes. That meant there wasn't room for the box of photographs of all Mum's Nerang relatives and us as babies, so the box had to go with the blankets and pillows for the six of us on the back seat floor.

The front floor on Mum's side was covered with *Women's Weekly* magazines and murder mysteries and Jackie's maps and Mum's overflowing green basket.

And yet still she kept rushing back up the stairs into the house and re-appearing with more items—missals for Mass, packets of tea, toothbrushes, bottles of soft drink, toilet paper, cups and saucers, spare shoes, presents for all the people we were visiting, face cloths, talcum powder, her yellow hair brush and mirror set, her sharp bread knife for any trouble, Kokoda for mossies, towels, a tin bucket to use as a toilet, rope for a clothes line, pegs, a couple of cushions for her back, a kerosene lamp, a hot-water bottle, and several hats. She also had the jar of cream with a rubber massager on the top which she had bought to stop Fred going bald. According to the advertisements on the wireless—in an American voice—all you had to do was rub this into the scalp with the massager and your hair would keep growing. I was very pleased to hear this because Mr Stewart had once remarked that I was the sort of person who went bald at a young age, and I was always worried he would be right.

It was the same American voice which advertised a powder

Mum bought once. And I used to imitate him: "I promise you that my new powder, Cream Puff, will make you lovelier than ever before."

By now the poor Zephyr was so full that there was just nowhere to sit in the car, except for the driver. No more could go on top: the rack was loaded so high that the Zephyr looked like the first double-storey passenger car. More and more was moved to the back shelf until Fred couldn't use his rear-vision mirror, and the luggage on the floor was as high as the seat, so there was nowhere for our legs to go. I perched up high on a bundle of towels.

Then Mum staggered out of the house carrying in both her large arms a long white bundle: the white debutante gowns she had made for Gay and Sheryl for some convent ball.

That was it as far as Jackie and I were concerned. This time Mum had gone too far.

"She can't be serious," I said.

"Don't call me 'she'—'she's' the cat's mother," said Olive.

With black-green afternoon summer thunderstorm clouds gathering rapidly overhead, and lightning coming closer, we told her the dresses weren't going. There was no room, and no argument. But, replied Olive, she wanted to show the relatives the bubble everglaze material and the large white flowers she had made from the same material and sewn on the front with sequins.

No deal.

This was the sort of situation where Mum would attack: we could take the cricket set, she said, but all she was allowed to take were work items like the clothes line and the camp oven so that she could continue her function as "Slave Number 42", as she called herself when she felt her wishes were being ignored in favour of everyone else's. It was over the fence for her to be the Wooden Water Joey for the trip but not to be allowed to take just two little dresses south to show her handiwork.

Well, if her ball dresses didn't go, then neither did the cricket set.

So in went the dresses.

For the first time in history we locked our house, Jackie making sure that there was absolutely no way anyone could get in while we were away. Amid loud claps of thunder, we climbed into the car to hide among our precious cargo.

I took up my traditional family seat at the back left window and searched in vain for somewhere to put my legs. Gay was in the middle, and Jackie at the right window, with Sheryl squeezed between Mum and Dad in the front. Jackie had filled the hessian water bottle we had tied to the front of the car so that the breeze cooled it as we went: and, with a few blasts of the horn, we set off down Ekibin Road, though it was disappointing there was no-one around to see us off.

We had barely got going when someone noticed that we hadn't seen Nigger around before we left. We kept going, for there was a long way to go and Jackie's plan was to reach Coffs Harbour on the first night. Then a loud blast of thunder prompted Jackie to suggest that maybe Nigger had rushed upstairs because he was scared of thunder, and we had locked him in.

If we didn't turn back he would die while we were away. The house was so well locked that, in the end, the only way in was for Gay to climb through the skylight above the front door and unlock it from the inside. And there was Nigger, hiding under a bed like a black rug.

Before we could again mobilise to leave, the storm broke, a fierce Brisbane storm which rattled so loudly on the tin roof of the house it was hard to hear the thunder. Since the house was again locked, we raced underneath. But the storm was so fierce the wind and rain blew right through and wet us even though we were under the very centre of the house. And, out in the storm, Mum's kapok mattress—now heavy with water—was starting to hang down over the sides of the roof rack like a giant melting ice-cream.

The storm stopped as suddenly as it had started, and it was late afternoon when we finally drove off for Melbourne, with Dad announcing proudly that we were all cashed up—he had brought twenty pounds along for the trip.

Once we crossed into New South Wales we felt we were on our way: the yellow line markings—instead of Queensland's white—seemed to tell us the adventure had begun.

The Zephyr was flying along despite the load on top, its big six-cylinder engine eating up the miles as we pushed on through the bush. Then, to our surprise, Gay said: "Dad, a policeman on a motorbike keeps following us." Even though it was bush, there was, apparently, a city speed limit, and Jackie said it must be to catch Queenslanders driving south. Fred didn't like this theory and put his hand out the window and waved it up and down to show he was stopping, and then bent it at right angles as he came to a stop. These were official hand signals, but Fred had his own extra one where he put his hand straight up in the air out of the window if he was stopping in a hurry. He told us to say nothing and stay in the car, while he got out wearing his white pith helmet to face the policeman.

You could never tell with Fred, but he said the policeman must have been from Melbourne because, when he heard that was where we were going, he let us off.

We didn't get far into New South Wales when we found a good camping spot next to the river opposite a shop at a place called Jenner's Corner at the Kingscliff turnoff. That was when Fred discovered that he had left his pith helmet on the lid of the boot after talking to the policeman—and it was still there! Yet we had just driven over a twisting mountain road. Everyone was impressed, and Fred said he should write a letter to Ford to tell them what a marvellous car their Zephyr was. In his elation at keeping his hat—which he said prevented headaches—Fred announced that in the morning he would drive home to get his shaving gear, which he had accidentally left behind. He didn't want to go immediately because, for once, he could genuinely go to the pub for a drink and not have to pretend he was a "traveller"—a strange rule that you had to be a driver on the highway who had travelled more than fifty miles before you could start drinking alcohol on a Sunday.

But Fred didn't go back, because Jackie pointed out that it was 1400 miles to Melbourne via the coast roads and that, at this rate, we would spend the whole holiday just driving to Melbourne.

146

So the next day we got Fred cracking for Melbourne shortly after lunch.

Fred was great at getting up early to go to work, and then he'd skite that he was "a Briton". He used to annoy us by coming into our room and yelling out orphanage phrases like: "Rise and shine for the Lunn line", or "Wake up, your King and country needs you". But if he didn't have to work it was impossible to get him out of bed. Olive then had to get him up by poking him in the ribs with her finger, and he would invariably say as he staggered out: "There's no rest for the wicked."

We discovered two things on that second day: that New South Wales had a much better ice-cream (Norco) than anything Peters or Pauls could produce in Brisbane, and their rivers were much wider than even the mighty Brisbane River which, we had always assumed, was one of the world's great rivers. They even had a creek—Wilson's Creek—which not only made our Ekibin Creek look like a drain, but was much, much wider than the Brisbane River.

One of these rivers was so wide that they hadn't been able to build a bridge across it so we had to queue up behind a truck to drive onto a ferry which was dragged across the river by a thick cable. It was a very small ferry and, once the truck was on, there wasn't much room for us. As Fred drove down the steep slippery slope onto the ferry he was too slow putting on the brakes and bumped into the back of the truck, making a dint as big as a fist right in the front of our beautiful Zephyr's cream bonnet.

Up until then the Zephyr didn't have a mark on it. Jack and I had especially washed and waxed it for the trip, and now it was spoiled. Yet Fred didn't care a bit. "You'll get all that sort of thing if you live long enough," was all the excuse he offered for his mistake. It was a sentence he used often when things went wrong. Or if he didn't like a picture, or a religious service, or a school fete, he would always say: "It was good for women and nippers."

When Jack and I told him how he could have avoided the accident, he gave his usual reply to being corrected: "Intelligence is rife."

It was often difficult to work out what Fred was talking about. He would warn Jackie to be careful of "isms and osims", saying they were what caused all the trouble in the world. But, just as I would think he was about to tell an interesting story, he would say: "Getting back to normal ...." and talk about ordinary things again.

If he was about to get back to isms and osims, he would start by deliberately interrupting the conversation with his usual "my uncle ..."—and waiting to see if we stopped to hear what he was about to say. If he thought someone was crazy he would say he was "whacky the noo"; if he was in trouble with Olive he was "in the gun". If he went shopping he "ran the cutter", and then "brought home the bacon". An untidy area resembled a "Chinese Pak-a-Poo ticket".

It was as if he had his own language, perhaps because of his education which he always described as "sadly neglected". He didn't listen to stories, he "paid attention", and he didn't go back to work but "boxed on".

To make up time for the late start, Fred drove on into the night, with Olive urging him to find a place to stop as we passed dozens of garages with the sign "last chance at city prices".

At last, in the darkness, we made camp in a park near the ocean, which we could hear but not see. We were awakened by the heat late the next morning and were all surprised to see we were almost on the edge of a cliff, looking down on the beach far below.

On the right was a giant cave running into the cliff face from the ocean. Jackie wanted to explore the cave but Mum was too smart to let him go, and I didn't want to go anywhere because my legs were aching from keeping them up under my chin for hour after hour in the car, so that I didn't crush the ball gowns.

Before we set off again, Olive produced a glass jar of "Malgic Adrenaline Cream" from her green basket and rubbed it into my knees, and it took the pain away.

When we reached a place called Taree, Fred said he had a stomach on him like a poison pup and stopped by the roadside and disappeared into the long grass. As usual, he told us that if a policeman came along, to say he was caught short. Olive looked out her open window and saw a dead cow. Slowly the rotten flesh began to stink us out. When Fred returned, she said he had provided a wonderful story for her to tell the relatives in Melbourne: how we had been trapped in the car in the summer heat between a dead cow on one side and Fred caught short on the other.

Dad had a certain cure for stomach upsets—port wine and brandy. So in Taree he went to drink this concoction at the local hotel. There he met a fellow who said he had never met a man wearing a pith helmet before. And he warned Fred to on no account continue on to Newcastle along the Pacific Highway because the road was just so bad. Instead, he provided us with a shortcut for the 100-mile journey on a better road.

The Pacific Highway must have been really bad.

This road became nothing more than a dirt track which wound up and up into jungled hills. The road itself was so narrow that, when we finally did meet a car going the other way, Fred had to back right up to let him get past.

I was in the worst position sitting on the left side because, looking out my window, there were lots of times when I couldn't see the edge of the road—just down into the jungle. So I guessed our left wheel must be right on the edge.

Then we spiralled down, first to the right and then a very sharp curve to the left. Jackie and I counted fifteen of these left curves in a row, and inside each was a palm tree so similar to the previous ones that we began to suspect we were going around in circles in the bush. And it was raining and getting hard to see because the windows were fogging up, as all six of us breathed uneasily in the car.

Also, because Fred insisted on giving hand signals even though there were no other cars around, rain kept blowing in his window.

It was very late and very dark when street lighting showed we had finally reached Newcastle. Jackie was asleep in the front seat between Mum and Dad as we searched to find the way through in the drizzle. Finally we found the sign we wanted—"Pacific Highway"—and the Zephyr picked up to its high-pitched powerful roar, and we set sail for Sydney, hoping to find a place to camp not far out of town.

When Jackie woke up he took a while to convince Dad that he was heading north on the Pacific Highway towards Brisbane—along the stretch of road we had avoided, from Taree. So we had to do a U-turn and drive for half an hour just to get back to where we'd made the wrong turn.

When we got back to Newcastle it was really teeming down, so much so that Fred couldn't see to drive and, in desperation to escape the deluge, he drove up onto a footpath under a shop awning. That was great for a while, but we were so cramped in the car that we drove off looking for shelter— any shelter.

Just around the corner we came upon a football ground which had a grandstand. "Perfect," said Olive. And it was too. We didn't need to put the tent up and there were plenty of dry places to lie—and Mum was able to spread our wet tarpaulins and blankets and her mattress over the tiered seats in the grandstand to dry.

We were awakened the next day by an angry galoot who was demanding to know what we were doing in the grandstand. He said we had turned it into a gypsies' camp, and said he would have us removed by the police. We all started to pack up the wet things to leave, but Olive—who used to tell Bible-bashers who knocked on our front door "Am I glad to see you I want to tell you about being a Catholic"—gave him a lecture on Queensland hospitality and small children and pneumonia and of an Australian family on holiday in dire straits: and he relented, and said we could stay and dry out.

We reached Sydney late in the day, with still just enough light to see what we had expected would be the highlight of our trip: Sydney Harbour. One of Olive's favourite stories was about a Yank officer during the War who criticised everything about Australia, except Sydney Harbour. Putting on an American accent, Mum would have him saying: "You Aussies might be twenty years behind us, but boy is that Sydney Harbour really something. You don't have the beauty of our countryside, but Sydney Harbour is the best harbour

I've ever seen. You Aussies might live remote from the world, but you've got a beautiful harbour." And then she would say an Australian soldier asked the Yank: did he want to know how to get a harbour like Sydney's in America? "Naturally we would," the Yank replied. "Well here's how you would do it," said the Aussie. "Get a huge long tube and put one end in Sydney Harbour and one end in New York—and if you Yanks can suck as hard as you can blow, you'll have it there in no time."

What a disappointment then it was.

I had expected something breath-taking. Something you couldn't see across. Instead it was much smaller than Brisbane's Moreton Bay. Olive was disappointed too, although Fred reckoned we were all one-eyed Queenslanders.

Whether or not Queensland was much better than the rest of Australia was the only point of disagreement between Fred and Olive: and Fred was hoping this trip out of the state would enlighten Mum to the delights of other states. But we knew it wouldn't.

Not much was said as we headed south looking for somewhere to camp. But it seemed impossible to get away from civilisation and street lights and, late that night, in desperation we stopped in the main street of some small town and looked greedily at their rotunda. It was like a giant tent just waiting to have someone sleep in it. So we parked the Zephyr next to it and made it our home for the night. Mum wanted privacy, so we had to erect the lean-to, which tied on nicely to the rotunda.

It was embarrassing, Gay said, the next morning when we woke up and lots of people were walking past, like at Annerley Junction on a Saturday morning. But they seemed to be mainly interested in the Red Indian painted on our lean-to (they couldn't see the cowboy).

That was the day when Olive surprised us all.

There was a small piece of park with several concrete seats, next to the rotunda, and Jackie and I decided we had better have some cricket practice. To our surprise, Mum—who had never played with us before—said she would like to have a bat, which seemed a bit ridiculous. But the more we derided the idea, the more determined she became. So we said she could have one go. I let Jackie bowl because he was a very good spin bowler, and I kept wickets. Mum was laughing loudly as she faced up with a right-handed batsman's grip, something she said Pa had taught her. She made the bat seem small, as if she was waving a hammer in her hands, but her large legs, swollen by thrombosis, looked vulnerable without the protection of cricket pads.

Jackie and I never used pads. He said we didn't need them. They were just for sissies. People stood and watched as Jackie gave the ball some air, spinning out the back of his left hand. Although she was big and heavy, Mum skipped forward with disconcerting speed and hit the ball on the full, transferring all her weight from the bluish right leg to the bluish left leg as she did so. The ball looked smaller and redder as it flew past Jackie's shins and crashed into a concrete seat where it took off again at right angles, without losing speed at all, to ricochet off another concrete seat, and another. Everyone took cover, until the ball finally hit the side of the white tent and came to rest under the car.

I don't know if it was a fluke, but Olive, even more proud of herself than usual, handed the bat back to Jackie and danced with her arms upraised and her forefingers pointing in the air as she sang her old song: "You'd better beware of the Duncans, you'll find that they're no pumpkins."

Mum was obviously no stone-waller, and, for the first time, I began to believe all those stories she used to tell about what a tom-boy she was and how she could swim the Nerang River. No wonder she didn't mind us boys buying knives and owning bows and arrows and canoes and a Daisy air rifle. She even talked tough, like a man rather than a woman. "What you see when you haven't got a gun," she would say if an over-dressed woman covered in lip-stick and powder and wearing high heels walked past the shop. Later she would tell Fred that she saw this woman "done up like a sore thumb". And, if you asked her where something was, she would say: "Use your eyes instead of your mouth."

While batting she got a prickle in her foot so she gave Fred a needle and "went like a horse", raising her foot backwards while leaning on the bandstand, with people watching. When Fred stuck the needle in too far, Mum amused the group by saying: "Have you got a miner's licence?"

Olive was so sure of herself that she didn't wear make-up or high heels, and she joked about women who "dressed up to the nines". If Gay asked what she was wearing to a do, Mum would say "my blue charmeuse and my pearls" as a joke. She wasn't interested in Kings and Queens like other women, and if a customer in the shop demanded too much attention, she would say later that he thought he was "Lord Muck". To her the rich were enemies—particularly the English rich—and the poor—particularly the bush poor—were her heroes.

Olive loved to quote from the poem about Saltbush Bill the part where he let the New Chum beat him in a day-long fist fight so his starving sheep could feed on the grass: "And the tale went home to the public school of the pluck of that English swell, how he fought with the drover man all day: but blood in the end must tell".

She was very competitive, so much so that if Fred cooked dumplings for dinner, and we said how great they were, you could bet chocolates that Olive would cook dumplings the next night: and sit waiting for someone to say they were better than Fred's. But she was still a bit of a lady, because she got so happy every time Fred said how beautiful she was: particularly when he said she was the most beautiful woman he had ever seen. Then Olive would start explaining about her fine skin.

Once again, it was after midday by the time we got the Zephyr loaded and on the road, but it was flying along and, where there were mile posts, Jackie and I counted off the seconds with the watch he got for passing State Scholarship, to see if we could reach the next one in under sixty seconds. And the Zephyr just kept on doing it over and over again. Fred decided the engine was so powerful that he didn't need second gear—and he only used first and third to save mucking around.

But Fred was too easily side-tracked.

A sign beside the road offered peaches for sale, and an arrow pointed up a side-road. Fred turned in, but the track deteriorated and seemed to lead nowhere. Just as we were about to turn back, there was another sign: "not far now". So we kept going for a few more miles until Olive was demanding Fred stop ... when we reached another sign which said "nearly there". And then another which said: "don't turn back now—you've come too far". Which was true. There was no way Fred would turn back now—he wanted to see who was at the end of these signs.

When we got there, the farmer and his wife sat us under a big shady tree out of the heat, and we stayed for hours and left with a big cardboard box full of peaches being nursed by Olive and Jackie in the front seat.

It was dark when we got back on the highway, and there wasn't much sign of civilisation as we headed along the Princes Highway south to Victoria.

Suddenly a giant shadow leapt into the headlights and propped backwards. But too late. Fred swung the wheel, but there was a bang and we hit the kangaroo with the side of the front of the car. Everyone got a fright and Fred pulled up to see what happened. It was totally dark when he turned out the lights, and we were all alone. The Zephyr was dinted on the left, but I wasn't worried about that. Fred was now walking back down the highway with the torch, with Olive following him and yelling out to find out what he was up to. It was obvious. He was looking for the kangaroo.

"Leave him alone—he'll attack you," called Olive through the darkness. But Fred, of course, kept looking. When he came back, he said he couldn't see the "poor fellow" anywhere. Olive asked what he was going to do if he had found the injured kangaroo. Fred said he was going to take him for help to the next town. No-one in the car could believe Fred. Where would he have put a wild, wounded kangaroo in our already overcrowded car?

Mum cooked a big delicious stew in her cast-iron camp oven that night by the side of the road, and the next day we drove and drove to make up time, with Gay and Sheryl both complaining Fred wouldn't even stop for a pee.

My knees were aching again from the effort of avoiding crushing the ball gowns, and I was sick of all the bad roads that were slowing us down. We hadn't even seen a mile post for hours. It was terribly hot, and the only thing to look forward to was the occasional drink from the canvas water bag which kept the water ice cold.

Then we came to a sign which shocked us all: "300 miles of bad road ahead" it said. What did they think the road was that we had just covered? But they were right. This so-called highway deteriorated into a narrow bullock track with a thin strip of old, broken bitumen down the middle. There were few towns and fewer cars. But, when we did meet people going the other way, Olive got really annoyed because they kept telling us "we believe the roads are really bad when you get to Queensland".

She soon put them straight on that.

To overcome our disappointment, we set our sights on the Victorian border and the town of Orbost. And we wrote in the dirt on our once beautiful Zephyr, "Orbost Or Bust". And Fred started us all singing: something we had never heard him do before, except when he was angry. He kept singing a song called "On the Road to Anywhere" and we all came in on the chorus: "We're on the road, on the road, to anywhere, with never a heartache or never a care; we're on the road to there, on the road to anywhere that leads to somewhere, someday". Which in our case seemed pretty true.

As we roared through the night, Mum sang us to sleep with her favourite song, which she sang so well: "Isle of Capri", about a boy who fell for this girl but, as he bent his head to kiss her hand, saw "a plain golden ring on her finger .... It was goodbye on the Isle of Capri".

The next day Fred taught us a song about driving a Ford to a place we were all looking forward to seeing on this trip: Gundagai, a famous Australian town where we learnt at school the dog sat on the tucker box: "Bless the Lord how we roared in that old-fashioned Ford along the road to Gundagai. With the radiator hissin' and half the engine missin' .... There was water in the petrol and sand in the gears, hadn't seen a garage in over forty years ..."

As he pushed on, further and further along that dirt track of a highway, Fred kept saying "this is Kin Kin country", which to Fred meant he was lost miles from anywhere. It was a reference to a story he told us about how Mum one night had made him drive Aunty Vera home to Uncle Bill's new police posting at a town called Kin Kin. It was after a long, hard day of work in the shop, and Fred didn't know where Kin Kin was—he hadn't even heard of it before—but Aunty Vera knew how to keep him going. Fred said that, as they pushed on north of Brisbane into the night in the old Hillman, Aunty Vera kept on saying "this is Kin Kin country, Fred" for hours before they eventually got there.

A few nights later we couldn't seem to find anywhere to pull off and camp. On and on Fred pushed, until finally we spotted a small road which led to a large clearing. We turned in and emerged through some bush into what seemed to be a cleared, if rough, camping ground. Olive got her mattress down and we set up the tent and, with everyone in a good mood at our luck, we went to sleep. But when we woke up in the morning we found we had camped on top of some town's rubbish dump. When we lifted up Olive's mattress there were old burnt cans underneath, but Mum couldn't feel them through the thick kapok cover. We couldn't get the mattress clean after that.

We were so pleased to reach Orbost that we stayed all day in a nice park, while Olive tried to clean things up to face the relatives next day in Melbourne. She had already done the ironing by using her favourite trick at home: folding the clothes under a towel and sitting on them.

Jackie and I were amazed when we challenged Fred to a race to some trees and he beat us. He seemed so old that I couldn't understand it at all. He also bowled very well in our cricket matches, and Jackie and I got to admire and like him. We knew he was good at marbles—he could fire them so hard he used to break ours in half. But we didn't know he was a sportsman who liked playing cricket and telling stories.

We had developed a habit in the car of saying "she's apples" to cheer everyone else up, and somehow Jackie and I started to call Fred "Herb", and he called us "Herb", and we developed our own special handshake where each person grasped below the other's thumb, and this became our standard form of address and greeting forever after.

We finally drove into Melbourne after more than a week on the road—twice as long as the four days we set aside when we'd looked at the maps. What a moment as we cruised down Teak Street, South Caulfield and pulled up outside Uncle Arnold and Aunty Alice's house at number 35. As they came out to greet us with their two daughters, Helen and Judith, I felt a surge of pride as I looked at our Zephyr which was twice the size of a normal car, and covered in mud, with dints in the front and side.

You only had to look at it, with Fred standing there in his white pith helmet, to see what an epic adventure we had come through.

It must have been great for the Victorians, too. Lots of people in the street came out to look at our car and at the five Queenslanders—and Fred—as we piled out on to the footpath, which was very neatly mown. In fact the first thing I noticed was that everyone's lawn was really short.

Fred was back where he was born, but it took a while for him to understand what they were saying, because they hadn't learned what we knew—that you had to shout at Fred to make him hear, though he could hear better with his right hand cupped around his ear under his pith helmet.

I wasn't sure what to do, because Olive had warned us to be on our best behaviour, that they weren't Catholics, and not to eat too much. I felt much better when she said at the dinner table what we had all been thinking: that Melbourne was a very flat drab place, with no views. And hotter than Brisbane.

Aunty Alice soon got to understand what Olive was like because, when she asked Mum what books she liked, Olive replied: "A good murder", which seemed to shake Aunty Alice a bit.

And Mum just had to tell her favourite story that night about the woman who used to say to her children when there were guests for tea: "Eat up kids—look how the visitors are eating!"

The relatives didn't seem to know what Fred was talking about when he kept referring in his stories to "the animals". They seemed to think he must be talking about our dog and rooster, and didn't realise that he always called us kids "the animals" if he wanted to refer to all four of us at once.

There were a few awkward moments, such as when Fred said things like "whatchamacallum helps those who help themselves", or when he found a cup with a crack in it and, without saying anything, put both his thumbs in it and broke it in half. Aunty Alice wouldn't have known that this was what Fred always did with cracked cups, anyone's cracked cups. He believed they were unhealthy. He didn't mind cockies or rats—you would always have those no matter what you did, he said—but cracked cups harboured germs. And he would never use a cup or eat off a plate until he had stood up from the table and rinsed it under the tap. That was when he knocked over the thin Holbrooks sauce bottle he brought with him because he used sauce on most meals, and Mum said what she always said when he knocked the sauce over at tea: "Never known to miss."

His relations also had to get used to his habit of involuntarily yelling out when he yawned, as if he were being stabbed. But I could see that Fred's cousin Uncle Arnold was so pleased to see him that he didn't mind what Fred did.

We soon got to like Melbourne, though it was difficult for me. Fred allocated Jackie and me sixpence a day each pocket-money which we gladly spent on Swallows banana-and-cream ice-cream sticks, which were better than anything in Brisbane.

It was terrific to be able to play cricket in the park with Uncle Arnold and his girls until nine o'clock at night, but the heat was so bad that sometimes I had to lie on the lino in the house to get cool. Yet an hour later we kids would be fighting over their blankets.

Then came the big day.

Mum took us in to town on a tram, and we went to a

museum to see the stuffed body of the great racehorse Phar Lap, which I had always wanted to see, and there were also lots of examples of snakes, with details of how many sheep their venom would kill: one snake had enough poison to kill 500 sheep.

Olive and I left the others there and went to a place where they kept all the newspapers—including the Brisbane *Courier-Mail*. She somehow knew that that day they were getting the *Courier-Mail* which contained a list of all the names of those who had passed State Scholarship in 1954. If you didn't pass nothing was said: they just didn't bother putting your name in the paper.

Olive kept telling me not to worry as she got the paper and rapidly turned the big pages, looking for the list of names. "Here they are," she said grimly. "Don't worry if it isn't here. You did your best. You can do it again next year."

She ran her right forefinger down the tiny columns of names, searching for the Ls, and then the finger slowed right down, and she moved closer to the page. All of a sudden she leapt back from the black page and a huge smile lit up her face, and I noticed what lovely blue eyes she had as she looked proudly at me. "It's here!" she shouted, breaking the silence of the long, high room. "It's here," she said more quietly, in disbelief. "You passed State Scholarship."

I felt good that I had made her so happy. And it meant that, like Jackie, I would get a wristwatch as my reward.

12
Brother Basher

The only way Olive got me to go to secondary school after passing State Scholarship was to threaten to put me into a boarding school if I gave any more trouble.

This threat really shook me up because I couldn't imagine surviving twenty-four-hours-a-day at a school far away from Annerley and the shop. Particularly after what Fred had told me about "institutions", as he called any places where children were kept.

I started to long for the convent: and I decided I would go up there and carve my name in a tree so I would not be forgotten. But I never did.

Mum took me across town to meet the headmaster of this boys' college locked in behind a series of rock walls. His name was Brother Adams, and he sat behind a wide desk with a statue of a boy in the school uniform behind him. I recognised the uniform because the statue was wearing the same clothes Jack had worn for the last year since he had left the convent: green-grey shirt, black and red tie, grey double-breasted suit, a broad-brimmed grey felt hat with a red and black hat band, and a red and black badge with a chalice and a star and some Latin writing which Jack said meant serving God always.

Brother Adams told Mum I would be admitted because I had a brother at the school, and he said how lucky I was, because so many boys had to be turned away each year. He didn't say anything about the low marks I got in State Scholarship but I felt that was what he was really talking about. Overall, I got 57.1 per cent, but in English I scored just 76 out of 150. Pretty good really, except that one mark less and I would have failed and my name would not have appeared in the paper, because if you didn't pass English you didn't pass State Scholarship.

I didn't think I was lucky to get into this college because I didn't like it at all. Ever since Jack had started school there he had changed. The school was right on the other side of town, where none of us had ever been before, and he was no longer interested in what happened at Annerley or the convent. He had even stopped playing marbles. Now Jack only cared what happened at this school, which he said was was one of the nine Queensland "Great Public Schools" and that was why it was a GPS school. And I said it couldn't be much of a school if it was named after the road outside— Gregory Terrace—instead of its real name, St Joseph's College.

Jack kept disagreeing with me on everything.

For example, when I said if you drove enough nails into a board you would strengthen it because it would be mostly steel, he said I was wrong. And he kept coming home with new words like "consch" for someone who always did his homework, and "bash" for the triangular shape he made in his hat with pencils, because that was what all the GPS kids did. And he told stories all the time about boys we had never heard of: like a new boy called Manners who was embarrassed when Brother Adams addressed all nine hundred boys at a school assembly and said: "The boy with manners is bound to step forward", and this boy stepped out of line and called out "here sir".

Jack said sports days were much more exciting than at the convent, and he knew this long list of Aboriginal words that made up the school's warcry: which we didn't have at the convent. He said the whole school used to practise at assembly, using a drum and megaphones, and they only started after the school captain called: "Warcry Terrace! One, two, three!" Whenever they won a race at inter-school sports or the first football team scored a try they gave the warcry. And they even had a long song called "Terrace to the Fore" which they all learnt and sang only when the school won.

"Terrace to the Back" I called it. It seemed like a lot of hooey to me.

But I had to admit their inter-school sports sounded much bigger than ours: even though I could see that with more than 150 boys in Jack's year in three classes they had lots of boys to choose from. They even got into the paper when I was in State Scholarship, because three GPS boys each jumped over six foot and one of them jumped 6ft 6ins at the GPS sports at the Gabba cricket ground, which Jack claimed equalled the Commonwealth record, "fair dinkum".

Jack used fair dinkum so much after he went to Gregory Terrace that Mr Fogarty called him "fair dinkum".

And he learned a new way of talking so that he said things he didn't mean. If I agreed to help him roll the pastry he would say "that's real curly of you" or "that's really big of you", when clearly he didn't mean it. He even became friends with a former State School kid called Paterson who somehow got into Terrace and who showed Jack a new way home by walking with him up St Paul's Terrace and down Wharf Street to catch a tram.

Yet I had myself seen Jack fight him outside their house for the honour of us Catholics.

So I started calling him "Big Boy" to show him what I thought of his new image. And he didn't like it. Every time I said "Big Boy" he would get stuck into me but I would scream "Big Boy" more and more and, short of killing me, there was no way he could stop me. I never ceased to marvel at how many different ways I could say "Big Boy".

Most of our fights were at night, when Mum and Dad were at the shop, but I got the better of him one day when I picked up a stone and let fly and hit him in the back of the head.

It might sound rough, but Jack didn't know how lonely it was for me having to get around Annerley without him. Not only had I been bashed up with no hope of calling on his help, but the whole class had laughed at me when Sister Vincent asked how Jack was doing at Gregory Terrace, and I said he had scored 96 per cent for bookmaking.

I didn't know then that the real name of the subject was

bookkeeping. Fred was always backing horses with bookmakers, but for some reason he used a false name: Tim O'Halloran.

Even though he now went to this GPS college on the north side of Brisbane, Jack still kept his promise to take me to see my first cricket Test at the Gabba just a week before Scholarship. Pa had told us what fun it was, and he had predicted a big future for a new batsman called Neil Harvey. We sat in front of the public stand, leaning over the white picket fence that surrounded the Gabba ground, and watched the new English fast bowlers Tyson and Statham being thrashed by the might of the Australian team. Harvey scored 162 and Arthur Morris 153, and I wondered why England bothered to come and play us because we were so good. We heckled the sun-burned, tired Tyson whose white skin had gone pink under our hot Queensland sun. He was nicknamed "Typhoon" because he was supposed to be so fast, but in the heat he trudged slowly back almost to the fence to begin his run-up, and Neil from next door, Jack and I called in unison "get a Taxi, Tyson".

Jack took me to my first day at Gregory Terrace: by bus from Annerley to North Quay and then a walk down Queen, George, and Adelaide Streets to the front of the City Hall—where there were a lot of tall palm trees and some statues of lions—for another bus to Terrace. It wasn't a good place to set out for school from, because it was opposite the Tivoli theatre which showed lots of good pictures and which had a big cool milk bar with rows of inviting shiny steel milkshake cans.

School started at 8.30 a.m. and so we had to leave home by 7.30 to get there in time, because it was so far away. That was why most of the boys on the southside went to the nearby Christian Brothers Catholic college of St Laurence's. Kenny Fletcher did. So did Johnny Summers. And so did my cousin, Johnny Duncan. And that's where I wanted to go too: but Mum wanted us to travel right across town just because she thought this was a better school.

Olive bought me some underpants to wear with the rough Nylange school suit pants, and laughed when I put them

163

on under my pyjamas thinking you wore them to bed. Of course, she still insisted I wear a singlet every day, and she made sure I took a handkerchief, because Olive always said that if you coughed up any phlegm—and I was what she called "chesty"—you should get rid of it and not swallow it.

Sister Veronica obviously agreed with Mum because once when I coughed some up, and spat it on the ground in front of her, she congratulated me.

The gate Jack took me through, that first day at Terrace, was so narrow only one person could walk through at a time, but it looked down over the vast play area between the three-storey verandahed classrooms and the stone-walled school hall which was the size and shape of a suburban church. As I slowly descended a long staircase, I could see the whole area was concreted and it was covered in a sea of people of all sizes in exactly the same uniform ... except for the occasional man in a long black smock or black trousers with a white jacket: the infamous Christian Brothers.

I immediately became very conscious of myself.

Where should I carry my hand that wasn't holding on to my school port? Should I do my coat buttons up or not, since my double-breasted suit was slightly too big because it was the one Jack had worn the previous year. Where should I go and stand, now that Jack had disappeared into the crowd? I couldn't go and sit next to him here: I was too old for that now.

I was small for my age and some of these boys were giants. I had only just scraped through State Scholarship and they would soon know that I shouldn't really be here at this famous place. I didn't know anybody and who would want to know me?

As I reached the middle of the giant concrete area, searching for the sub-juniors—as our year was called—a familiar voice from behind me said: "Hello Lunn." I swung around and there, to my eternal surprise, was Jim—waving his right hand stiffly, palm out, from left to right as if saluting. Of all people, Dima Egoroff!

What was he doing here? I was so surprised, I asked him

how had he passed State Scholarship English. How did he get into this exclusive place when he was a Russian who had only a few years ago arrived in the country?

"You low mongrel dog Lunn," he said. "You bastard boy. Of course I could get in here easily. Do you think I shouldn't of have? Anyway, how have you been going these couple of last days?" Well, with English like that, I was surprised to see him. But I never ever corrected Jim's English: I liked the way he turned some of his sentences inside out. It made talking to him different.

The one thing I knew for certain was that Jim never mentioned to me that he was thinking of going to this college: and yet he certainly knew I was, if I passed.

The sub-juniors were all called beneath a verandah and divided into three classes of between forty and fifty each.

This was done on the basis of your Scholarship pass: with the top passes going into the "A" class, so they would not be held back by dumb boys; the next group into the "B" class, so they could all progress through the text books together; and all of the dunces into the "C" class.

So, naturally, I was in the Cs.

We filed quickly down two steps into adjoining classrooms on the ground floor of a three-storey brick building. We could sit where we liked, so I sat over near a window towards the back on the right-hand side, to be as far from the teacher as possible. Some other boys got the two back rows before I could get there.

Seating was divided into rows of two desks, just like at the convent. And, when I sat down, I looked around and there was Jim sitting next to me. He mustn't have got much of a pass either, but I didn't ask him because I knew Jim would just hate to admit to a low mark.

But he didn't have to: you didn't get into the Cs unless you were almost an idiot.

Overall, I was pleased that Jim had turned up again, as Mum would say, like a bad penny. He had a hypnotic, resonant quality to his voice which helped me to daydream because, knowing him so well, I didn't feel the need to listen closely to him. If it were really important I would pick it up in his change of tone, or he would poke me hard in the ribs with his massive right forefinger. And we could help each other cheat.

Also, looking around the airy room, I could see that Jim would be a good man to have around in this C class, which seemed to have more than its fair share of big tough-guys.

The only negative was that I knew that being Jim's friend would also mark me out as different. And that could mean a lot of trouble.

Not only was Jim a Russian but he was a self-conscious, aggressive, interfering Russian who would—like his countrymen—as soon seek confrontation as peace. And this class did not seem to be the place to start looking for trouble. Many of these low-mark thugs made the chaps in the A class and the boys at the convent seem like little girls.

In contrast to the As and Bs, the Cs seemed to overflow with New Australians: Romeo, Cantarella, Chimenti, Pennisi, Davissen, Stankunas, Tamer, Malisauskas and even a Chinese bloke. I couldn't guess how they got into Australia, let alone this elite college—most looked too rough and surly for such scholarly and religious surroundings. But it was my lack of brains that put me there, and so I had to put up with them: unlike my convent friends Sam Aherne and Terry Callaghan who had also turned up here but were in the A class, and so we hardly ever saw them.

The classroom had an altar in a front corner of the room, and prayers were said frequently during the day, winding up with a two-minute-long litany before you could go home which began: "Lord have mercy on us. Christ have mercy on us. Lord have mercy on us. Christ, hear us. Christ, graciously hear us." Then the Brother would begin the litany of praise to Jesus and Our Lady to which we answered at least fifty times "pray for us": "God, the Father of Heaven .... pray for us; God the son, Redeemer of the world .... pray for us; God the Holy Spirit .... pray for us ....."

With buses, trains and trams to catch, the class would go faster and faster as the dirge wore on. Barely would the Brother finish, than the class would say "prayfrus". This would speed the Brother up, because we would finish our bit so quickly he would have to come in faster and faster with his lead until, towards the end, he would just be starting his phrase of praise when the class would say "prfus".

Each day for fifty minutes there was religious instruction about the Mass, the Gospels, the Saints and the Church … and none of these tough guys ever dared to mock anything. Before going to class each morning, you were supposed to go and say a prayer to a statue of Our Lady at the school hall, and many of these tough boys not only did that, but also succumbed to the pressure to walk up three flights of stairs to the area where the Brothers lived, to "pay a visit" to the Blessed Sacrament in the school chapel: something you were supposed to do every lunch hour. There wasn't much time, though, after you had queued at the tuck shop and gone to a sports team meeting.

We had twenty-five minutes less time off than at the convent and non-Catholic schools: just ten minutes for little lunch and forty-five for big lunch. Which meant we did more than six hours a day in the classroom learning: with no free periods, because we were studying more than twice as many subjects as for Scholarship: English, Physics, Chemistry, Latin, Bookkeeping, Maths A, Maths B and Religion—though the C class didn't do French.

We weren't considered sophisticated enough.

Religion though was a proper subject. In fact it was far more important than the others, and boys who did well at Religion were forgiven a thousand other sins. Each class was awarded a Religion prize, and this was listed before the title "Dux of the class" in the school's annual magazine.

In the school hall there were rows and rows of long timber seats, and the walls were lined with photos of classes and football and cricket teams going back to 1875 when the school started: the year before Custer and all his men were wiped out by the Red Indians. There were honour boards for Rhodes Scholars and for the school's seventy-five priests. We were told that the Archbishop of Brisbane, the Most Rev. James Duhig, was the school's most famous old boy, and that he had just reached the mark of fifty years as a Bishop.

After religious instruction, university entrance seemed to be the aim of the school.

Our grades were not called Junior or Senior but "Junior University" and "Senior University", and the school kept track of how its past pupils fared, years and years after they had left the college. The school magazine carried photos of all the medical graduates for the previous year—nine—and a listing, course by course, of all the "Terracians" at Queensland University. Most were studying medicine: thirty-seven compared with only nineteen in dentistry.

The college also listed its passes in public examinations the previous year: with boys finishing fifth, tenth and thirteenth in Queensland in Senior. But it didn't do as well as Sister Vincent with State Scholarship, the college entry reading "number of passes: 66 out of 67 presented". (How many were not "presented" was what I would like to have known.)

But none of this fooled anyone in sub-junior C. We could easily work out that these were the results of the A classes, not the C. And I could see that we were all stuck here together—the dumb, the foreign, and the unruly—so that the bright boys could do better for the college and, of course, the church.

Not that the Brothers had given up on us.

Far from it.

They tried their best to teach us geometry and chemical equations and Newton's Laws of physics. And, if we wouldn't learn, they tried to beat it into us with a strap.

Toughest of all was a Brother whose nickname was "Basher".

At first I wondered why they called him this. He was a handsome, tough man like a movie-star hero and, although he looked like he could run through a cement wall, he had a nice smile. When he was bemused by a strange answer, his nose would shine as he kept his lips together and tried not to laugh. He was teaching us maths, and at first I liked him until I realised the shouts I had been hearing from classrooms far above—and the whacks that followed—were his shouts, and his whacks.

Basher was determined that we were going to learn something about maths despite our low level of intelligence.

He expended a lot of energy pacing around the room, drawing on the blackboard, setting homework, correcting papers, asking questions: he even tried talking about the films to get us interested. "You know how they say this is the picture of the year? Well this is the Theorem of the Year," he would say while trying to teach us about circles in geometry.

But few of us could see the point in knowing the area of a circle.

To try to induce greater interest, Basher would continually ask questions—especially about homework—and, if you didn't know, sometimes he would come and stand next to you and flick you across the bum with his strap to try to encourage thoughtfulness. But with me this just led to total mind block. I soon found that being hit on the bum was more to be feared than on the hands, which were used to taking blows from cricket balls and bat handles.

Thus I came up with a plan.

Knowing I had not done my homework, and would not be able to answer any questions, in desperation I pushed a blue-and-white check covered exercise book down the back of my Nylange trousers to soften the blows.

Although he wielded the strap more than any other Brother, the boys liked Basher the best because they respected his power and his straight-forwardness. Unlike some other Brothers, he did not bear grudges, had no obvious favourites, and would talk nicely to you a couple of minutes after having given you four of the best.

We also knew that he was going a bit easy on us because, although he was more powerfully built than other Brothers, his strappings hurt less. He also talked a lot about sport—Test cricket and Test rugby—and gave every boy a nickname instead of calling him formally "Master Lunn" or "Master Egoroff".

The day he gave me a nickname was the day I couldn't answer a question.

Basher came and stood by me and flicked my backside with his strap. It made a much louder than usual thwack. His nose began to glow, his lips could not be contained together.

"Huggles, Huggles, Huggles my boy, what have we here?" he said, and I knew the game was up. He pulled the exercise book out of the back of my trousers. "Huggles what have you been up to? Don't tell me you are that frightened of a little tap on the backside?" As he said this, he held up the offending pad for all to see. And all the class laughed at me. But I was glad when they did, because whenever a Brother could raise a laugh it usually meant you would get off without any cuts: and I did.

But, inevitably, a few days later I was in more trouble than ever.

Basher gave us an unexpected test and, since Jim and I were too scared to try cheating in front of him, I got only two out of ten right. Instead of asking individually for results, Basher asked all those with less than six to move to the right-hand side of the room—and about a dozen boys shuffled reluctantly across. Then he asked anyone with less than three to move to the left-hand side near the wide doorway.

I stood up alone, and walked to the left side: the bottom kid of the bottom class in the bottom grade of the secondary school.

To say the least, Basher was upset that his learning instructions had been so comprehensively ignored by so many of the class. He harangued the whole class and then, questioning the dozen boys individually about their study intentions, he concluded each interview with two cuts. As I watched this from the other side of the room, I wondered what would happen to me. At least four, possibly six of the best I decided. The longer it went on, the more nervous I became. With the last of the failures strapped and back at his seat, it was my turn. But Basher first addressed the class about the importance of study habits and of homework. Then the bell went: a signal to end the period and, no doubt, finally to deal with me.

Basher walked back to his desk, picked up his briefcase, and strode across the front of the room in my direction. But he veered off towards the exit.

With one pace to go, he spotted me, stopped and looked, frowned as if he were puzzled—and left the room.

I don't know if he took pity on me or just forgot what I was there for. But Basher didn't seem to like having a reputation for hurting boys. One day, when Trevor Davisson got four of the best from Basher (who, like most of the Brothers, hit lengthways down the hand rather than across), he turned to the bloke next to him and said "that's twenty from him this year". Basher heard this remark and again his face began to glow: "What's that, Davo? You call those cuts do you? You go around telling people, I suppose, that the bad Brother has given poor little Davo twenty cuts with his big strap. Well let me tell you something, Davo. They are just taps that I give you when you're a naughty boy. Just soft taps. Hold out your hand and I will show you what a real strap feels like."

He only gave Davisson two on the right hand but, although Davo was pretty tough, they seemed to make him shrivel up. Yet Basher seemed to put no extra effort into these two. They were short sharp cuts which hardly made a noise, whereas usually he leapt about and raised the strap high in the air and appeared to swing furiously for little result. Except to make us all very scared.

Even Egoroff.

Because Jim was strong and tough, I thought Basher's antics would not scare him. But how wrong can you get?

One of the things about Jim was that he always had many excuses if things went wrong. But who could blame him? If admitting a sin meant the cuts, then a lie—any lie—was worth the effort. Thus, with us, undone homework was always left at home; lateness was always due to the Brisbane City Council bus failing to keep to schedule; and lack of knowledge was always due to some temporary failure of memory cells. So, when Basher asked him to recite the theorem we were supposed to have learned the previous night, Jim got up and, after stalling as long as he could, said he knew it—but could not remember it at this particular moment in time.

The Brothers, of course, never accepted any of our excuses, because they had heard them a thousand times from a thousand boys.

Basher deliberately and slowly put his hand into his briefcase on his teacher's desk, and said menacingly: "I'm coming Egg". At this, Egoroff became flustered and almost incoherent: "I could have known it," he said. "I'm coming Egg," said an unimpressed Basher, pulling out the strap and waving it like a wand. "I would have known it".... "I'm coming Egg, I'm coming," said Basher as he swept down between the rows to where we were sitting and raised the strap above his right shoulder. "I should have known it," said Jim wistfully, automatically putting out his hand to meet its fate: as we all did so willingly.

Down came the inch-wide, thick, weathered, tapered, stitched, stained, leather strap, as I leaned around behind Jim's back to see it hit. Suddenly I felt a pain in my right eye as I was knocked backwards. Jim had piked out at the last moment and pulled his hand back—and the strap whipped through the air, hitting nothing.

Basher could hardly believe it.

He was one of those people who would look into your eyes when he wanted you to know something, and I watched him look deep into Jim's eyes as he said: "Oh Egg, you're in big trouble now."

Actually I had already seen other boys do this, but not Jim, and not to Basher. One boy did it to Brother Keenan, a small nice man whose thin black leather strap hurt much more than anybody else's. He didn't give the strap very often, but when he did, lots of people got it as if to make up for lost time. He could give four of the best to a dozen boys in incredibly quick time: turning and hitting outstretched hands with mechanical precision—two to one hand, two to the other, turn, lift, whack-whack, again and again, as if he were marching through the task.

In the middle of one of these bursts of staccato activity, a boy pulled his hand away and Brother Keenan had so much follow-through on the strap that it whipped through and hit the middle of his smock below knee level and pieces of a black button ricocheted across the room.

No wonder he hurt.

One of the boys who had a particular reputation for pulling

his hand away did so because he had skin that peeled off his hands. When the strap hit, it left a strap indentation in his hand for an hour afterwards. To counter this, one Brother used to hold the tip of this boy's left hand tightly and only let go as the strap was about to connect. But the boy would still pull his hand backwards. Thus the Brother aimed further back, and one day, when the boy left the hand in position, his steel watchband exploded as the tip of the strap flicked down his wrist, and the watch fell on the floor in several pieces.

The second time around, Jim took his medicine from Basher like a man, and promised to learn the theorem.

Not all of the teachers gave the cuts.

One who didn't was a non-Brother lay teacher we all called "Wimpy". Because he didn't give the cuts or blow us up, lots of the boys gave him a tough time: so much so that after just two months of teaching us he said that—after decades of teaching without a strap—we class C boys had forced him to get one. And he held up the new tan-coloured strap for all to see. He warned that, if he were ever forced to use it, he would strap everyone who deserved it.

For the next week all of the tough boys went looking for the strap, but to no avail. Then one day, when Wimpy was writing on the blackboard, I thought he was in error and called out helpfully: "You're wrong." To my surprise he immediately called me to the front, opened his briefcase, got out the unmarked tan-coloured leather strap, called out the names of about twenty boys and lined them all up behind me, and gave us all four of the best.

They were the weakest cuts I ever got.

We also had a young woman who came in specially to teach elocution and, naturally, she didn't give the strap, though she let Brother Keenan give it for her once.

She was trying to teach us to pronounce things correctly and she asked the class what was the most important part of the body in pronunciation. No-one raised their hand. "Come on boys," she said, with her cultured accent. "What moves in my mouth when I speak?" And she said this slowly and distinctly, curling her lips and rolling her tongue around like it was a boiled lolly. But she was too obvious, and again no-one in our C class would raise their hand. It was as if we were on strike. But she wouldn't give up. "Come on boys. Look at me closely. What moves in my mouth when I speak?" And she stuck her tongue out at the class and wiggled it about.

A boy called Anthony Pollard could take it no longer, and raised his hand. "At last," she said. "At last a boy in the C class who actually knows something. Now tell us, what moves in my mouth?"

"Your false teeth, Miss," said Pollard.

At the roar of laughter Brother Keenan came bursting into the room with his trusty strap to deal with Pollard.

The C class's reputation as dumb, rowdy, no-hopers had been preserved.

13
Winning respect

Inside or outside the classroom, Jim and I failed to make any impact on college life.

Most of these boys had been at the school since they were eight, competing at athletic carnivals in satin pants, and playing cricket on turf pitches instead of dirt grounds. They played a game called handball which involved hitting a ball into a wall after it had bounced.

They had never even heard of tunnel ball.

The first big sporting contest on the agenda—unfortunately for us—was swimming. Gregory Terrace was the champion swimming school in the GPS competition and, of course, in the whole of Queensland. If you were fourteen and you couldn't swim fifty metres in under twenty-eight seconds then it was no use diving in the school pool.

Jim and I were unlucky that the Brothers had this stupid idea that all boys should compete in everything, unless you had a medical certificate: so we had to swim at the school swimming carnival, even though this was not our speciality because there was no public swimming pool anywhere within miles of Annerley—only Ekibin Creek, which was about eight yards across at its widest point.

Not only did we have to swim against our classmates, but we had to swim in front of about three thousand people under lights at the pool where Australia's Olympians trained in Brisbane: the Valley Baths.

I had never seen a pool with ropes in it. I could see what they were for: they were there to keep the swimmers apart, because swimming in a straight line was impossible with your eyes closed to keep the water out. What really surprised me was how long the pool was—so long that you could hardly see the other end. There was no way I could have made it that far but, luckily, Jim and I ended up in the bottom division race: as did all the convent boys. This meant we only had to do half the length and reach a rope strung across the middle of the pool.

When the races started, I was shocked to see that all of these experienced Gregory Terrace boys dived head-first into the water from concrete starting blocks high above the shallow end of the pool.

The Brother doing the starting was a huge man with grey curly hair who taught the seniors, a fierce-looking man called Brother Campbell. I was so scared of hitting my head on the bottom that I went straight up to him and told him of my fears. To my surprise, he understood immediately and suggested I start from in the water.

It was embarrassing to be the only person at the carnival to climb down into the water for the start. The crowd went silent, and all my classmates saw me. And what I didn't realise until the race started was that the people who dive in get a tremendous start in a swimming race. I thus kicked off so far behind that I had no chance of beating Jim. But at least there was no fear of drowning because two of the college champions from senior were standing next to the pool ready to help anyone who got a cramp. They didn't have to rescue me but, after I made it to the rope in the middle of the pool, one of them was kind enough to help me get under all those ropes back to the side.

This public display of incompetence—the Brothers never made us swim in the annual carnival again—did not help Jim and me win respect, even among the C class. In fact it became increasingly obvious that the tougher boys, even some from other classes, didn't like us very much at all.

The major reason for this was probably that Jim and I preferred to play handball the opposite way round—by hitting the ball into the ground on its way to the wall and on the full as it came off the wall: this was called downball. I suppose my background didn't help: particularly my tap-dancing background.

When the winter football season arrived in May I told a crowded football meeting of all three classes that, although I didn't have a medical certificate, I wouldn't be able to play because, unfortunately, the under fifteens played on Saturday morning and that was when I had to go to my tap-dancing lessons.

I was startled by the reaction. It was much worse than when Jim asked if they had any three-legged races at GPS.

I wouldn't have minded if they had all laughed, but they just looked at me and shook their heads and curled their lips as if I was an idiot. Even the Christian Brother gave a funny sort of half-laugh and said he didn't think tap-dancing was a very good excuse. No, he said, I would have to play.

He asked everyone to state what team they thought they would make in the under fifteens, to help the Brothers pick the trial teams. I had nothing to go by, as Jack still could not play because he had had the fever. I knew I was pretty good at the convent, but there were a lot more boys here, and they were much bigger.

I generously said I would be prepared to play for the Bs.

The Brothers were obviously not impressed with boys who came from the nuns, and I was put in with all the also-rans in a trial, and was then selected in the absolute bottom team in the whole secondary school: the under fifteen Is: six teams below the lowest team to get their photo in the school magazine, the Cs.

I didn't mind so much for myself, but what would Jack—who wasn't allowed to play rugby—think of his brother only making the Is? What would happen to the old warcry: tackle low?

Anyway, I needn't have worried. They played a different game at this college, called rugby union—not rugby league, which was the game Jack and I had always followed because the big matches were played at the Gabba near Annerley. This was where we saw Queensland nearly beat England, except the stupid ref disallowed a winning try by our hero, a centre called Ken McCaffery.

Rugby union was like rugby league but it had fifteen men in each team instead of thirteen. For the first match against

Nudgee College, they put me in the second row because that was where I had played at the convent. But here they pushed harder and, every time the ball came through the scrum our way and I lifted my foot to let it past, the scrum fell over on top of me. But if I didn't lift my leg, the ball went back into the middle and the other team got it and scored a try.

After just one game I was dropped from the Is and, since there were no Js, I had nowhere else to go. My college football career was over before it had started. But at least I had talked Mum into letting me stop tap-dancing classes.

As always, with Egoroff around, there were other battles to be fought. This time it was not Jim's Russian background that got us into trouble—no-one in the C class seemed to worry about those things: too many óf them were foreigners themselves. It was the self-conscious, stiff, rolling, truculent, pleased-with-himself, arm-swinging, happy way Jim walked around. It was as if he was trying to draw attention to himself: "Here I am, waiting to be picked on, come and get me." Also, when introduced to someone he didn't know, Jim made no attempt at a warm welcome. While others shook hands, Jim waved his hand palm-outwards in an arc from left to right as if to dismiss the person from his presence.

Knowingly or unwittingly, Jim refused to adopt the low profile expected of a convent new boy who was no good at study or sports. And he could not help making remarks that upset those boys who expected some respect because of their sporting prowess or their straight-out meanness. I tried my best—for my own sake—to keep Jim quiet, but it was almost as if he went looking for trouble or, more likely, didn't know when he was getting up people's noses.

Thus every time someone asked him "how are you going, Egg", Jim would say: "One foot over the other, otherwise on a bicycle."

This was Jim's Russian version of how he was getting from one place to another, but it was also a cheeky answer: especially to older boys. He also let himself become upset by the much worse swear words used by these C guys, and would even intervene in private conversations if he heard someone use these words.

By now Jim was a much more sophisticated young man than at the convent, and he even allowed himself a "bloody" or "bugger" occasionally. But he tried to police those who used four-letter words.

Inevitably, this led to threats.

Perhaps because English was not his mother tongue—he spoke Russian whenever he was at home—Jim tended to learn off complex phrases and use them often. Thus he began most sentences with "In any case" or "Cutting a long story short". When confronted by a group, he loved to repeat Mark Antony's "You blocks, you stones, you worse than senseless things". And, when told to nick off or keep his nose to himself, Jim's standard reply—spoken very rapidly, as was his way when he had learned something by heart—became: "Do you want to go down in a screaming heap and come up spitting out teeth by the dozen?"

I tried to get him to drop this one, but he reassured me that he only said it "to upset them". This did not seem to be the place to be doing it.

Already one member of our C class had robbed the school armoury of .303 rifles, smashed a window at Wallace Bishops and taken jewellery, stolen a car, and been arrested enjoying himself down the Gold Coast. One foreign boy claimed to have a revolver in his port and, after picking the port up one day, I believed him. And another foreigner carried a knife: one day I watched him sharpening it in class. He said he didn't like the Brother who was out the front that day at all.

In the class was a large youth with a permanent scowl on his face. Together with his quietly deliberate tone and shifty eyes, this gave him the appearance of a criminal. So much so that when one Brother was asking what various students planned to do after leaving school, this boy replied, so softly that hardly anyone could hear: "A job in a bank." Pretending he couldn't hear him, the Brother raised a huge laugh by saying: "Did you say 'a job on a bank'?"

This scowling youth was on a collision course with Jim. Supported by a couple of boys who had previously piked out when they felt the steel in Jim's hands, he cornered the

Russian in the area below the upstairs verandahs, next to our classroom. He quietly told Jim some of the boys had had enough of him: and he shoved Jim back a yard.

This caused much delight among his gang.

I was getting uneasy. There was no question here of gathering enough support to help Jim in a fight. Even with Johnny Summers and the whole of the convent class, we wouldn't have stood a chance against this lot, whose eyes all focused into a confident meanness. But Jim was unmoved. We had been studying Shakespeare, and Jim had learned a new phrase:

"You are a wretch," he began quickly, as the eyes of these boys opened in disbelief, "who, having seen the consequences of a thousand errors, continues still to blunder." And, as the boy thrust his hand again into Egoroff's chest, Jim folded his arms over the hand and leaned forward—forcing the big boy further and further down on his knees as the hand was bent ever backwards towards the wrist. Not content with this display of strength, Jim had to continue to show off. He kept his arms folded over the hand, and continued to talk to the group as if nothing at all was happening, ignoring the pleas of the boy on his knees, and commenting—as he so often did—"as I was saying before that rude interruption".

Shortly afterwards, Jim easily disposed of the boy who owned the knife, grabbing him in those iron hands, bending him slowly backwards over his own spine onto a desk and saying: "Are you a perverted little agent or something."

But Jim always let them go when they gave him best, and never hurt anyone unnecessarily.

Probably because he didn't have to.

Jim knew he was stronger than any boy his age. It was obvious to me and to him, and he didn't have to prove it.

But one day he inadvertently did.

Many of the boys who were already strong wanted to make themselves stronger in the arms so that they would be better at sport and defending themselves. To do this some carried a handball—a small, very hard black ball—or a tennis ball, and squeezed it as hard as they could all day with one hand, making the forearm muscles stand out. One of the boys had sent away for a special new device for strengthening forearms, and he brought it to school. It had two green wooden handles, held apart by a piece of thick sprung steel which looped around from one to the other. The idea was to try to squeeze the two handles as close together as you could.

I was having a go with this device after watching a dozen other boys try it, but none of us could get the two handles to go anywhere near touching: even by cheating and using two hands. Then I gave it to Jim.

Jim took the green handles in that iron brown grip of his right hand and, as he started to squeeze, the muscles in his forearm stood out like the irregular bulge in a Coca-Cola bottle. The two handles came inexorably together and there was a loud crack as the steel spring snapped in two. A dozen boys stood gaping as Jim said: "Who owns this. It's too weak." After that, we didn't have any trouble with the other boys.

But we were having a lot of trouble with schoolwork. Probably one of the main reasons for this was that not only did Jim and I sit together but, if we did any homework at all, we did it together: usually over the phone by him ringing me on 48 1425, or me ringing him at his place on 91 1652. Once, we were on the phone for three hours trying to work out how to analyse the following sentence: "One thing was the smell of fish." We couldn't imagine a more stupid sentence, and for hour after hour we tried to make sense of it, instead of both going away and talking to someone who might know. But we had so much fun that, decades later, we only had to say "one thing was the smell of fish" and we'd both burst into laughter. For us the sentence took on a special meaning: that the whole world had gone mad.

Sometimes I went to his place because it was between Annerley and the college, at a place called Kangaroo Point. But I didn't really like going there because I was a bit scared of his brothers who, if anything, were more frightening than Jim. The older brother, George, lifted huge weights silently under the house, and the two younger Russian brothers— both as strong as Jim for their age—had a chrome-plated knife that made my bowie knife look small and they waved this around just a little too close to me. Plus they had a home-made pistol which they reckoned fired a ball-bearing into their steel incinerator.

There were many ways for me to get to Gregory Terrace from Annerley Junction. Besides the two buses to town, I could catch a tram, which was slightly slower but much nicer, particularly because I had learned the GPS boys' trick of sitting in the vacant driver's cabin at the rear of the tram. Here was a nice little round seat that swivelled left or right, and you could swing the big shiny brass steering handle around as if you were driving, though it made no difference to the tram. And most of the time the conductor never looked in there, so you didn't have to pay your fare.

Anywhere in Queen Street you could get off that tram and catch another one up Wharf Street and along St Paul's Terrace to within two streets of the school.

Another way was to catch the tram to the Gabba and hop on one of the new quiet trolley buses—which had poles up to electric wires like the trams—across the Story Bridge to the museum. I often went this way because I could arrange to meet Jim when he jumped on the trolley bus at the stop before the Story Bridge. Then, as soon as we got to school, we could start copying someone's homework down for the morning periods—the rest could be left to the lunch breaks.

Sometimes we went home this way and I would spend a few hours at Jim's place in Shafston Avenue. They didn't have a lounge or much other furniture, except for a piano, and Jim was always swapping piano lessons with his brothers. His mother would still be at work. His father— who worked at Peters Ice-Cream factory repairing engines— didn't come home anymore. But Jim didn't talk about that at all. If he talked of his home he talked only of his mother who was beautiful like a young woman. And Jim always said she was beautiful and told her she was beautiful. She had dark hair and eyes and a big smile, and always made us Ham Delight sandwiches when she came home. Jim said she had carved statues for buildings in Russia, and he showed me some photos of them. But he said no-one wanted statues in Brisbane, so his mother made money sewing.

That was why Jim was always so immaculately dressed

compared with me. His mother made sure all his clothes fitted him exactly, and he was the only boy in the school with a silk school tie.

Jim used to make money for the family by buying really thin copper wire and wrapping it around magnets, and somehow he made burnt-out electric motors work again for washing machines, electric drills and refrigerators. He used to claim he had been doing this since he was eight or nine, but I found that a bit hard to swallow. Still, when we were at the convent he fixed Mum's washing machine after the local repairman failed to get it going twice in a row. So he must have known something.

There was one day every week when such visits were out, because after school we had to stay back and be in the army cadets.

Joining the cadets was compulsory for every boy over fourteen, but although Jim and I were only thirteen they still picked us. The Brothers didn't worry about things like age—they just worked out they needed 105 new army cadets and lined us all up in order of height and I was very unlucky because I was number 104.

I was 5ft 2ins, but when we walked over to Enoggera Army Barracks to get out-fitted with our military uniform, the man gave me a pair of trousers marked "5ft 10ins", saying "you're growing like a horse, pink cheeks". Even though I could see they looked ridiculous, there was nothing I could do about it. But I liked the army belt we got—which operated on a similar principle to the scout belt—and the gaiters and the brown slouch hat with the side turned up.

That weekend I tried everything on, big black boots and all, and was marching around the back yard when Neil's mother saw me and rushed over to the fence and started to abuse me for joining the army and for "wanting to kill".

I was taken by surprise, because she had always been such a quiet, nice old lady who couldn't do enough to help me. I tried to explain I was not in the army, only the cadets. She said it was all military, and everyone in every country should disarm. This worried me for weeks. I told Fred about it, and he said he only knew one thing about all the nations in the world: "They will all kill you .... quick."

I ended up in a different cadet platoon from Jim, Nine Platoon, one of the school's infantry platoons, as opposed to other units like Vickers machine-gun or the mortar platoon, which got Jim.

Every Monday we all did the same thing: marched around the school's concrete grounds or were given a .303 rifle from the armoury. We learnt the parts of the rifle and how to clean it and put it together and load it with dud bullets, as well as important things like "first pressure": though we didn't get to fire any bullets. But we did learn the eight one-word rules for shooting—"musketry" they called it—including even three rules for after you had fired: "reline, reload, and relax".

That August the hundreds of army cadets from Terrace set off in buses for Greenbank, in the bush west of Brisbane, for a week-long camp to learn how to be soldiers. I was allocated to a four-man tent with my platoon and given a hessian bag to fill with straw as a mattress, and five blankets. Five didn't seem many in the middle of winter in a cold place like Greenbank, but we were taught how to intricately fold them into a narrow bed, where each blanket was used twice, either above or below your body. The straw mattress was called a palliasse and we were warned not to put much straw in or it would be too uncomfortable to sleep on.

We were told to keep our rifle bolt out of our rifle and hidden in the tent so that if someone stole it he could not fire it, and we each got a steel dish to eat out of which was squarish in shape with high sides called a dixie, and we were issued with a greatcoat: a big warm wool khaki coat from the last War to go with our winter uniforms, also from the last War. Then we were told to strip off and put our greatcoats on and join a long queue which led to an army doctor.

When I got close I could see he was telling the boys to cough, so at least it wasn't an injection. When it was my turn I couldn't believe it when he reached in through the folds of the front of my greatcoat and wrapped his hand around my balls and said "cough". If I hadn't been so surprised I would have objected. No-one was supposed to be allowed to do that—it was the sort of thing saints died to stop. But I froze, and coughed. Next to him was a cadet corporal, and the doctor asked my name and the corporal wrote it down. This had not happened with the boys in front, so I spent the first night in my tent believing he had found something wrong with me—perhaps to do with impure thoughts. But nothing was ever said.

The next day we marched a few miles to a rifle range where hundreds of cadets were lined up in rows of ten to shoot at targets from a mound. I had been looking forward to this. Mum had told me I was from a long line of good shots, and Jack had shown me how you used the sights to aim the rifle with our Daisy air rifle.

What I wasn't prepared for was the loud explosion every time one of these guns was fired. It was much louder than any cannon in the pictures. It broke the air and threatened the eardrums and, as my row moved closer to the mound for our turn, it got even louder.

When we were one row from firing I could see the boys in front of me being driven backwards by the recoil of their rifles each time they fired, even though they were lying down.

I fondled the brass bullets and marvelled at how big they were: how smooth and shiny.

Then I was on.

"Limber up" was the command, and we threw ourselves forward as we practised every Monday, taking the impact of landing on our left hands. A regular army soldier kicked me in the bum and said to get it lower: "Only parsons are allowed to leave that up in the air," he shouted. (He must have known we were all Catholics.)

I raised my gun above the sandbank, pulled back the smooth, well-oiled bolt (we had oiled it a hundred times with the pull-through and oil hidden in the butt), and watched the golden bullet arise magically and thrust into the black steel hole of the barrel as I slammed the bolt home and down. I released the safety catch. Raised the butt into my right shoulder. Took aim. The boy to my right fired, and hot oil hit me in the face and my ear rang. Then the boy to my left fired. Then the boy on my right again. I had to fire. I knew it would hurt my shoulder, so I held the butt slightly away, even though for eight months we had learnt to hold it in tight. The explosion tore my mind and the rifle my shoulder. I had fired, but could I stand it again? I was shaking. I fired again. My shoulder ached. Five to go. I took first pressure, squeezed and the gun went click. It wasn't supposed to go click.

The bullet had not gone off.

Mum had told me how Pa's gun had once exploded in his face, so I hurled the rifle over the front of the mound, down into the dirt where it rolled harmlessly into a ditch. No-one knew why I had thrown the rifle away but all firing stopped as a regular army officer ran along the back of the mound abusing me all the way. As I stood up, rifleless, I was removed "never to shoot again".

I was glad really.

Being in the army didn't seem like a very good idea. On the parade ground that morning an army officer drilled us and shouted: "You'll be fighting for that land you're standing on within a year." Fighting who he didn't say. And no-one was game to ask him.

I don't know that we would have been much use. Basher was a captain in the cadets, and after our first day on the range he addressed us: "How is it," he asked, "that ten boys can get up on the range and each fire seven bullets and only one bullet hits a target?"

No war could have been worse than this. The toilets were all timber thunderboxes in one large tin-roofed shed with no walls so that you sat among a lot of boys in two rows facing each other, which gave me severe constipation. The showers—in long rows in another wall-less shed—were buckets with holes in the bottom which you pulled up above your head with a rope. Brother watched over us to see nothing else went on.

I lived in fear of being set upon and having my balls nuggeted with boot polish as happened to some others, but Jim arrived in my tent just in time to save me.

I had to run around a parade ground with a rifle above

my head as punishment for having the worst-made bed in the daily inspection which awarded points to decide the best tent and the best platoon.

The only thing I enjoyed about that first camp was the speech Brother Hodda, who was a major in the cadets and in charge of the college corps, made to the whole camp on the first night. He told us we had come to learn how to defend ourselves, our nation, and our Catholic religion by learning to fire rifles, mortars, and machine-guns. And we would be living in the bush for the next ten days.

"Boys, remember," he said, "kill no birds, touch no nests."

14
Something like the truth

There was so much to learn at this new college, right down to a study book that taught us things like which hand to use to raise your hat when greeting a lady—the hand away from the side on which she approached.

This tip was contained in a book called *Christian Politeness and Counsel for Youth* which also told us the correct way to greet men, women, priests and bishops. It contained just some of the things we had to learn to be good Catholics, but there were hundreds more which had to be picked up from where the nuns left off.

New words had to be learned. Words like "devotions", "special dispensation", "infallibility", "vocation", "transubstantiation"—the process by which the bread and wine became the body and blood of Jesus Christ.

Iniquity was simple. It was sinning.

You could have Devotion to an apostle or, say, the Sacred Heart of Jesus, by saying special prayers, while a Vocation was a thing in the mind that students like us got at about age fifteen when we decided to become a priest or a Brother. They were considered so important that once you said you had one of these Vocations you could be sure of favourable treatment by all of the Brothers, both in class and even down to selection in a good football team.

The Pope himself handed out special dispensations. For example he had long since ruled that Lent fasting did not apply on St Patrick's Day (March 17—and such dates always celebrated the death, not the birth, of a saint). The Pope could allow you to eat meat on a Friday for medical reasons, but he would naturally never allow a worse sin, like, for example, attending the church of another religion.

There were a hell of a lot of other religions, and it turned out that the members of these were the State School kids, who went to schools paid for by the state, while we Catholics built and paid for our own schools: but the Brothers said we also paid for theirs, which seemed very unfair. No wonder we weren't allowed to marry these Protestants, who came in many guises: Anglicans, Lutherans, Presbyterians, Methodists, Seventh Day Adventists, Baptists .... so many that it was easy to see why they couldn't be the one true Church like we were. Some Catholics did get special dispensation to marry Protestants, but only if the Protestant promised the children would be brought up Catholic. They couldn't marry in front of the altar, they had to marry at the side.

Whatever the Pope said, was right, because he was infallible. But it wasn't as clear cut as that, once you started to learn the ins and outs of our religion properly. He was only infallible if three different circumstances applied: if he was speaking as head of the church; if he was binding all the faithful; and if he was defining doctrines of faith or morals. We were told it was very important to make this distinction because Protestants, particularly the Anglican breakaway ones, loved to say we treated the Pope as if he were God.

In our second year we had to join the YCS (Young Catholic Students) and spend every Friday—after school of course—talking with an older team leader about our religion. Jack was a YCS team leader.

Many boys also became members of organisations with high sounding titles like the Crusaders of the Blessed Sacrament; the Pontifical Society for the Propagation of the Faith; and the Catholic Literature Crusade, whose Terrace members sold the *Catholic Worker* newspaper in the streets in opposition to Communists selling the *Tribune*. While some good boys joined almost everything, I didn't really want to join anything, but ended up in the St Vincent de Paul Society and used to have to visit old soldiers in the Greenslopes Military Hospital on a Sunday morning, and talk to them and hand out religious magazines given to me at school.

The funny thing was that they never complained about these visits, though I could tell they weren't interested either.

There was also Holy Sodality which involved going to Communion once a month on a Saturday at your local church at 7 a.m.: and the Brothers often asked whether we had been, which was difficult for me because I rarely made it. Not because I didn't want to go, but because I had trouble getting out of bed in the mornings. No matter what happened, I never ever felt really awake—Sunday or school day—until after lunchtime.

Another thing we were supposed to do was to attend Mass and Communion on the first Friday of each month for nine months. If you could do this then, the Brothers said, Saint Joseph would ensure that before you died you would live long enough to ask for, and receive, forgiveness. Not only for venial sins but all mortal ones as well. It was a certain way to Heaven but so difficult that I never went close. That was why you had to do it nine times in succession, because then it became an almost impossible task: you would always run into a freezing morning, a failed alarm clock, a missed tram, a lolly left out to tempt you to break the fast that was required before Communion, or an impure thought the night before in the warmth of bed—with no chance of attending Confession before Mass at 6 a.m.

We also learnt about scores of saints who died for the church. But mostly we learnt about Our Lady and how she could help us by saying prayers such as the Rosary or other beautifully expressed appeals like one that finished: " .... for never was it known in any age that anyone who implored thy aid or sought thy intercession was left unaided". And we learnt about her various feast days: like Our Lady Help of Christians, patroness of Australia, and Our Lady of the Seven Dolours (sorrows), a feast day started in 1667 by the Order of Servites and extended to the whole Catholic feast-day calendar by Pope Pius VII—in thanksgiving for his liberation from captivity by Napoleon in 1814.

That was where Jim was lucky. Being Russian Orthodox he didn't really have all these worries.

There was so much to learn about our one true Church that there was no time to study for the Junior University examination to be held at the end of my second year. But the Brothers didn't mind that: "Education is more than instruction. It involves a development of right attitudes towards life and its problems," they said.

This Junior exam, like State Scholarship, would decide whether the state would pay money to help send you on to Senior, where you would do another series of public exams to see if you could go to university. Presumably, people there did more examinations. But I didn't know because I had never seen the University. I didn't even know where it was.

The Christian Brothers held a fake Junior Public Examination at the end of sub-junior—with foolscap-sized examination pads and supervisors and all—so that we would get practice for the Junior exam twelve months later. I just managed to pass everything except, of course, Latin.

Latin was a subject I just could not do, no matter how many times I got the cuts for not knowing my vocab, or no matter how many declensions I learned off by heart, like "*amo, amas, amat, amamus, amatis, amant*". We used to say in the C class: "Latin is a dead language, dead as dead can be; it killed off all the Romans, and now it's killing me." We sang hymns in Latin, like "*Tantum Ergo*"; we said Mass in Latin; and we even said whole prayers in Latin—but still I knew nothing about the language. I just memorised sentences, like when I first learned to read at the convent. *Mea culpa, mea culpa, mea maxima culpa* I knew was "through my fault, through my fault, through my most grievous fault"—only because both the Latin and English versions were said when beating your chest with your right fist.

The good boys from the A class used Latin whenever possible, to show how superior they were. Even school reports on football matches contained Latin phrases. When our first fifteen disastrously lost a rugby union match to Brisbane Grammar in my Junior year, the school magazine said: "*Fluctuat, nec mergitur*", whatever that meant.

There were also lots of hymns to learn. They were mostly to Our Lady—Blessed Mary Ever Virgin—and were sung in the big hall with the As, Bs and Cs all in together, for once, because hymn singing had nothing to do with intelligence: just like voice-speaking where the reading aloud ability I learned at the convent got me into the combined class voice-speaking choir. We competed in an inter-school eisteddfod, reciting "Reynard the Fox" who was chased "till his tongue hung out and his feet were dragging, and his belly and brush were filth'd from dragging".

We didn't win anything.

I enjoyed the hymns more than the recitation because you could yell out as loudly as you wished and yet not be noticed. And it was nice to be surrounded by song instead of study. We sang them so slowly and with so much feeling that it made me feel flushed with pride. I still know all the words:

> Hail Queen of Heaven, the Ocean Star,
> Guide of the wanderer here below,
> Thrown on life's surge, we claim thy care,
> Save us from peril and from woe ...

It was like having a second mother:

> Mother dearest, Mother fairest,
> Help of all who call on thee,
> Virgin purest, brightest, rarest,
> Help us, help, we cry to thee.

These hymns taught you to love Mary with words of praise like: "Oh mystic rose, what tree? Oh flower, ev'n the fairest, is half so fair as thee?" or "When wicked men blaspheme Thee, I love and bless Thy name". Protestants, apparently, thought this showed we adored Mary too much. But there was a hymn that answered this:

> But scornful men have coldly said,
> Thy love was leading me from God;
> And yet in this I did but tread,
> The very path my Saviour trod.

Just in case we were not learning enough religion, each June for three school days the college had a "Retreat" during which we concentrated solely on religion. So much so that

192

we were not allowed to talk, though Jim and I managed a sentence or two every time we lifted our desk lid to get something out.

This would have been very boring except that each year some special order of priests—in my Junior year "the Oblates of Mary Immaculate"—would come into the school and, in between lots of prayers, hymns and a seemingly infinite variety of services, they would give us interesting talks which often got away from straight religion.

One of these priests was particularly entertaining, beginning the first day with the announcement in an Irish accent: "Boys, the stories I am going to tell you over the next three days are the truth, the whole truth, and something like the truth, so help me God."

During this Retreat I learned that the Christian Brothers were an Irish order devoted to teaching Catholic boys. I also began to realise that the main religious concern at this college did not seem to be "the Conversion of Russia"—as it had been at the convent—but "the Conversion of England" which, we were told, would one day once again become "Our Lady's Dowry"—as it had been before King Henry the Eighth defied the Pope to get a new wife, and made priests into bishops without the sacrament of "Holy Orders" because he didn't use bishops, thus breaking the apostolic line back to Jesus Christ.

At these Retreats we learned that it was idolatry to worship false gods like money, or pleasure, or power; how the Devil was a fallen angel called Lucifer who rebelled against God because of the sin of pride; how our souls were spirits in God's likeness and leave our mortal body when we die; and how we should practise "self-denial"—to keep saying "no" to things we were allowed to have—in order to strengthen our will to resist things we were not allowed to have.

These visiting priests also helped solve some of the mysteries of the church, explaining our belief in the "Assumption" of the Blessed Virgin Mary into Heaven: that after Our Lady's death, unlike anyone else, her earthly body was taken to Heaven along with her soul.

All of this was difficult for Jim and I to understand. But

it was no harder than another thing the Brothers often talked about: something they called "School Spirit".

It took me two years to get this School Spirit.

In my first year I hadn't cared if we won at sport or not. Jack dragged me along to the Valley pool for my first GPS championships and, while the whole school was ecstatic that we won our fourth consecutive championship, I sat up the back embarrassed by all the shouting our school did. They even did warcries every time one of the Brothers entered the Valley Baths: particularly for Basher and Brother Campbell, clearly the school favourites.

Brother Adams urged us to involve ourselves in sport, saying the Pope had said sport was "an efficacious antidote against weakness and an indulgent life". But it was very difficult to get into a good team because everyone seemed to have this School Spirit, and they were dying to get maimed for the college.

Because of this, Rugby Union was by far the most important sport and the only one everybody played: it was the only way you could almost be guaranteed to spill blood for the school, and every Monday in winter a new batch of boys limped around school or bore new plaster casts as proof that they had School Spirit.

It was supposed to be compulsory for the entire school to watch the first fifteen play at 3 p.m. on Saturday afternoon. Unlike Jim I used to go every week, but I refused to join in the warcries on the hill and instead stood up on Gilchrist Avenue in my black and red school blazer, with an umbrella in case it rained, and watched silently.

Apart from swimming there wasn't much to cheer. The football team lost half the time, despite what the Brothers predicted.

In my second year, one of our boys in the squad for the Melbourne Olympics that year, Peter Andersen, got appendicitis and Ross Murray nearly drowned, swimming all of Andersen's events as well as his own.

For Terrace to win the GPS carnival, Ross Murray had to win the last individual event, the 400 metres, after already winning the 100 metres freestyle in record time, finishing second in the 100 metres breaststroke, and second in the 50 metres freestyle: four big races within a few hours of one another. Ross had a fantastic new thing called a "tumble-turn". While the others swam up to the wall and pushed off with their hands, Ross flipped over and pushed away with his legs and gained a couple of yards every time. But, as the race wore on between the ropes, I could see him gasping for air out of the side of his mouth in the water and, with two lengths to go, he stopped tumble-turning and finished second.

We lost, but I could see that what he had done was School Spirit.

Our rowing team was also supposed to win the Head of River, which started at the Grey Street Bridge and finished at the Regatta Hotel, but one of our blokes caught his oar on a crab—of all things to strike in the deep muddy river, I thought—and we lost that too. This was such a disgrace that the only reference to it in the school annual was: "We were leading at the Gasworks."

By the second football season, unlike a lot of boys in our class, I was still under fifteen and this time I made the under fifteen Es. The more I played the more I began to understand the game, and I started to enjoy watching the firsts play in their distinctive all-black jerseys with two red Vs—so different from the butcher-striped red-and-black tops of the dozens of other college teams.

We had a magician at five-eighth for the firsts called Harry Roberts who quickly became my hero when Terrace beat Nudgee College—the other GPS Christian Brothers College—for the first time in many years. The match was at Nudgee, and Harry scored two tries in which he out-witted practically the whole Nudgee team. This was an outstanding feat because, unlike Terrace, Nudgee was a boarding school with thirteen rugby ovals. Terrace was in the middle of the city and we had to play in the nearby parks along Gilchrist Avenue. And while we cheered from a steep grass bank, they had their own timber grandstand which echoed and vibrated to their warcries.

We only had to beat the Anglicans—Churchie—in the last

match of that season to win the premiership, but seven of the firsts were out injured and Harry broke his collarbone in the first ten minutes and was carried off. By half-time we were down 13-nil, and early in the second half our goal-kicking lock, Peter Stevens, split his head open. No replacements were allowed after half-time so the Brothers bandaged his head and he went back on.

With the pupils, the parents, the Old Boys and the Brothers going berserk, Terrace came back and beat the Anglicans 14-13 and won the premiership. That was School Spirit.

Although Jim was not the type to join the crowd, deep down he seemed to have caught some of this spirit as well. To my surprise, he said he had an idea for Terrace to one-up everybody else at the annual athletics carnival in October 1956 at the Gabba cricket ground. That afternoon I caught the trolley bus with him and he took me into a bedroom at his mother's house where I was surprised to see the floor covered in beakers and pipettes and glass jars and bunson burners and rubber tubes all tied together like a science laboratory in a picture. It wasn't like Neil's chemistry set which he used under his house to distinguish between chemicals. Everything was much bigger: like the real thing.

And something else was different about this room.

The blue paint on the vertical VJ wall boards was all peeling off, from the white ceiling downwards, as if eggs had been thrown at the ceiling and the yoke had dribbled down the walls.

"Cutting a long story short," said Jim in agitated excitement, "these couple of last days I've been making Hydrogen." And, for once, it really did look like a long story.

"I've got some balloons," he said, "some red and black balloons."

Jim's idea was that we fill these red and black balloons with Hydrogen from his apparatus, and on Saturday release them at the Gabba with a big sign saying "Terrace" underneath. "Everyone will see it," Jim said. "In any case, they will wonder how we did it."

I liked the idea, but I didn't like the look of the walls.

"There was a bit of an explosion," said Jim, sensing my

196

trepidation, "but it won't happen again. I know what went wrong."

The following Saturday morning Jim set up his Hydrogen-making equipment in the old timber garage at the front of the house. His mother had kicked his experiment out of the house, and the garage was the perfect place because they didn't own a car.

Within minutes, the triangular-shaped bottles were leaping about as their contents bubbled profusely up through rubber corks into glass stems. Hydrogen steamed off into the balloon Jim was holding as he leaned perilously over the apparatus, his brown leg muscles standing out below his shorts. The longer it went on, the more the bouncing bottles rattled and clashed, and the liquid bubbled and boiled until I backed out the garage door.

"Quickly," said Jim, who was still leaning over his jumping experiment, "cover everything with that newspaper."

No way.

I seemed to spend more and more time now, refusing to carry out Egoroff instructions, because I knew he would get us into trouble: like the day we were supposed to bring the flowers for the class altar.

The last thing I had wanted to do was to walk through Annerley carrying a bunch of roses, so I left the flowers to Jim, who also refused to be seen walking down the street with his hand full of flowers. "Don't worry Lunn," he said. "I know where we can get some flowers," and he raced out of the school grounds into Spring Hill, which was against college rules.

The trouble with Spring Hill was that very few of the people in the old timber houses bothered growing flowers, and we had only minutes to get back to class with flowers for the altar.

I urged him not to do it, but nothing could stop Jim once he had made up his mind.

A small house with a table-sized garden sported pink and red roses, and Jim, ignoring the thorns, reached out to break one off—just as the old lady who owned the house looked out: exactly what I had expected to happen.

"What beautiful roses you have, madam," said Jim, putting on the very soft, innocent voice he used for people like his mother and Sister Veronica, as he raised his hat with his left hand because she was on the right. "Cutting a long story short, we were having a special May Altar for Our Lady, the Virgin Mary, and I was wondering if you might like some of your beautiful roses offered up to her on her Altar?"

Luckily for us, she gave Jim a bunch of roses.

"The newspaper won't make any difference if it explodes," I warned Jim as he filled a third balloon: I knew just enough about chemistry to know that Hydrogen was dangerous—they wouldn't have named bombs after it if it wasn't.

"I know the paper is no protection," Jim said, as the bottles threatened to explode, "but I will feel better if I can't see it."

Typically, Jim hadn't made the cardboard sign. But we put each of the balloons into a cardboard box—which stopped the balloons floating away—and took them to the Gabba. In the middle of the championships we left the Terrace section of the cricket grandstand and took our secret weapons over to the grass hill in the outer and let them go.

It was a proud moment as thousands of boys from nine colleges started to look up at the red and black balloons rising slowly above the ground. No-one had ever seen anything like it before, not even at the Test cricket.

There were loud murmurings from the grandstand, and the officials even stopped the start of a 100 yards championship to look.

It was a big success: at least until Monday when, as I suspected might happen, a Brother who didn't like Jim or me enquired: "Who released those balloons?" Of course he knew it was us—he was already getting out his strap. But Jim said he had checked with Basher who had said it would be alright.

Now we were really in trouble. I knew Jim hadn't done any checking. Not Jim. But the Brother believed him.

"Well why didn't you say so," he said, and put his strap away: now we had to hope like hell he didn't check with Basher. This particular Brother hit really hard. Not only was his strap much wider than usual but, as he raised it to bring it down, the end stood up like a cobra and accelerated downwards, making the tip bite into the flesh.

His reputation had spread to classes he didn't teach. Once he caught a boy talking in an adjoining unattended class, and handed this wide strap to the boy and told him to stand out the front of our class with the strap: "When that clock gets to three I'm going to give you the cuts."

The boy gave a nervous half smile.

By ten to three the boy started to look uncomfortable. By five to three he couldn't take his eyes off the clock. With a minute to go he broke down and wept—and was sent back to his class in disgrace, but without getting the cuts.

That was the thing about the Brothers: they were all so different. Some were saints, some devils.

In Junior we had two new teachers. One was thick-set, balding, red-faced and aggressive, while the other was pale, thin, quiet, and so sensitive-looking that we called him after a flower: "Tulip".

Tulip went out of his way to be nice to all the boys, liked me, and only gave the cuts under extreme provocation—like the time Jim passed the thin copper wire he used for rewiring motors all around the room until a web of wire was created which Tulip, who wore thick spectacles, got caught up in: and still couldn't see what was holding him. But even then he did not hit hard.

Tulip didn't even give me the cuts when I used one of Jack's essays. It was an essay on "Hats" and, to save time, I copied it out: though I didn't understand what he meant by a girl looking "chic" in a hat. Most other Brothers would have given me the cuts, but Tulip merely wrote on the bottom: "Nice try, but a certain Jack Lunn wrote this first." What I didn't know was that the Brothers had been so impressed by Jack's essay that they had passed it around to read on the weekend: and that was why we were set the subject.

Tulip tried really hard to teach us C boys some science, and only smiled when one brave boy yelled out "hav-a-hearts" when Tulip walked past, looking like an ice-cream salesman in his new white starched three-buttoned summer jacket.

He became my cricket coach and was always asking me if I had yet got a Vocation. I always said no, because this was not the sort of thing you lied about, even to get favourable treatment.

In complete contrast to Tulip, the thick-set Brother was vicious. Though he did not give the cuts often, when he did he sometimes made boys bend over and thrashed them across the bum. When he was really angry with some particularly tough boy, he made him put his elbow on the desk, with the hand stretched out, so the boy's arm wouldn't give way beneath the impact of the strap. And, while six cuts were often talked about but rarely seen, his normal tally was six. This made even the toughest boy in the class cry into his palms.

His presence made it a nerve-wracked year for the whole C class. The few good boys at the top were feverishly trying to work their way up out of it; the tough boys at the bottom were copping the thrashings; and those of us in the middle were just trying to survive.

The Junior Public examinations went on for weeks. Writing in special foolscap books at individual desks, we were watched over by lots of non-Brothers. For each subject you either got an A, B, or C—or a fail. I got four C passes, and a B for English. Unfortunately this was not enough. One more B instead of a C and I would have qualified for a state-subsidised Senior education.

I prayed to everyone I knew so I wouldn't have to go back analysing sentences with a new group of Junior C boys, without Jim by my side. My prayers were answered when Brother Adams's annual report arrived in the letterbox: "The appreciation of the gift of Faith reaches its highest realisation in a Senior Boy," he wrote. "He goes into the world convinced that he has a unique personal responsibility to spread the Kingdom of Christ on earth. Parents should remember that the Senior class is the completion of a Catholic education and not merely a pre-requisite to a University course. A boy will benefit tremendously quite irrespective of success or failure .... there is much to be gained by boys of ordinary ability, who have not a University course in view, remaining for Senior .... not too much should be asked of these boys."

So Olive agreed to pay the extra school fees for me to go on and do Senior.

15
Bill Haley's cousin hits the Gold Coast

Now that Jack and I were on our way to Senior, and I was going to be sixteen shortly, every man who came into the shop asked the same question: "What are you going to do when you grow up?" Because an accountant, Joe Noonan, often came into the shop for dinner, I once made the mistake of saying that I was going to be an accountant.

I said this to a man who wore a suit and a waistcoat and a small hat. He seemed to know a lot about the world and was disgusted with this piece of information. He dragged me over to our big pile of cases of used soft drink bottles: "You see all these bottles?" he said. "Well, there are more accountants than there are soft drink bottles."

So I decided not to become an accountant.

Jack pleased this man greatly by saying he was going to be a dentist. That was great, he said. There was more money in dentistry than anything else.

It sounded interesting, but I couldn't become a dentist because you had to go to university and study for years and years, even after Senior, and you wouldn't start work until you were pretty old. Fred had the same idea, because when Jack told Dad he was thinking of becoming a dentist, Fred's only reply was: "I've always said I'll have to nurse you till you're forty."

That was the good thing about Fred: he never ever asked us what we were going to be, though it must have occurred to him since we kept going to school while others all around us got jobs.

All Fred ever told us was that it was best to keep busy by working at something because it would keep you out of

202

trouble. That was why he always said he kept his "head down and bum up", though he did take time off one Saturday to take us to the races. I put my money on Lancaster, which won the Brisbane Cup, and Jack kept the money Dad gave him and didn't have a bet because he said the odds were against the punter.

Fred said he could not tell us about learning because he had always been too busy to learn. And he said it was no use telling us anything about work because his father could never get him to work hard when he was our age. Even if Fred did start to do some work Grandpa Hugh used to tell him to "sit down and watch the snails rush by".

It wasn't often we got a chance to talk to Fred. He was always in the shop and we were mostly at school. We always got off the bus two stops early, to visit the shop on the way home from Terrace, but there wasn't much chance for talking: Fred was so committed to the shop that he was hard to talk to when he was working.

One Sunday, a man in a big Chevrolet pulled up outside and came in to buy a large apple tart. But we were sold out. Fred heard him express his disappointment, and offered to make one for him: imagine, one apple tart in Fred's huge oven. It was like one player on a football field. Fred told him to come back in an hour.

An hour later the man turned up and Fred checked the oven by turning the silver handle to the right, and dropped the wide grey door down until it stopped level with the floor of the oven. He got his stick with the hook at the end and pulled the long black tray out, prodded the pie with his right forefinger, smelt it, and pushed it back in with the stick and shut the door. "It'll be another ten minutes," Fred said. "You told me to come back in an hour. I can't stand around all day waiting for you to make an apple tart," the customer said, and walked out.

Some nights Fred would padlock and re-padlock the front door a dozen times as people rushed up—seeing a shop closing—and ask to buy a packet of cigarettes or a bottle of milk. Mum always said the best way to get customers was to start to close the front door.

When he did finally make it home, Fred liked to have someone to talk to, but it was always very late. So anyone who was still up would try to sneak off to bed before Fred could catch them. That was why Olive christened him "Dracula", a name Fred enjoyed immensely. "Dracula got me last night," became a common remark for explaining tiredness at breakfast. Fred said he liked catching someone in the kitchen at midnight because he disliked being left sitting alone "like a Mopoke" at the kitchen table.

If Dracula did get you, he wouldn't ask anything about school or football. Instead he would talk about life.

He would often say how, until he was thirty, he never knew you died. And he would tell things he had heard women say in the shop, his favourite being: "It's been great since the old man died." He liked to talk about how women loved spending money and how they enjoyed having "all their money on their backs". If a store had advertised a sale, he would say sarcastically: "Look, they're giving them away!"

He was no real comfort. If you said some boy had pinched your rubber, Fred would say: "If they need it bad enough, let them have it"; if you complained about Jack or Gay or Mum, he would say "don't make yourself hard to love"; and if you asked him where he had been, when he left the shop for a few minutes, he gave answers like "I was off to see the wizard" or "I went to see a man about a dog". These evasive answers usually meant he had been to the pub for a beer or to place a bet on a horse.

When he finally did go to bed, if it had been a big day in the shop, he would wrap his trouser braces around his arm because all the money was in the trouser pockets.

Because we were always up so late, Fred bought a new type of alarm clock: an electric clock you didn't have to wind. You just plugged it into the wall and the buzzing high-pitched alarm would not stop until you got up and turned it off. This clock was always kept twenty minutes fast to try to help everyone run on time. Though we all still ran late, the buzz of the green clock on Mum's duchess ruled our lives. Every Wednesday morning this green clock went off at 6 a.m. because I had to go for a piano lesson before school to a little old lady four blocks away in Venner Road: even though it was obvious that I never improved from one year to the next. And on school days it went at 7.20 a.m. (7 a.m. real time), but I still could never get out of the house until I heard the Tarragindi bus struggling up the hill in first gear outside our house, loaded down with people.

With my brown school port in hand and Sammy the Sparrow arriving on the wireless and Olive calling out "have you got your wallet, a handkerchief, football shorts, homework", I would race the bus two blocks up the hill for the next stop. If I missed it there, it was another long block to the Annerley Junction stop. Often I couldn't catch it and then I was late—mostly because the bus drivers didn't like GPS boys in smart uniforms with their big ports, and football or cricket boots attached, that took up a lot of room on a crowded bus. When they saw me they went faster. Sometimes in the afternoon, at the bus stop outside our house, they simply refused to wait until I could make my way through the crowd to the front of the bus to get off.

"The bus was late" was my favourite excuse for turning up after the bell at school. Jim was always early, but on the one day he did arrive late several of us were kept outside until the Brother was ready. We then filed in with our excuses: "The bus was late"—sit down; "the bus was late"—sit down; "the bus was late"—sit down; then Jim—"the bus was early"—sit down. "What! Get back out here Egoroff! What do you mean the bus was early?"—"It left before I got there!" said Jim.

Olive too started asking what I wanted to be when I grew up. She should have known, because it was pretty obvious. That was why I kept walking around the place imitating the wireless announcers, calling imaginary rugby league matches between Queensland and New South Wales like George Lovejoy: "Out the ball comes Queensland's way. Payne gives it to Tyquin, Tyquin to Davies, Davies to McGovern who's going for the corner. He's over. He's scored. Queensland has won. I'm crying, everyone's crying .... Time for a Coke." Although I never saw men like McGovern, they were—like Mickey Hill—my unseen heroes. I stayed up after midnight to listen as McGovern almost scored a try in a Test in England, even though the wireless reception was so bad that it was difficult to hear what was being said, the volume rising and falling while what sounded like a cyclone played in the background. This was made even worse by the English announcers who were so matter-of-fact they didn't make the game exciting like Lovejoy did.

Though I didn't have one, when asked the time I always said: "The time by my Wallace Bishop Loyal watch is ..." and I announced imaginary Melbourne Cups: "Around the corner into the straight, and as they straighten up for the home turn with two furlongs to go you can put your glasses down, it's London to a brick on Bernborough." And I rattled off the advertisements: "Drink Fourex beer, it takes one X to mark the spot .... but it takes four Xs to mark ... the perfect spot."

Finally, Olive took some action.

She bought me a new gaberdine raincoat and took me into the ABC's Alice Street office where I saw an old man in a dark suit. But when he asked me questions I became totally incoherent and, for some unknown reason, I kept saying "you reckon?" He told me to go away and practise reading editorials from the papers, but we didn't know what they were.

Then Mum took me to the Vocational Guidance centre behind Parliament House. They got me to do hours of tests and the man in charge announced proudly that they had worked out exactly what I should be. It stood out very clearly, much more so than was usual. And he held up a piece of paper with a series of short thick lines and one long thick line that ran almost right across the page to the word he announced triumphantly: "Architecture".

Olive looked at the man in disbelief and took me home, saying a decision on what I wanted to be could wait until after Senior.

Now that Jack and I were nearly grown up, Mum thought we should get to know our father better. So we were told to take our new lean-to tent and go down the Gold Coast for a "boys only" holiday. Particularly now that she had just bought Jack and me some togs made out of a new material which meant they were so small they could fold up into their own pocket.

Jack and I cleaned the Zephyr and we were so happy that, as Jack rubbed the special wax polish on, he whistled Slim Dusty's "A Pub with No Beer". At least that was what I thought he was whistling. But as the rubbing made him breathless, and his whistling slowed, it sounded more like Stephen Foster's "Beautiful Dreamer". We had the music for both upstairs, and I raced up and checked the two and I was right: the music was almost the same. This was one of my proudest moments, but it worried me because I couldn't understand how the rest of the country hadn't noticed.

I was really pleased to be going with Fred because I had gained new respect for him recently. He had finally got sick of Jack trying all his wrestling holds on him, and threw him straight over his shoulder so that Jack landed flat on his back. He got the fright of his life.

In the afternoon we practised putting the tent up in the back yard, and late that day the three Herbs left the three girls at home. We pitched our tent on the wide expanse of grass in front of Kirra beach which, we were surprised to see, was deserted. What could have happened—or be about to happen?

Jack and I had fold-up stretchers, and Fred slept in the Zephyr on the fold-down bed which had been installed. You just dropped the back of the front bench seat.

After we went to bed and blew out the lantern, a storm blew up which was lifting the flaps and blowing water in on us. Jack and I got up and tied it down more securely. But the storm worsened. Soon the sand floor of the tent was covered in several inches of water and the drains we dug would not carry it away because the land was so flat. The ground became so water-logged that the flapping tent pulled the heavy steel stakes out of the ground, and slowly the tent collapsed around us. All our blankets were wet. Though my stretcher was an inch above the water, pieces of wet tent kept landing in my face. We had to do something, but we couldn't wake Fred up: he was snoring in the car.

Eventually, Jack and I sat up under the one remaining

tent pole waiting for dawn and the storm to stop.

Despite the storm, Fred slept in, while we tried to re-establish the tent during a brief respite from the rain. But then it came again.

When we finally got Fred up, he looked at the weather and the black sky and said his usual "no rest for the wicked". He tried to help us keep the tent up, but the wind was so strong the rain was blowing through the thin white sides. "This tent's about as good as a two-bob watch," said Fred, so we sat in the Zephyr, out of the sea spray now whipping across the wide, green, deserted camping ground, unable to see through the misted windows and listening to the car wireless—where we heard that a cyclone was lashing the Gold Coast, and all the roads to Brisbane were cut off by flood waters.

There was nowhere to go. We were stuck.

Late that afternoon—as we once again tried to fix up the tent for the night—a man in shorts and bare feet came walking across the flooded plain towards us with an umbrella. He introduced himself as Mr Keen and said his friends called him "mustard". He and his wife had been watching us all day from their rented brick flat across the road. "I couldn't take it any longer," he said. "You can't stay out here. You had better come and stay with us."

We didn't argue.

In twenty-four hours in the storm, we had forgotten what it was like to be inside and warm, and to smell things cooking on the stove and to be drinking hot Milo. How wonderful it was to get into a dry bed with dry white sheets. The Keens clothed and fed us for two days before we set out at night to try to get back to Brisbane. We were doing well until we came to the Logan River, which had overflowed its banks on the southside of the bridge. A lot of cars were queued up, waiting to head north, but it didn't look all that deep so Jack and I urged Fred to drive through. He hesitated for a couple of hours, and then we took off into the flood. Other motorists said to stay in a low gear and keep revving the engine and riding the clutch.

The water must have been over two feet deep in the middle

and Fred didn't rev hard enough and we conked out. It didn't seem to matter, until we noticed the flood water was slowly pushing us off the road. Jack said we should open the doors to let the water flow through the car, which seemed a drastic idea. Just then a truck appeared behind us, wanting to get through, and he pushed us out.

It was such a close call that we were exhilarated to be on our way home, and Fred took off over the bridge and sped away until he suddenly realised that he didn't have any brakes. So we had to drive slowly home to the girls to tell them of our adventure.

The Gold Coast had become my favourite place to go during school holidays. Mum and Dad had bought ten acres of farmland at the end of a dirt road a few miles north of Southport, because Olive had always regarded the south coast as her ancestral home. She always told with great regret the story of how Pa had given her brothers two blocks of land at Surfers Paradise, but they were unable to keep up the rate payments.

Not that the farm was very nice. It was miles from any of the Gold Coast action, and it was covered in scrub with one small clearing and a large swamp which was full of snakes and mosquitoes. I tried to talk Olive out of it but, once she had made up her mind, there was no chance of changing it. It was the same with her decision to buy a floor polisher instead of one of the new mowers that were driven by a motor. I explained to her that the yard at Annerley was much bigger than the floor of the house, but still she went for the polisher, even though it made little difference to the appearance of the house. Mum's answer to the motor mower plea was to buy a goat which butted us and wrecked the plants.

Owning a farm was what she had always wanted, and she dominated it more confidently than Lawson's "Drover's Wife". Not only was Olive by far the biggest form of life among the trees, she was also the deadliest: she killed snakes one-handed, while cooking meals in her camp oven. (We camped out, because there was no farmhouse at the farm.) She knew how to get rid of mosquitoes—she threw sugar on our camp fire; she treated insect bites with a bag of washing blue; and she applied sliced tomato, cold tea or metho to my frequent sunburn. She didn't worry about our wounds, unless she could see a red streak emanating from the cut.

Apart from exploring the bush, the only thing to do on the farm—since we weren't allowed to listen to the car wireless for fear of running down the battery—was to talk. Olive would tell us that we all thought she was as "old as Methuselah", and that our policy was to make her do all the work "to kill the old ones off first". She told of the dangers of eating pork (tape worms) and advised us never to eat it unless she had cooked it herself.

When she talked of cricket she always reminded us of Pa's words—"if you can't be a good cricketer at least dress like one"—and she often said that Queensland had missed a chance to win the Sheffield Shield because someone down south had "drawn the colour bar"—whatever that meant— against our black fast bowler Eddie Gilbert. If she didn't like a sportsman, it was because she thought he was too thin and looked like "a chewed up piece of string". She often said a chap from near Nerang, Mick Madsen—one of the "pigs", as Olive always called forwards—was the biggest, toughest footballer ever to play for our home state of Queensland, of which Mum was very proud.

If she found you in her old cane chair, she would call you a cuckoo. If you said she was doing something wrong, she would tell you not to tell her how to suck eggs. And she was always telling Fred to "go easy on the condiments", because he put a lot of sauce on his meals. Whenever I let her down by failing to run a message, she would say "anyone who leans on you is leaning on a dead stick".

For our first holiday at the farm, Neil from next door, Jack and I were going to ride down on our bikes from Brisbane, but we were stopped after a debate in the back yard between Olive and Neil's mother. So we put the bikes on the train to Southport, and rode to the farm from there.

It was a miraculous sort of place, the farm. Strange things often happened there.

When we first got it, we took our boarder Mr Stewart

down. Being an American, he had been raving about how he had never seen a snake in the wild, and so we told him there was a snake under every log on our farm—and he was stupid enough to believe us.

There was an old log near one of our two tents, and Jack and I told Neil to lift it up so Mr Stewart could see a snake. Neil was laughing as he struggled to lift one end up high. We were struck dumb when we saw a big snake crawl up the side of the log towards Neil, with Mr Stewart saying, "Well, well—that's a fine specimen." Jack warned Neil, but Neil was still laughing and saying: "How many heads has this one got Jack?" It showed Mr Stewart that Neil was no squib.

Though we had three bikes, we only had two working headlights. And Olive said we could not ride into Southport after dark unless we all had lights. That was why we had brought along an old rusty bike light from under the house which didn't work. But it was a light and, if we left before dark, we figured Olive would never know the difference. But Mum was not fooled. She insisted that each of us show her our light was working before we could go. Neil shone his, Jack his, and I was left with the light that didn't work. This, I knew, would call for some acting so, as I turned the rusty tin switch on top, I prepared my little speech: "Gosh, it was working before. The battery must have gone flat." There was no hope of it lighting up: it hadn't worked for as long as I had lived at Annerley. Yet, as I said a prayer and turned it on, the bulb flickered and the torch shone brightly.

Though snakes were our biggest problem, the most dangerous thing happened the day Fred decided to shift the Zephyr by rolling it down the slope without the engine on, while he was only half in the car.

We had two tents on the farm: the one with the Indian on the side, and the lean-to. Fred got the car rolling just as Olive walked out from between these two tents, heading for the table that our lunch was on. This was the collapsible table Jack and I had spent hours making, for the Melbourne trip, out of a wooden cake tray with "Websters" written up the side. When Fred saw Mum he slammed the brake on with his left foot, but nothing happened. He hit it again, and the pedal went straight to the floor. He swerved and drove straight into the table, sending our lunch into the air, and finally the car hit a tree. It turned out he had been pushing the clutch instead of the brake, and for years afterwards Fred told the story of how, if Olive had been killed by his run-away Zephyr, no jury would have believed him and he would have spent the rest of his life in jail.

The farm was alright, but my first holiday with Jack and his mates in a fibro flat in Vista Street at Surfers Paradise was more fun: though Jack had to tip me off—now that I had turned sixteen—not to continue Mum's trick of wearing a hair-net to bed to keep my cow's lick hairstyle in place overnight.

These boys were so old they went to dances, and fell in love with girls. One of them kept walking around all the holidays singing "Hey There", a hit song about a bloke love made a fool of.

The only time I ever came close to girls was at peak hour on the buses and trams, when everyone was jammed in together. I got to looking forward to lucky days when I would be crunched up close to a nice girl on the bus, inevitably brushing against her when the bus swerved around a corner or as people pushed past to get out. And it wasn't even sinful pleasure since, under the rules of sinning, I wasn't doing anything deliberately wrong: I was merely standing innocently on the bus and getting shoved around. Though I guess it was sinning to look down the front of women's dresses when I was standing on the tram—drawn by the white lace and shiny satin which covered sinful regions. Of course we always had to stand up and let everyone else sit down. It was one of the rules of the school, and many boys got the strap after it was reported back that they had held a seat while an adult stood.

Even if there were spare seats down the back of the bus I found it best to stand up because the vibrations sitting above the engine led to impure feelings and an embarrassingly obvious, growing pleasure.

I got to see plenty of beautiful girls in the pictures, so

I knew the type I liked: Doris Day or Debbie Reynolds. Now that the pictures were all in colour, and in wide Cinemascope, going to town for a film was just about the most exciting thing you could do—to see famous shows like *Ben Hur* or *The Robe* or *The Greatest Show on Earth*. There was the Regent theatre, which was like a palace, or the Wintergarden which created a lot of excitement because its carpeted entrance seemed as long as a football field, or the Saint James or the Tivoli. Neil, Jack, Kenny and I loved the pictures in town so much that one Saturday we worked out all the times so that we could see three movies in one day at three different theatres including: *The Man Who Never Was* and *The Man Who Knew Too Much* with Doris Day.

It was so exhausting we never did it again.

Gay was at a big Catholic girls school called All Hallows, and she had some nice looking girlfriends. But Gay and these girls—including her best friend, Pipsy—talked their own special language, called "arpy-darpy", which I couldn't understand. It involved putting an "arp" or a "darp" before every vowel in a word: "Darpou garpodarping tarpo thdarpe sharpop"—or something like that—meant "Are you going to the shop?" But they used the language so fast I couldn't understand anything they said to each other.

The only time one of them ever showed any interest in me was when luminous socks came in. I was wearing a lime green or a tangerine pair under my grey school trousers, and she yelled out "Where did you get the socks?" I didn't answer her because I knew these girls were so frightened of boys. They had reputedly even been told not to polish their leather shoes too much, because we would look down to see the reflection from under their dresses.

Even Olive was becoming obsessed with modesty now, and every time I walked around the house in a long singlet to stay cool in the heat, she chased me with her jar of mustard ointment, threatening to put some on me unless I put my pants on. She used the mustard ointment on chests for colds—and, now that we were older, used brown paper soaked in vinegar on the forehead for a fever.

One of Jack's best mates, the college handball champion

Mark Fogarty, was in our Surfers flat, and he suggested I go with them all to the big Sunday night dance at Father Brick Shannon's Catholic church in Surfers. The priest was called "Brick" because he was always asking for donations of bricks (in the form of cash) for a new church. I wasn't keen to go because I had no confidence in myself. Everyone in the family was on to me for slouching around, and Mum kept saying "shoulders back". They said I was round-shouldered, so I knew I wasn't going to get a girlfriend.

I told Mark I had only been to a dance once in my life, and had not enjoyed it at all. It had been held at the big new secondary school the government had built at Salisbury, out at the end of our tram line. A lot of these girls, in their red uniforms, used to come into our shop after school for a milkshake, and Jack got friendly with them. So when it came time for them to have a dance, he went to the Salisbury school in his red and black Terrace blazer and asked the stern headmaster, Mr Mackie, if he and I could go to the dance—even though it was for Salisbury High pupils only. The headmaster said Jack seemed like a good boy, and agreed.

There was a new material called "nylon" out, and it was used for making shiny white shirts which didn't need ironing, and dried almost immediately after being washed. Mum was so impressed with this idea that—although they were much more expensive than ordinary cotton—she bought Jack and I one each to wear to the dance. As there were only two brands of these shirts, we got one of each (mine was an HG; Jack's a Bisley) so Olive could work out which lasted better.

As soon as I arrived, I saw a beautiful student called Jenny and fell so much in love with her that I couldn't ask anyone else for a dance: and, naturally, I wasn't game enough to ask her. I found out that she lived down at Fairfield on the other side of Ipswich Road, and on a Sunday morning I would walk over there and stand in the park and wait to see her go by, on the way to what Protestants called Sunday School. Once, as she went past, I took a photo of her with Mum's Kodak box camera, but she didn't seem to notice. Some athletes used to run in the park, and I watched them while

I waited. Then one Sunday they sent a runner over to ask if I was interested in joining. So I had to stop going there.

Mark Fogarty dismissed this story as something that had happened nearly a year ago—when I was only young. Anyway, he said I should go to the Surfers Paradise dance because I bore a surprisingly strong resemblance to Bill Haley, whose song "Rock Around the Clock" was top of all the hit parades. He said all I had to do was alter my hairdo and I would be a dead ringer for Bill Haley: and he got a comb and a glass of water and some hair oil, and carefully re-did my hair with a Bill Haley curl in the middle of my forehead. Every one of Jack's mates in the flat agreed that I was the spitting image of Bill Haley: so much so that they suggested I should tell everyone I was related to him in some way—his cousin—to sort of explain away the strong resemblance.

At the dance I did as they suggested, and lots of people were very impressed to have Bill Haley's cousin in their presence. Every lie made the story far more complicated, as people asked me about Bill and his song and his band, the Comets. But after a while I started to enjoy it. For the first time in my life, people were taking notice of me, even though you could see my singlet through my white nylon HG shirt. They were waiting to hear what I had to say, and agreeing with whatever I said about hit tunes. I was a big Doris Day fan, since seeing *Calamity Jane*, and I said Bill's favourite songs were Doris Day's latest "Whatever Will Be Will Be" and Kay Starr's "Rock and Roll Waltz".

Everyone agreed they were great songs.

Yes, Bill was thinking of coming to Australia soon. No, he didn't like Pat Boone. Yes, naturally, he was a Catholic and went to Mass and Communion religiously every Sunday.

It was such a successful charade that this really pretty girl in a red skirt, which swung up around her waist when she twirled, kept asking me to dance with her. Here I had an unexpected advantage in this ruse. Jiving was the only dance I knew how to do, because some of the steps resembled tap-dancing. Also, Gay was an expert dancer and the first dance she came across—when she was old enough to learn something other than ballet and acrobatics—was jiving to rock and roll. And she had to practise with someone, so of course it was me.

Gay was such a talented dancer that she invented new moves and steps. Being able to bend backwards to the floor, she needed someone who could catch her as she went down, and who had the timing to throw her back up and spin her around. So, for the first time ever in public, I knew what I was doing when I hit the floor as Bill Haley's long-lost cousin with his hair plastered down with Spruso hair oil, dancing and swinging and spinning with this short-haired blonde in the red skirt.

Soon the others stopped to watch us, and I started to wish more people had turned up for this dance. But my moment of glory ended when Brick arrived, as he always did at some stage of the night, and intervened, telling the girl in the red skirt she had to stop dancing rock and roll with me, because every time she swung around, or tipped over, she showed her pants. I tried to explain that I couldn't see them from where I was, but he just wouldn't listen.

So we sat and talked about rock and roll. She seemed to believe everything I said to her, which gave me a strange sense of power. She was about the nearest thing to a date I had ever had, but after that dance my forehead curl washed out and I went back to being just Johnny Duncan's cousin from Brisbane, and never saw her again.

16
The boys in the band

The best thing about going on to Senior was that there was no C class.

Most of the Junior Cs had gone off to get jobs, and four of the As and Bs had already joined the Christian Brothers at the "Juniorate" at Strathfield in Sydney. So there were only two Terrace sub-senior classes: A and B.

Thus Jim and I had gone up in the world, without even trying: we were now in the Bs, and there was no big supervised end-of-year exam to face for two years, our first respite since Scholarship. The only cloud on the horizon was that all of the Brothers agreed that Senior, in two years' time, would be the hardest exam any of us would ever do: more difficult than university, even more difficult than State Scholarship.

Perhaps because most of the Cs left after Junior, the Brothers gave the strap much less often. And Jim and I felt more comfortable, now that we no longer had to analyse strange sentences. Now a sentence was just a sentence. And I was very pleased when our new English teacher, Brother Campbell, announced on our first day as Seniors that, as far as he was concerned, the perfect English sentence was: "The cat sat on the mat (semi-colon) it was a fat cat"— because, he said, everyone could understand it.

On top of all this good news, I had managed to make it into the cadet band, and now had my own silver cornet and a special uniform: white webbing with white gloves; arm badges with a tiny brass trumpet and lyre on a red felt background; and, on each shoulder, red and black epaulettes with TERRACE in polished brass. Boy it was good to march through Annerley and the city looking like that.

I appreciated being in the band more than most, because the boys in the band didn't have to go shooting. We didn't even have a rifle.

Also, it had been really difficult for me to get a place in the band. For a year all I had was an old brass army bugle to practise on, to learn to play "calls": traditional army tunes with a limited range of notes, because the bugle did not have the three valves which gave the cornet so many additional notes.

Some other school cadet corps had bugle bands, but Terrace was the only one in Queensland with all trumpets and cornets: so we were the only band that could play any tune we chose. Terrace had this champion cadet band because one of the boys in the band was a top musician who played both the violin and the trumpet with something I thought was called the Queensland Sympathy Orchestra. His name was Brian Buggy and he taught the other boys in the band to play, not by teaching the boring theory of music, but with numbers—showing which valves to press down to make a tune. For example, to play "Waltzing Matilda" we didn't need to know about the flats and sharps and the crochets and quavers, all we needed to read was: "1/2 1/2 1/2 0 0 0 1 0 1/2 1 1/3 1/2 1, under the shade of a Coolibah tree".

One of my problems with the bugle was that it was very hard to find a place to practise. I was immediately barred from blowing it in the shop or the house, and so retreated up into the mango tree, until old Mr Reeves, who never usually spoke to me, threw up his sash window and stuck his head right through and yelled out: "Cheese it Hughie, cheese it", and slammed the window down again. Thus I only really got to practise after school on cadet day, picking up various calls by listening to the others.

At cadet camp the previous year, I'd been attached to the band, but not really part of it, since there were no spare cornets available. So I was in a sort of no-man's-land. Unfortunately, Jim missed out altogether when he applied to be a drummer. He auditioned with a drum roll they called "the black cat piddled in the white cat's eye", and the drum skin bent visibly as Jim pounded it with both hands, the drumsticks threatening to fly off and ricochet around the room. And Sergeant Brian Buggy had to try to explain that, even though a drummer is required to make a lot of noise, he is supposed to let the drum do it for him.

The band was so special that Sergeant Buggy asked for, and got, a special marquee as our camp headquarters: something no other unit had.

When we arrived at Greenbank army camp that year I was sitting outside my tent in the middle of the day when a couple of older boys who played the tenor drums—swinging large white drumsticks above their heads for show—came over and asked me how I was going. They said they had been listening to me practise at school and, though they were drummers, they felt I "had the necessary" to be the very next person picked for a cornet. All I had to do, they said, was to bring Sergeant Buggy's attention to my unique blowing ability. "Why don't you blow that call you kept practising at school—now, while everything is quiet—and he will hear it?" one of them suggested. Eager to please, I raised my short brass bugle to my lips, pursed them, and blew as hard as I could: "Da dum da da de da dum dum, dum da da de da dum" .... and I noticed all the cadets diving into their tents, grabbing their dixies, and running down to be first in the long queues for lunch.

"Sergeant Buggy," the voice of Brother (now Major) Basher boomed out through the long rows of green-brown canvas tents, "send over the cadet who did that." Did what? I thought, just as a sinking feeling hit my stomach.

Sergeant Buggy appeared in front of me, with a forced smile on his face and his right hand outstretched, his index finger wiggling me towards him. It was me. I had played "Come To the Cookhouse Door Boys" without realising it. Now I knew why I knew that tune: I had heard it last year in camp.

Major Basher looked even more fierce in his full army uniform, under one of those officers' caps that make people seem four inches taller than they really are. I saluted and stood at attention: "So, Huggles," he said, "we meet again

.... Been playing tricks on everyone have we boy?" No, Sir. "Been sending three hundred people to lunch before lunch was ready have we son?" Didn't realise, Sir. "Been trying to upset the Major?" Just practising a call like at school, Sir.

The Brother looked carefully into my eyes, with his pupils of steel, and waited for me to crack. But my innocence was profound. "Dismissed, Cadet Lunn," he said, and I saluted, about turned, and marched back to my tent much relieved.

Because Terrace had the best band in Queensland it could do what it liked and so, while the rest of the cadets practised marching or taking bren guns and mortars apart, we marched off into the bush to "practise". Often this meant sitting around telling stories while one boy hit a drum or blew a few notes on a trumpet. Some of the boys would even have a cigarette: which risked instant dismissal, because no-one at Gregory Terrace was supposed to smoke.

The band was also the medical corps in our cadet unit, and we had to practise putting each other's arms in a sling, carrying one another draped over our shoulders with the fireman's lift, and learning how to secure a broken thigh bone by using the wounded man's rifle in what the army called a "John Thomas splint", a phrase which always caused everyone to snigger. When our families visited on the Sunday, and there was a mock battle with smoke grenades and troops firing blanks, we had to scout around the bush battlefield on our bellies in groups of four with a stretcher, repair the wounded (after they told us where they were supposed to be hurt), and carry them off—to loud applause from hundreds of parents and brothers and sisters who seemed to love seeing their children shot in army uniform.

Even Olive could be seen applauding. But not, of course, Fred, who was disgusted that he was paying for me to learn this, and said he was pleased Jack was not in the cadets—again because of the fever.

One day, when Sergeant Buggy wasn't with us, we marched a long way into the Greenbank bush before settling down on some logs in a small clearing of gums and long dry grass. After a while the tenor drummers came over to talk to me. They said they were sorry about what happened the other day. And they said that, though it had been the wrong time to play the bugle call, it had certainly been played very well. That was why all the cadets had instantly recognised it. Now that we were safely out in the bush, what about demonstrating it again so the other trumpeters could hear it?

I was very reluctant, but all the trumpeters were keen, and hadn't I spent the last year walking around saying "tick-a-tee" to get my tongue ready for the day I got a cornet? So again I pressed the bugle to my lips and blew for the right to have a cornet.

Within seconds of the last note being blown, an angry under officer from the Senior class crashed into our clearing— which turned out to be very close to a parade ground. "Who did that?" he demanded. "The major just lost a whole parade ground of first-year cadets he was drilling. They ran right out from under his nose."

Well now I'd done it. I could only think of what Brother Campbell had told us Richard of Bordeaux said to the King after losing a battle: "When there is no excuse there is only apology." But I could see that not even an apology would suffice now. When Basher found out it was me, he didn't even want to see me. I was just detailed to clean the latrines for the rest of the camp.

All that was behind me now. Several members of the band had left since then, Basher never bore grudges, and so I had got my silver cornet and now I could play marching tunes like "Dog Faced Soldier", "Pack Up Your Troubles in Your Old Kit Bag", "Stars and Stripes", "Colonel Bogey" (including the alteration for "March on the River Kwai"), and even some classy waltzes—like "Carnival of Venice" and "Mocking Bird Hill"—which we played when the band slow-marched, or while an army officer inspected our troops.

We learnt complicated formation marching, where parts of the band would branch off and intermingle, and we would come out magically in formation at the end. There was one tune we played which lasted just long enough for fifteen paces to be taken. This was a trick we performed at every cadet passing-out parade when, with parents watching, the under officer would call to the 350 cadets stretched in platoons across the entire football field: "Parade will advance in Review Order." The drummers would give two drum rolls as we pursed our lips to our mouthpieces and, when they finished, we would blow this fifteen-beat tune as the whole parade marched fifteen paces forward and all stopped together on the last note, with perfect precision.

We were the only school band able to play a difficult Protestant hymn called "Nearer My God to Thee", and so we played it at Greenbank for the Protestant GPS cadets at some flag-raising ceremony they had each afternoon. I was surprised it wasn't a sin to play one of their hymns, since they were always threatening to invade our lines for a fight with army belts, and we Catholics were barred from attending their churches.

Back at school we had some nice teachers—Brother Adams for maths, and big Brother Campbell for English and logic: a man Senior boys had always affectionately known simply as "Doc".

Doc was a very devout man, whose favourite saint was the Little Flower—St Therese of the Child Jesus—a French Carmelite nun who had been dead more than sixty years. Perhaps he admired her because she had one outstanding quality that he did not: St Therese was said to be so self-effacing that she lived unnoticed by most of her sisters in religion before dying of consumption aged twenty-four, after a life dedicated to prayer. Doc was the opposite of self-effacing, and he was famous among his colleagues for his intellect and for his ability to communicate with students.

Logic was an unusual subject for anyone to do in Queensland for Senior, but Brother Campbell insisted that every boy must do it because, he said, he would ensure we passed: and that would put us a quarter of the way to a Senior pass. And the more Catholic boys who passed Senior, the better for all Catholics.

Doc was certainly unusual. He once told us that he bathed seven times a day, and he got us to throw the textbook—written by a professor mate of his—away, and each day he stood in front of us like a black-clothed giant and read out the notes he had written himself on the subject, saying that the next year he would teach us logic from these notes in just one year. As he did this, he told stories about himself and his life, and there was such an aura around him that no-one ever played up and he never had to give the strap.

Doc, who had been at Terrace seventeen years, and had coached the first fifteen until he got too old, told about the Latin and Philosophy classes he sometimes taught at night at the university, and he warned the smart boys that "if you can't pass English you won't get to look through the paling fence at the university".

He told us never to use our common sense: "Common sense is that which tells you the world is flat." He used lots of big words, but always told us what they meant. Doc admitted to us that he was a misogynist, but despite this he loved his mother who, he said, had ankle-length hair at his insistence. He talked of mothers with such great respect that he said the only excuse he would accept for being late for school was if your mother was sick. He dwelt on poems about mothers. He read us one where the poet compared his mother to a mountain "who none but faith could move", and it reminded me of Olive. And another about Stonewall Jackson who warned his men to leave an old mother alone: "Who touches a hair of yon grey head dies like a dog. March on, he said".

He referred to non-Catholics generally as "callithumpians", and warned us to stay well away from "the girls on the hill"—the St Margaret's Church of England Grammar School girls at Albion, who caught the same buses from town as we did. If Doc did get angry he would say that he was going to "spiflicate" us: but then minutes later he would say the word meant "to smother in kisses", whereas the dictionary defined it ominously as "damage, hurt, punish, kill or destroy utterly".

Once I thought he went too far, when he was reading from a radio play we had to study called *Fire on the Snow*, a poetic story about Scott's failed expedition to the South Pole, which Doc said had a beautiful descriptive start: "The world is spun between two giant hands of ice". In the play, Scott was worried that a Norwegian explorer, Amundsen, would beat him to the Pole, and he said to his men: "We must beat that Norwegian Walrus there". But Brother Campbell read out: "We must beat that Norwegian Bastard there". I thought I must be hearing things, and the whole class looked up as one, making Doc pause. "What does your book say?" he asked. Then he explained that our books must have been censored by the state, and "Walrus" substituted for the swear word.

Only three things could really upset him: boys who got their hair crew-cut (very short, so it stuck straight up on top), being late for school ("punctuality is the courtesy of Kings"), and failing to learn by heart four different lines of poetry every night.

Poetry was Doc's favourite thing, and each day he would call on several boys to recite the four lines they had learned the previous night. But you had to watch which lines you learned. Once I got up and recited a piece about a woman who "made the bar she leaned on warm", and he demanded to know why I had chosen to learn this—I couldn't really explain that it gave me pleasure.

But any anger—and guilt—was very soon gone.

Doc could even joke about proposed punishments. Once, when someone called Wordsworth's ode on the "Intimations of Immortality" the "Imitations of Immorality"—a perfectly understandable mistake—he said that if people didn't get the names of poems correct he wouldn't use a strap, he would get a fence paling and give the cuts with that. He said he would bring it into our class—and he showed where he would lean it against the wall ready for use. But, despite the serious look which was always on his face, you could tell he was only joking by the soft look his dark eyes took on. When he couldn't believe our ignorance, he would shake his head from side to side so that his wide creased jowls swung independently.

He was adored at Terrace, not just because of his large stature or curly grey hair or thick inquisitive black eyebrows, but because it was said he had once punched a spectator at a first fifteen match against Churchie. This Protestant had yelled out when we were losing: "Come on Terrace, where are your Rosary beads now?"

As terrific as Doc was, he could not make up for the new Brother from Waverley College, Sydney, who made life miserable for all of the dumbest kids. His nickname, I don't know why, was "Freddie", and he was our chemistry and physics teacher. Freddie had a string of letters after his name as long as the big row of upper teeth he showed with his smile, the reason some kids called him "Shark". From the day he stepped into the classroom, just as I could see there were some boys he liked, I could tell he didn't like me at all.

We were now in the school's newest classrooms, which featured roll-around blackboards, and Freddie knew so much that, along with Oliver Goldsmith, I wondered how one small head could carry all he knew. He would often start writing a chemical reaction on the blackboard and still be writing equations when the board had rolled right around to where he had started. Even then, Freddie would not stop to address the class. He would merely start rubbing out the beginning and keep on going: not realising that people like me had no idea what it all meant.

I suspect he was showing off, because the first thing he did when he met us was to prove mathematically that naught equals one. And the first story he told was how one of his former chemistry students now sold the headache powder "Sitruc", which was the main competitor for Bex and Vincents APC. It was advertised on the wireless with the promise—"Take Sitruc or Suffer".

Freddie said the pupil's name was Curtis, and he spelt it backwards for the headache powder.

We had to do experiments for him in the physics and chemistry laboratories and then write them up in science books which had lined graph paper for drawings. He would have to sign each experiment when it was completed and written up—and he was always refusing to sign mine. Which meant I had to do it again: like calibrating a pipette or proving Archimedes' principle.

We also had him for religion. But, unlike Doc, he wouldn't discuss things. Once, when someone asked him who Cain married after killing Abel, he went to the chemistry library and brought back a big book and started reading it to us. When it became obvious that no-one understood a word, Freddie said: "Only a scientist could understand this book. And that's why you need theologians to interpret the Bible."

It took only a few days for him to reveal his true personality. He told the class he would be leaving for twenty minutes, and he didn't want anyone to talk until he got back. As he walked through the door of the chemistry laboratory to leave, a boy called Sam Tamer whispered something. Freddie swung around, his teeth glistening: "Tamer, did you talk?" Yes, Sir. "Come out here, son," said Freddie, getting his strap from the drawer and addressing the class: "What you are about to witness from now on shall be known as 'the Tamer treatment'. Anyone who talks in class will get this treatment." He then started hitting poor Sam's right hand with the strap, over and over again, as everyone in the class counted silently. As he passed six, the whole class seemed to gasp. No-one had ever heard of anyone getting more than six altogether, or more than three on the one hand. Seven ... eight .... Even one hit with a strap bruised and numbed the hand so it curled involuntarily inwards and burned. Sam's hand must no longer belong to him anyway. When would he stop?

Nine ... Ten ....

And he finally stopped.

After that, no-one spoke when Freddie left a classroom.

Jack was now in his final year in the class ahead of me, and certain to pass Senior. Brother Campbell was noted as a tough marker of English papers and, when Jack wrote an essay on the International Geophysical Year, Doc announced to the class that he had given Master Lunn 29 out of 30. "The reason he only got 29 was that I decided 'surely no-one is good enough to get 30 out of 30'."

Not only was Jack doing well at school but doctors had cleared him to start playing sport: in fact they now had a totally new theory that exercise was good for people who had had rheumatic fever. So it was lucky that Jack ran and jumped and fought for all those years.

As I expected, Jack quickly made his mark.

We already knew he was very fast because, not only could he murder me in a race, but he was faster than Kenny Fletcher, who won races at St Laurence's. Jack started on the wing in the sevenths against Nudgee and soon found himself in the seconds. The seconds had lost badly to Brisbane Grammar at the start of the season: so badly that the headmaster, Brother Adams, criticised their School Spirit at assembly. So when the two teams were to meet again, he called on them publicly for a special effort.

Scores were even at six-all, with a minute to go, when Grammar's fastest player escaped near his line and looked certain to score at the other end. But, with Olive cheering wildly, Jack chased the boy down the sideline in front of the big crowd—waiting to see the firsts—and brought him down with a diving tackle just a foot from the line, to make the match a draw. As Jack lay flat on his back, with his legs being pumped up and down, Olive rushed proudly and apprehensively to his side, because of the fever: a disease we learned at school was caught primarily by poor children who lived in crowded quarters. But Jack soon jumped up, and was made reserve for the firsts; all that barley water must have worked.

Fred—who usually went for a walk in the park instead of watching the football—saw Jack's heroic tackle, and turned to me and said football was "like war". He also unwittingly insulted me, saying he was pleased to see I was staying well out of the game—"down the back" as fullback for the sevenths.

Not being a Queenslander, Fred didn't understand the game at all.

Fullback, in fact, was probably the toughest assignment on the rugby ground. If anyone broke through, the fullback had to stop them when they had reached top speed. The fullback also had to catch the ball when they kicked through, which meant keeping his eyes on the ball while knowing fifteen of the enemy were charging through to get him.

I had changed to fullback after Olive had invited some relatives—a newly married couple—to live at our place. Since Mr Stewart and Mr Clark had gone, there were only six of us living in our house.

The husband, Les, was an Australian Rules footballer who had been paid to play in Melbourne. He told me I wasn't big enough to be a rugby forward, and I wasn't fast enough to be a back: so I should be a fullback. And he took me down to the park and showed me how to kick with either foot.

After that, I never feared a football match: but I dreaded ever having to stand up and speak in front of the class.

Doc liked debates, which were usually done by the smartest boys in the A class. But one day he picked me in a team of three, for my first and last debate. It was on compulsory unionism, and my job, he said, was to argue for the affirmative. I had no idea how to do a debate, or even what compulsory unionism was. All I knew was that unionism was an "ism" and had something to do with politics—because two Old Boys had come back to talk to us in religion period one day about Commo unions trying to take over Queensland.

I knew better than to try to get something out of Fred. But Joe Noonan, the accountant, was in the shop for a pie so I asked him because I knew he had been in politics. In fact I had stood outside a hall all day one Saturday, handing out how-to-vote cards for him at an election, though at first I had been reluctant to help him because he was standing against the premier, Vince Gair, who had driven me to football matches when I was at the convent. But Joe explained that the real reason he was standing as a "True Blue Liberal" was to take votes away from the real Liberal candidate and help Mr Gair who, he said, might otherwise lose.

Joe seemed more than happy to help, and proceeded to dictate what I was to stand up and say in the debate: "Imagine yourself in a rowboat," he said, as we sat in the varnished eating alcoves of the cake shop, with me writing it down in my exercise book while Biddy, the drunk, kept interrupting. "Imagine the rowboat is out at sea with little food or water and miles from land," said Joe. "And imagine how you would feel if some of the men in the boat refused to help row the boat to shore." "That would be unfair," I said. "Right," said Joe, while Biddy said we should all drown.

Joe spoke so quickly, and with such conviction, as he argued with Biddy about the need to stay with the boat, that I got little more written down.

It would have been a waste of time and effort anyway. By the time it was my turn to speak, my body was trembling, my voice was gone, and I was so self-conscious standing up addressing both classes that after "Imagine yourself in a rowboat ..." my speech trailed off rapidly to nothing, because I didn't understand what I was talking about.

But Doc didn't go crook. When I finished, he came across and congratulated me, saying: "Always remember son—to be brave is not to be without fear, but to overcome it."

17
Impure thoughts

The Brothers often remarked on how, once boys reached sixteen, they started coming to school with their hair done and their clothes ironed neatly to impress girls. But Jim had always done that, even at the convent—and he hadn't met any girls. And it must have been obvious to the Brothers that I hadn't been that lucky either.

Not only was my hair all over the place since I stopped using hair oil or a hair net, but I now had soft white hair on my face which men coming in the shop insisted on calling "bum-fluff". Olive was too busy in the shop for ironing and, anyway, I don't think an iron would have made any difference to my big, baggy Nylange grey trousers. Now that Jack had left school, I had inherited his pair which he had got someone to peg-leg by taking in the bottom cuffs. The Brothers didn't like this sort of thing because it was what lairs or bodgies would do, but the cuffs were still just wide enough at the ankles to get away with it.

The more experienced older boys had a scoring system for things they had done to girls, made up of even numbers from two to fourteen: from two for touching their bust on the outside to fourteen for "all the way".

I had only the vaguest of notions what "all the way" meant. I knew it had something to do with impure actions but I wasn't even sure how, or exactly where, a boy and a girl got together: though I knew what with, and that they both had to take their pants off.

I also knew—though Jim and I never discussed such subjects—it somehow created babies and would be extremely pleasurable, and my mind alternated between thinking it would be a pity only to be able to do it six times in your life for six babies, and rejecting the entire act completely to concentrate on a clean, wholesome, pure life. I was swayed towards the latter by a quote from the knight Sir Galahad that Doc told us about: "I hold my sword with a steady hand, my lance it thrustest sure, my strength is as the strength of ten—because my heart is pure." But Doc said that while courage, courtesy and virtue were the ideals of knighthood, it was well to remember that knights must face their dragons and their "Valley of Desolation".

My friend Saint Anthony—whose holy picture I now carried in my wallet with "please call a Catholic priest" written on the back of it in case of an accident—was said to be the "model of chastity, which ennobles the body and imparts to it a charm of grace and beauty elevating the soul to make it queen of body and heart".

So much so that Saint Anthony, Doc told us, was "like an angel in the flesh".

I wasn't sure if purity was possible for me, since I had now grown hairs there. Did these strange hairs each represent an impure action? Were they then abundant evidence of Mortal Sin? I resolved to cover up.

Freddie did give us a talk on the human body in religion once, and he—and everyone else—seemed embarrassed when he came to what he called "nocturnal emissions". He said these were not a sin, because it was a normal bodily function which was necessary, and therefore pleasurable. Because you were asleep, they did not knowingly or willingly happen. But, if they did happen knowingly and willingly—that is, if you happened to be awake—they were a Mortal Sin: the equivalent of killing somebody. Which seemed like rough justice to me.

Freddie also warned us about the dangers of being taken in by the bodies of girls—though, of course, Doc put it much better, quoting some saint as having said: "Look not upon a maiden lest her beauty be a stumbling block to thee", and "many have perished by the beauty of woman".

I was so impressed I wrote these down in my notebook.

Freddie said if you thought a girl was wonderful, "have

a look at her mother and you will see what she will look like in twenty years' time". I got Gay into trouble when I narrated this story at the tea table. "Don't you go spreading that story around," Gay said—and Olive immediately wanted to know why Gay would worry about being compared with her.

Brother Adams, who very rarely gave the strap although he was headmaster, strayed onto sex when he gave a lecture about the dangers of rock-and-roll, now that Elvis Presley had everyone all shook up with "Jailhouse Rock", which made people involuntarily want to shake their bodies to the music. Brother Adams warned that jiving with a girl could break down the respect you had for her. I could never understand this. The government hadn't banned any rock-and-roll songs, but a few years before, they had banned a really slow number which began: "When you're dancing and you're dangerously near me, I get ideas ... I get ideas."

I didn't tell anyone at school—not even Jim—but at the end of sub-senior, Christmas 1957, I finally met the girl of my dreams down at the coast.

While Jack was waiting for his Senior results we took the lean-to tent to the camping ground at Southport for a two-week summer holiday. We had a little bit of money because Jack had sorted Christmas mail all night at the GPO, and Jim had got me a job at his post office, delivering telegrams. I had to swear an oath before getting the job. Jim delivered telegrams all the time, but I only lasted one day because it was so hot pushing a bike around in the summer.

Since Fred owned a shop, Jack and I could buy our food wholesale, so we went to get provisions at the Tickle Warehouse at Fairfield. We liked Tom Piper's Irish Stew, so we saved time by just buying fourteen large cans of this, figuring that would make two meals a day for the fortnight.

A couple of other boys shared the tent with us: Ian Lynagh from my class, who I remember well because he cleaned his teeth every night; and Jack's Annerley friend Ricky Kidston, who had also just done Senior.

The first day we arrived, Jack met this girl whose father managed Allan and Stark's store in Queen Street. The store had Brisbane's only automatic donut-making machine, which squirted out little round bits of dough into hot fat, and a wheel moved these in a full cicle, turning them over half way and then dropping them onto trays which went through a sugar shower while they cooled off. Then they dropped automatically into a bin—and GPS boys queued up for them after school.

These people had a flat at Surfers Paradise overlooking the sand dunes you had to walk over to get to the beach. We often went for a walk through these dunes at night to spot the dozens of couples hugging and kissing on blankets in between the dunes.

The great thing about this girl was that her father used to pull Jack aside and give him thirty shillings so that Jack could take his daughter and all of us hangers-on to the pictures. And that included her beautiful blonde girlfriend who was staying with her from school (unfortunately, the Protestant "school on the hill" Brother Campbell warned us about). The blonde's name was Desley, and I instantly recognised her as a dead spitting image of Grace Kelly.

But I was too young, and Ricky Kidston got to sit next to Desley. He boasted that he had taken her to the pictures in Brisbane once, and he had everyone jealous when he said that, after taking her to the pictures at Nundah, her father picked them up in a big Austin, drove them home for coffee, and then drove him back to the Clayfield tram terminus, with him and Desley snuggled up in the back seat while the wireless played Grace Kelly singing "True Love".

One night after the pictures, we all walked through the deserted streets of Surfers up to the beach, and Desley and I ended up walking on ahead and talking together. We seemed to be able to talk easily and I could tell she liked me, even though she insulted me by saying I was the only boy on the Gold Coast who wore a singlet under his shirt.

I was walking on the road and she was between me and the gutter—as it advised in our Christian Politeness book. As we neared the beach I coughed up some phlegm, and when I spat it out into the gutter ahead of her she got a big surprise. She thought it nearly hit her. What she didn't know was that over the years I had learned to spit very accurately and had never hit anyone.

Desley said if I was ever going to take girls out I couldn't do things like that: and, without saying anything to Jack or Ricky, I resolved to take her out.

Other than that, it was a terrible holiday. After a few days neither Jack nor I could face any more Tom Piper's Irish Stew, and we lived on two-bob banana thickshakes from the Bikini Bar in the middle of Surfers. This was a famous place because a sexy older woman worked there, and her shakes were so big they always overflowed on the electric stirrer—so she would invite you to suck some out to prevent any more spillage on the counter.

Knowing Fred would be the only one at home, I hitched back to Brisbane a few days early, and rang Desley up and arranged to take her to the Nundah pictures just like Ricky had done. Then I told Fred I would work hard all day in the shop if he paid me ten shillings, which he did.

The trouble was, when I got home at the end of the day I realised I had no clean or ironed clothes to wear, and I wanted to call the whole thing off. But it was too late for that, so I tore off some bum-fluff with Jack's Gillette razor, had a few practice goes at kissing in the bathroom mirror by leaning my head to the left, and put on my worst Nylange school trousers, which were far too big, and an old dirty shirt, and caught the tram to the Clayfield terminus.

It was just as Ricky had narrated: driven to Nundah, upstairs at the pictures, coffee at her house, the ride in the Austin back to the Clayfield tram terminus, the father humming to the wireless, and Desley and I sitting almost touching in the back. Except I felt most uncomfortable. She was just too beautiful and pure, and I began to think how little I had to offer. I couldn't bring myself to embarrass her by trying a kiss.

It was almost a relief to get on the last tram back to Annerley, and I never saw her again, though she was kind enough to send me a Christmas card in which I was disappointed to see she wrote "Merry Xmas", dropping the Christ from Christmas.

18
Egoroff stockpiles poetry

Jack surprised everyone in the family by getting a job as a cadet reporter on the *Courier-Mail*. This was in 1958, and it was most surprising because when he came home from the interview, in his short-sleeved green shirt, Jack said the editor-in-chief had asked him who he knew on the paper.

And Jack didn't know anyone.

Our whole family didn't know anyone.

But he got the job and, within a week, he showed us the phrase "dire straits" in a story. Jack said he had suggested these words to the reporter who was training him, and the reporter had used them.

I didn't really believe him. How could Jack start dictating what was going into the paper?

But soon he proved me wrong.

There it was in the *Sunday Mail*, "By Jack Lunn"—"I Saw the Evil of the Bodgies". He had followed the bodgies and widgies around near Yeronga Park one night to see what they were up to.

It seemed to be a great job.

Not only did he get free tickets to the GPS swimming, and get paid to go and watch rugby league matches, but he didn't start work until 2.30 in the arvo, so he could sleep in while I had to get up to go to school to study for Senior.

And he got to wander around in the city until late at night.

He had plenty of money, too, and soon bought an old green Vauxhall car which sometimes jumped out of second gear. And he came home with lots of funny stories about reporters, like one called O'Shea who upset the editor by appearing in an advertisement for some laxative salts. And the editor called him in and said: "Now listen to me, shit-a-day O'Shea ... "

Doc was really pleased that Jack had taken a job where he could use his writing ability and, now that I had replaced Jack in Senior, Doc often asked me what Jack thought of the job. Doc said newspapers were very important because people loved others to read about them, or to see their picture in the paper: "That last infirmity of noble minds", he called it. But, more seriously, he told me that Jack's success made his heart glad because it confirmed his reason for having become a Brother.

Doc said that, when he was a young man in Sydney, he had once helped with a class of young Catholic boys. That afternoon he went for a brisk walk. He hurried down a few back streets, across a park, up over a bridge .... when he started to wonder if the small boy from the school running behind him was trying to catch him up with a message.

Doc stopped as the breathless boy approached.

The boy was from the class. "Do you have a message?" asked Doc. "No," said the boy. "Do you live this way then?"— "No."—"Then why are you chasing me?"

"I just wanted to see how you was," said the boy.

"That was when I knew I wanted to teach young Catholic boys good English, so that they would not start life with an all too obvious disadvantage," Doc told me.

Doc described himself as "an incorrigible Christian Brother". He was the only Brother who always taught in the long black habit, no matter how hot it was, and he never sat down while teaching. Instead, he stood with one or both hands tucked into the black cincture of his habit. Though he had studied physics and chemistry at Sydney University in the 1920s, his first love was English.

In his English lessons, he concentrated almost exclusively on poetry, saying it was "the finer expression of all knowledge". Instead of writing that a man bent on a crime soon finds a tool to commit it with, how much better, Doc told us, to write, as Pope did: "But when to mischief mortals bend their will, how soon they find fit instruments of ill". And instead of writing that a wife was too interested in other men, see how Browning wrote: "She had a heart ... how shall I say? ... too soon made glad".

And he interspersed the lessons with funny poetry of his own.

When teaching us how to scan a poem—to work out the recurring beat in the lines—he told us about:

> There was a young man from Japan,
> Who wrote lines nobody could scan,
> When told this was so,
> He said, "Yes I know,
> But I always like to get as many words in the last line
>   as I possibly can."

One of his favourite poems was "Christabel", even though parts of it were impure: like when Christabel took all her clothes off in front of the evil lady, Geraldine:

> Her gentle limbs did she undress,
> And lay down in her loveliness.

I had never heard anyone talk of these impure things openly before, but Doc was not fazed at all. This, he said, was a terrific example of "poetic restraint". "Coleridge shows he is a great poet by resisting the temptation to go into detail: and yet creates the entire scene—and the atmosphere of it— in two beautiful lines."

Then what would Doc say about the next stanza, which failed to show any restraint at all when the other lady, Geraldine, got undressed beneath the lamp?

> Like one that shuddered, she unbound
> The cincture from beneath her breast:
> Her silken robe, and inner vest,
> Dropt to her feet, and full in view,
> Behold! her bosom and half her side—
> A sight to dream of, not to tell!

No-one in the class dared make even the slightest adjustment. But Brother Campbell said this was not what Coleridge originally wrote. Coleridge had changed the last line on his original manuscript purely to increase the poem's power of suggestion. And he asked us to write in the margin, next to "A sight to dream of, not to tell!" the line Coleridge had originally penned: "Are lean, and old, and foul of hue!"

It was a bit of a pity, because it sort of ruined the poem.

Since English poetry was so complicated, I thought it would give Jim—with his Russian background—a lot of trouble. As it was, he seemed to have trouble translating his Russian sayings into English, confusing everybody with phrases like: "If anybody's cow should moo, your cow should keep quiet!"—which I think meant "You should talk!" But Doc made English poetry so interesting that Jim quickly stock-piled vast passages of complex verse and, in fact, could quote poetry faster and longer than any other boy in the class.

Though his choice of poems was unusual.

For example, even though Doc told us George Crabbe's long poem "Peter Grimes" was doggerel—a poem that lacked inspiration, dignity, and a sense of humour—Jim concentrated his efforts on it. And he used this poem in arguments as a substitute for physical confrontation:

> The boat grew leaky and the wind was strong,
> Rough was the passage and the time was long;
> His liquor fail'd, and Peter's wrath arose,
> No more is known—the rest we must suppose ...

On and on he'd go, devastating his opponent with a curtain of words.

Though his English was now very good, Jim relied heavily on an escalating arsenal of phrases from the great English writers to win arguments. If someone went to answer him with a sentence beginning with "but", Jim would surely say "But me no buts". Or if someone answered that they were doing nothing to him, Jim would quote King Lear: "Nothing. Nothing will come of nothing, speak again".

If cornered in an argument where he had no answer, Jim would ask: "Do you still carry a gun in your suburb?" or "Have you stopped beating your wife/mother/girlfriend?"—because Doc had taught us that such questions could not be successfully answered.

This Berlin Wall of words seemed to give Jim great

confidence with the language, a confidence I felt was misplaced. But how were others to know, since Jim had a well-modulated voice and such a perfect memory?

Though sometimes he overdid it, like once at the Rex picture theatre in the Valley.

Every now and then Jim used to get a small piece of pink paper which allowed two people to go to the pictures at the Rex for free. So, after football or cadets, we would walk down to the Valley and see some old black and white film in the near-empty Rex. He would never tell me how he came by the free double passes.

After several such visits, we found a different man was in charge and he queried the pink slip. Jim, of course, gave no ground and said—tilting his head to the left, with his head pulled back, as he always did when he knew he was in for a serious argument—that it was none of this man's business. The pink slip was either a valid pass or it was not a valid pass. Not surprisingly, the old man took exception and said he would not be spoken to like that by a schoolboy.

Jim replied straight from his English lessons with his favourite quote: "Surely this is the object of either abhorrence or contempt and deserves not that your grey hairs should secure you from insult."

"Rightho laddie, I'm going to report you to your headmaster," said the man. Now we were for it.

"What for?" said Jim, "The atrocious crime of being a young man, and not of that number who are ignorant in spite of their experience?"

The old man, I could tell, was not sure what Jim was talking about. But he must have been impressed, because he motioned us into the theatre saying he didn't have time to stand around arguing all day with the likes of us.

My taste in poets was different from Jim's, and that of everybody else in the class. I didn't know why, but I found myself most attracted to the atheist poets like Algernon Charles Swinburne.

I often chose Swinburne's poetry to learn off by heart, while always ready to explain to Doc—who said Swinburne was "a decadent poet"—that I did so in admiration of the rhythm and rhyme, which even Doc admitted was "supreme". Though he said all this meant was that Swinburne was "all dressed up with nowhere to go". My favourite Swinburne stanza was:

I am tired of tears and laughter,
And men that laugh and weep
Of what may come hereafter
For men that sow to reap:
I am weary of days and hours,
Blown buds of barren flowers,
Desires and dreams and powers
And everything, but sleep.

This was what Doc called "Potatoes when I'm hungry, Whisky when I'm dry, Peggy when I'm lonely, Heaven when I die" poetry.

His other least favourite poet—Edward Fitzgerald—also seemed to echo my innermost, unexpressed thoughts:

Oh threats of Hell and Hopes of Paradise!
One thing at least is certain—This life flies;
One thing is certain and the rest is lies;
The Flower that once has blown for ever dies.

It was easy to see that this was not the sort of view to appeal to a religious man like Doc. But he still spent weeks going through the poem with us, explaining the above stanza: "Up until here, Fitzgerald has only been agnostic. Now he comes out in the open with this nonsense which disregards the rational man for the irrational flower."

To counter such heresy, Doc had the great Catholic poets to teach us for the exams. Like Francis Thomson, who wrote "The Hound of Heaven", an account of how he tried one thing after another to flee God, but eventually came back into the fold of the Catholic church. And Gerard Manley Hopkins, who wrote lines like "The world is charged with the grandeur of God". And G.K. Chesterton, who, Doc said, became a convert to Catholicism.

Chesterton, we were told, was against "the narrowness of puritanism"—"wowsers" we Catholics called them—and this showed in lines like: "And Christian hateth Mary that God kissed in Galilee", and "The cold Queen of England is looking in the glass" (cold, Doc said, because Queen Elizabeth was unmarried). Not that Doc was against royalty: though he did say that the national anthem was "fantastic music, and very bad poetry" as he quoted some of the other lines from "God Save the Queen" that you never hear, like "Confound their politics, frustrate their knavish tricks". He said poems written by the British Poet Laureate were invariably bad because they were always "written to order as propaganda".

But he was aghast when, after Terrace won the GPS swimming carnival, we sang our school song while, unknown to us, "God Save the Queen" was being played at the other end of the Valley Baths. We had given the Protestants ammunition, he said, to accuse us of being against the Queen. Next year the school song was not to be sung if we won.

Doc's enthusiasm for the Catholic poets did not rub off on Jim, who seemed to take very much the Russian view of English poetry. Almost, I thought, a subversive view.

At special Saturday morning poetry classes Doc enthused about lines like "As Kingfisher's catch fire, dragonflies draw flame", and "The full-juiced apple waxing over-mellow drops in the silent autumn night"—and I enjoyed the bravado of "For sudden the worst turns the best to the brave", and the sensual description of a girdle "Had I but what this ribbon bound, take all the rest—the sun goes around". Jim, on the other hand, became the only boy in the school to learn the entire four hundred lines of "Peter Grimes" off by heart. The only boy in the whole state to do so, I expect.

This was by far the drabbest poem in the book, with no set stanzas to make it easy to read, and a poem specifically written to show the opposite side to the beautiful picture of village life usually portrayed in English poems. Therefore it was a horrible, bleak, depressing, frightening poem about a cruel, crooked fisherman who slept in a mud-walled hovel while beating and starving to death the young orphan slaves he had procured from a workhouse.

And Jim could recite it all, though he raced through the

barrage of unhappy lines, as if slowing down might force him to forget them:

The trembling boy dropp'd down and strove to pray,
Received a blow, and trembling turn'd away,
Or sobb'd and hid his piteous face;—while he,
The savage master, grinn'd in horrid glee:
He'd now the power he ever loved to show,
A feeling being subject to his blow.

Though I knew Jim as well as anyone, I could not understand his unusual attraction to this ugly poem—this madman's tale.

Despite everything Doc taught us, "Horatius Defends the Bridge" remained my favourite poem because of the great courage of Horatius who faced the entire Tuscan army alone and wounded. The description couldn't have been more vivid: you could see him lean on his friend Herminius when wounded by the giant, Astur.

He leaned one breathing space;
Then, like a wild-cat mad with wounds,
Sprang right at Astur's face.
Through teeth, and skull, and helmet,
So fierce a thrust he sped,
The good sword stood a hand-breadth out
Behind the Tuscan's head.

Surrounded by his victim's bodies, Horatius held out just long enough for the Romans to pull down the narrow bridge behind him and stop the Tuscans from crossing the flooded Tiber River to take the city:

Alone stood brave Horatius,
But constant still in mind,
Thrice thirty thousand foes before,
And the broad flood behind.

Horatius, his job done, then leapt bleeding into the river and sank under the weight of his armour ... only to reappear above the torrent as both sides watched from the banks. By now, even the Tuscans "could scarce forebear to cheer" their brave opponent as Horatius again rose to the surface. Even the Tuscan King, Lars Porsena, admired Horatius for his fight:

> "Heaven help him!" quoth Lars Porsena,
> "And bring him safe to shore;
> For such a gallant feat of arms
> Was never seen before."

So imagine my surprise when Doc told me that I shouldn't be too hard on Jim's choice of poetry because, like "Peter Grimes", Horatius too was considered by many to be doggerel. My only defence was that I could see a lot of similarities between "Horatius Defends the Bridge" and one of Doc's favourite poems, "The Man from Snowy River".

Doc agreed both were wonderful stories, beautifully expressed, even if they weren't great poetry. After all, they were easily parodied, he said. And Doc himself had written such a parody, on the hunt for a runaway rat at Terrace:

> There was movement in the Monastery for news had spread apace
> That the rat that troubled Terrace was at bay
> Behind the Wick and Oil Press he had sought a breathing space
> So all the Monks had gathered to the fray ...

On and on it went to the final verse ....

> And now beneath the Dressing Shed his listening youngsters gape
> And he oft at deepest midnight will disclose
> How he passed through air and water in effecting his escape
> And won the Terrace Steeple by a nose.

19
Jim goes over the top

It was in our last year at school that Jim—who, despite his record, had really always sought to avoid confrontation—finally developed what he thought was the perfect trick to prevent fights.

If an argument developed, he would draw a line on the ground and dare the other boy to step across it. With his scar down the middle of his nose, and rumours of his feats of strength, for months no-one dared ruffle this iron curtain, though many were left red-faced enemies at their reluctance to do so.

Then, of all people, Jim did it to this forward from the first fifteen who I knew would have to step across the line.

And so did he.

And he did.

When he did so, Jim played the trick he had told me would keep him out of fights.

As the footballer stepped over the line, Jim patted him on the back and, with a big laugh which showed Jim's strong, straight, white teeth, said: "Good on you, now you're on my side."

The only trouble with this Egoroff exercise was that—though a group of boys laughed—the footballer didn't get the joke. He grabbed Jim in a bear hug, with the strength of a man who had contained himself too long: Doc's observation that "a man will be criticised, but he will not be laughed at" was correct. "This is it, Egoroff," the footballer said.

That was why Jim had to pick him up and throw him away.

As this forward sailed over a row of desks, he must have wondered why Jim himself was not in the firsts. But Jim was too much of an individual to excel in team sport. He was all right the previous year when we were both in the sevenths, because down there one strong boy could successfully take on fifteen others. But higher teams required ball skills—passing, kicking, catching—to penetrate the opposing fifteen.

Now that I had learned to be a specialist at fullback, and had some of these skills, even I was in a higher team than Jim. In fact, I had graduated just about as high as a convent boy could expect to get—the thirds—and, as we waited for Jim's fifths to finish one day, I marvelled, as I listened to the sound of their bodies colliding, that I was in a higher team.

I was sensitive enough never to point out to Jim that I was in a higher team than him. Not only because I knew it would injure his pride, but because I also knew he would bombard me with inexplicable explanations.

Anyway I wasn't in a higher team for long.

After his match, Jim stayed to watch me play and—because we had had a couple of injuries—our coach, Brother McMahon, sent Jim on: not realising that he had already played a full game.

We were being soundly beaten by Brisbane Grammar because their fullback could kick the ball much further than I could, and he kept forcing us right back by kicking over my head. Well it was no use having Jim on the field if you didn't use him, so I pulled him aside and explained the problem. Jim nodded his face up and down, as if it were made of wax, and without looking at me. This was a very good sign.

Once again Grammar kicked past me, and once again my return kick was very short. So short that their fullback had to run so far forward to catch it that he was standing among all our forwards, just twenty yards in front of me. This meant that none of our team, except me, could tackle him because they were all offside in front of the person who kicked the ball. Now the Grammar fullback could attack me at full speed, untouched by anyone else.

Well, almost.

Jim was standing next to the fullback as he caught the ball, like a spy inside the enemy's camp. And he reached out and wrapped his arms around the unsuspecting fullback and swung him in two complete circles, picked him up until he was horizontal to the ground, and threw him into the concrete-hard Grammar dirt which had recently been packed down over a filled-in rubbish dump.

Not surprisingly, the Grammar fullback lost the ball with the impact.

Jim picked it up—while the rest of the Grammar team, our team, and the referee, watched, wondering what game this Russian immigrant was playing. Getting over his shock, the referee started blowing his whistle, as Jim—chased by an imaginary hoard—raced seventy yards to make a spectacular dive over their line and score a try beneath the goal posts.

When he saw no-one else had moved, Jim—looking very aggrieved—raced back up the field with the ball to where the referee was standing, his right arm upraised, awarding a penalty to Grammar. But Jim, never one to listen to logical explanations, wouldn't hand over the ball for the penalty kick. "I scored a goal," he said. "It was a goal. I scored a goal." The ref couldn't believe it. Not only was this boy arguing with him after being in blatant breach of the rules, but he didn't even know enough about rugby to be claiming he scored a try, not a goal.

Grammar kicked the penalty goal for three more points, and I knew Brother McMahon would be mad at Jim. But at the thirds team meeting to discuss the match at lunchtime on Monday Brother McMahon—who also coached the fourths—got up and announced that Jim was being promoted from the fifths straight into our thirds. "Sure, Egoroff doesn't know the rules, and he won't pass the ball, but he's got one thing none of you has got: he's tough. The rest of you are all afraid to get your jerseys creased. You're scared of mucking up your hair. But Egoroff will mix it with an entire team if he has to. And did you see the way he dusted up that glamorous Grammar fullback?"

At training that Tuesday afternoon, Brother McMahon made the rest of us dive head first into some mud patches so we would stop being afraid of getting dirty. Of course, what Brother McMahon didn't know was that, tough as he was, Jim was incredibly scared of fleas. If he got any on him, he raced out of a house as if he was on fire.

Jim was also making some surprise advances with his schoolwork now that we were far enough into physics and chemistry to be learning about electric motors and refrigerant gases—things Jim seemed to know about like we knew about cricket.

To encourage boys to take an interest in science—because it was going to cure society of all its ills with new chemicals and big industrial processes—there was a competition for the best scientific work done by a Queensland schoolboy. Jim decided to enter. I thought he was mad. What hope would he have against all the boys in the A class? And all the boys in all the A classes in all the schools in the whole state?

I thought he was going to at last build the jet engine he had drawn up years before, and re-drawn and re-drawn in class until I was sick of hearing about it, and having to admire his colour drawings of the engine parts when he should have been learning Latin vocab so he could help me as much as I was helping him.

He "branded"—as he put it—the first one "JE1" but changed the next design to "AZ1" for some reason. Jim said it would be powerful enough to power a car, and at one stage I had invested four shillings and sixpence in it, so I was pretty keen to see it built. But Jim said titanium was too expensive and, besides, he had a much better idea.

This time he was going to build a refrigerator that was more efficient than the ones in the shops. He said it was ridiculous that mothers had to open and close the refrigerator door with their bare hands. They needed, Jim said, both hands free while putting things in, or taking things out of, the fridge. It was the same for shopkeepers. Particularly butchers, who carried huge loads into and out of refrigerators.

So Jim set about building a more efficient refrigerator with a voice-activated door which opened when you said "open"

247

and shut when you said "shut". This news thrilled Freddie, our science teacher, and, for the first time since Sister Veronica, we had a teacher who doted on Jim and had reason to dislike me.

Actually Freddie didn't seem to need a reason to dislike me. Obviously, he didn't like the fact that I was a poor student. But he got on well with at least one boy in the class even further down the scale than me.

No, there was something more.

About the worst thing you could be caught doing was smoking cigarettes. I didn't smoke, but my mate Rod had been smoking since he was at Moorooka Convent when we played them cricket. He smoked so much he had nicotine stains on the end of his fingers: yet Freddie just made jokes about it when he handed out the weekly pay cheques from the Education Department to the boys who had promised to become teachers after Senior, and so relieve the shortage of teachers. Freddie would always say he didn't know what they spent all the money on. Then, when he came to Rod, he would say: "Well we know what he spends it on," and everyone would laugh dutifully.

I hadn't even been caught wagging it from school like Rod and a couple of others. I was lucky the one day they did it because I was late and missed them and—with nothing else to do—went on to school. Somehow the Brothers found out and Rod copped a lift under the lug from one of the Brothers.

Yet, despite my comparatively clean record, Freddie clearly disliked me.

Naturally I wasn't even considered when it came to choosing prefects, or class captains. Nor was I promoted in the cadets. And Freddie appointed thirteen boys to run the college bi-annual newspaper *The Terracian* without me even hearing it was coming out.

"The dignified grey is a suitable background for the red and black of our tie. No doubt the designers intended it to be so. Then why spoil the effect by wearing coloured sox?" wrote the "Chief Editor", echoing exactly Freddie's view of luminous socks, and showing why he had been appointed.

"Didn't we agree to submerge some of our individuality in the interests of self-discipline when we came to Terrace? .... An honest man with his head held high prefers people to look him in the eye, not to stare at his feet."

What rot. But Freddie would have loved it.

Mind you, despite my good record, I had had a few close calls with Freddie at Greenbank cadet camp the previous year.

Diarrhoea swept through the camp and I was lucky not to be among the ninety per cent of boys who were sick. At parade Freddie called for all those not sick to fall out and see him. I did as instructed, but when he said that we would have to shoulder all the work for the sick while they rested, I ever-so-slowly inched my way back to the huge ranks of the sick. "Cadet Lunn, where are you going?" Freddie called. "To the sick parade, Sir. I thought there were so many there that they must be the group who were well." Freddie marched across and gave me the big smile treatment. "You bear watching, son. I'll be watching you. You're an interesting case."

A few weeks later he spotted me again.

It was the day before the Terrace Passing-Out Parade. Sergeant Buggy was missing and we trumpeters were saving our lips as all the hundreds of Terrace army and air force cadets marched in full dress rehearsal on the football oval for the General Salute in the presence of His Grace, Archbishop Duhig. Freddie couldn't understand the lack of volume from the band, and kept complaining about our performance: comments none of us liked, since three of our trumpeters had played on the Amateur Hour on radio. One of the Senior trumpeters then hit on a brilliant idea to show what we thought of his unfair criticism.

The call at the start of "Dog Faced Soldier" was always blown with all valves up. What if, he said, everyone pushed down a combination of his own choosing when the drum major signalled the next change of tune by holding his stick high in the air?

The resultant cacophony sounded like all thirty trumpeters were being strangled. It brought Freddie running. "That was all out of tune," Freddie said. "I think you're right, Sir" said the Senior trumpeter, explaining the difficulties experienced once too much spittle blocked the pipes. "Buglers, check your instruments". And we all dutifully opened the drains at the bottom of our cornets and trumpets and blew out the bits of spit that were always there when you played.

We would have escaped this incident unharmed, except that someone else had an even brighter idea. What if, he said, we played Glenn Miller's really fast jazz piece "In the Mood" next time the drum major signalled with his stick—instead of "Waltzing Matilda"? "Don't be silly, no-one could march to that," I said. "Exactly," he replied.

So, when the drum major's stick went up and the drummers played two drum rolls—as they always did to signal exactly when to start blowing—we all pressed down the first and third valves to start "In the Mood".

The hundreds of marching cadets might as well have been at Cloudland Ballroom as they struggled to decide which foot to put down next. A platoon of sub-juniors—foolishly thinking they could keep time with the music—raced across the field like a troupe of Charlie Chaplins in a speeded up film.

But they didn't move as fast as Freddie. He was beside us within a few bars.

The rehearsal was over, the Senior trumpeter of the day was taken away, and, as he left, Freddie turned to me and said: "Cadet Lunn, wipe that smile off your face or I will wrap your bugle around it."

My poor relationship with Freddie had to reach a head sooner or later. I thought it would come with some failure in class as we readied for the Senior Public Examination.

Instead it came at a football match.

The Terrace firsts were getting beaten at Brisbane Grammar School, not only on the scoreboard but on the field of play. Grammar had a huge forward with the apt nickname of "Bull", and they cheered as he raced around the field knocking much smaller Terrace blokes into the dust. To me, he seemed old and balding, like a man playing boys, and he was the first footballer I had seen who chose not to kick for the sideline when awarded a penalty: rather he kicked high in the air and ran through to personally knock our poor fullback flying as he stood defenceless, looking skyward to catch the ball.

Against this onslaught the Terrace supporters were curiously silent so—for the first time at a football match—I started to try to lead a lift in Terrace morale. Standing on the hill overlooking the ground, next to the shouting Grammar boys, I called out things like "C'mon Terrace. Take this bull by the horns!"

On Monday Freddie called me out, got out his strap, and told me my behaviour at the match was a disgrace to Terrace and accused me of making "dirty" remarks. He seemed to be shaking with rage, so I didn't defend myself and just took the punishment on both hands.

But that was not the end of it.

Freddie was a captain in the cadets, which presumably was why I was the only Senior boy in the band who was not awarded even one stripe: traditionally given to Seniors so they could stand ahead of the hundreds of O.R.s (Other Ranks) in the meal queues at camp. That was why I was so reluctant to go to the August cadet camp in my last year in Senior. In fact, if Jim—who was the only other Senior cadet without even one stripe—hadn't rung at five in the morning I would never have made it to the buses to Greenbank. There wasn't much incentive to go, except that it was compulsory.

Every year they showed the only two movies both the army and the Brothers could agree were good for us—*Goodbye Mr Chips*, about an old school teacher much admired by his boys, and the *Lavender Hill Mob*, about a band of nice gold robbers who get caught. The cocoa they gave before bed on the freezing nights was said to be full of bromide to stop any impure thoughts. And the queues for meals were incredibly long.

But at least this time I had come prepared. Believing I was worth some stripes, and was more sinned against than sinning, I had stopped in at Allan and Stark's one afternoon on the way home and—after half an hour searching the store—they came up with two sets of sergeant's stripes which I bought. Plus some Durex tape. Now that I was seventeen I wanted to exert some authority, to see what it was like— for the first time in my life—to order other human beings around.

This new zeal grew partly out of winning a college .303 rifle-shooting competition after asking Major Basher if I could go and try again, four years after my first abysmal effort. "Do you blow a bugle or shoot a rifle, Huggles?" he asked. "Actually, Sir," I said, "I blow a cornet." Basher said he would think about it. And a few days later he announced that anyone who volunteered from the band could take part in the shoot.

I still don't know why I won—or why the three volunteers from the band, without benefit of army training, finished first, third and fourth. It was not an easy competition because we shot over three different distances—100, 200 and 300 yards—testing grouping, snap-shooting and application. Perhaps I had just accidentally picked up one of the few good rifles among the hundreds of old World War I weapons kept padlocked under the school hall. Or perhaps it was because I had since discovered that the system Jack used for aiming the Daisy air rifle was wrong: the top of the front sight had to be in the top of the V sight at the back.

It was dark at Greenbank at night among the tents in the bush. Only a few lights were sprinkled around among the trees, and most of what little light there was, came from the glow of lantern flames flickering from hundreds of tent flaps. So one night I pulled my stripes out of the bottom of my kit bag, stuck them on to my greatcoat arms with the sticky tape, and emerged from my tent—scared but exhilarated—to swagger powerfully through the scattered army camp as a sergeant.

I imagined myself shouting at first-year cadets and telling them to smarten up, using the unusual aspirated language of the army which the good boys who were promoted very soon learned to imitate: "Haaatension, by the leff .... kweak Ha!" I was dying to find some cadet with long hair so I could address him the way I had been when I first went to camp as a thirteen-year-old: "Get that hair cut, cadet. Are you planning to play the violin on it?"

The trouble was I couldn't seem to find any isolated first-year cadets.

Eventually I discovered why.

They were all off to the open-air theatre to watch the *Lavender Hill Mob* on a bit of white canvas strung between two trees, and all 120-plus of them were lined up as a company dressed in their greatcoats ready to go.

Awaiting orders.

I don't know what came over me but, before I really thought about it, I emerged from the shadows of some trees into the dimly lit area and shouted "Kumpanny! Haaatension!" To my eternal surprise, all 120 boys leapt into the air and brought their heels together with a resounding thud.

"Kumpanny, Leff Hern!"

And they all swung 90 degrees to the left.

"Kumpanny! By the leff.... Kweak Ha!"

And away they went, though I had no idea where I was going to take them—or even which way it was to the sheet of canvas. But, luckily for me, not knowing where you're going is not a problem in the army. "Kumpanny! Haabout Hern!"—and suddenly we were going back from whence we came.

With no questions asked.

I was feeling really good. I liked the way everyone reacted to my every word: so long as I imitated my masters. I was warm in my greatcoat; I was invisible beneath my brown slouch hat; I was somebody. The somebody.

Soon we were marching back through their company lines and two cadet under-officers—recognisable by their peaked officer's hats—emerged from the tent lines and walked slowly towards our group. "Kumpanny! Halt!" - and my long group pulled up in front of them at attention, as I planned my quick exit.

But just then, from under a tree walked none other than Captain Freddie, looking for all the world like Rommel in the war films—his hands clasped firmly behind his back, his head thrust forward, the gleam of light along the rim of his glasses and his tooth-line sending a cold shudder down my spine. "Sergeant," he called, as I tipped my head down to seek shadow. "Good work. They're ready for you now."

The one thing I knew about myself was that I had two things everyone commented on: pink cheeks and a distinctive voice, exactly the same voice as Jack's. People could tell our raspy voice a mile off. To speak normally now was to die in action. So I saluted and turned away.

Which way to take them?

"Kweak Ha!" I shouted.

I don't know when they eventually stopped, because I disappeared at a treed turn-off and ripped my stripes off and never wore them again.

A few nights later, I was relaxing in my tent just before lights out when the flap burst open and in marched Jim from the mortar platoon. He didn't appear to realise he was in my tent. "Hand over your greatcoats. Jim's been cold these couple of last days. If you don't, I will run over your tent," he said. He claimed to have already collected half a tent full of greatcoats.

Running over a tent was considered nearly impossible because they were big four-man tents, covered with a thick fly with steep 45-degree sides. Jim was famous for having done it once, but had confided to me later that the speed and effort required had nearly killed him. Now he just pretended to run over tents, coming back down the same side in the dark: but the people inside did not know the difference, and still got a fright.

"Jim," I said, "it's me. Don't run over our tent, run over the one next door"—and I named the four members of our class who were already asleep in there, including my mate Rod. Jim agreed, but said he would just run up and down the one side. As he walked away to get a run-up, I looked down at the steel spikes in the ground and—I don't know why—pulled a few of them halfway out of the ground.

In the dark, in his overcoat and heavy army boots, Jim came racing up beside the long line of tents like a Cossack on a bayonet charge, and leapt high in the air onto the tent fly. Boots slipping, he fought dew and gravity with momentum, friction, and sheer strength as he strove manfully to get to the top. For a moment he made it, appearing silhouetted against the sky like a trapeze artist in an overcoat—clawing the air for balance, tip-toeing in his boots on the edge, and then disappearing with a crash as the whole tent came down.

There was chaos and commotion from under the flattened tent as Rod and the others searched for a way out of their suddenly dark, smothered world.

As cadets rushed to the scene, and a drummer crawled out from under the flap, I saw Jim walking away purposefully into the dark. In unfamiliar fashion, he held his hands pseudo-nonchalantly behind his back, trying to look as inconspicuous as possible. Only then did I realise the possible consequences of our actions. At that very moment, a big torch beam split the area as if it were rifle fire.

"What's going on down there?" boomed Freddie's voice from behind the light.

I slipped behind our tent and entered from the other side, jumped into my blankets and pretended to be asleep. Suddenly a torch was in my face. And, though I hadn't yet opened my eyes, I knew whose torch it was. I started to stir. I yawned. I blinked. I squinted. I slowly sat up. I stretched. "Who is it? What's wrong?" I asked, blinded by the light.

"Why are you in bed in your army clothes, Cadet Lunn?" asked Freddie. "It was too cold and I was tired and I couldn't be bothered changing, Sir."

The torch went out but the flap was still held open. Could I see a row of teeth? Yes, I could see a row of teeth. They disappeared as the flap fell back.

I could tell Jim was angry, as soon as I saw him the next day at breakfast, by the pose he always adopted when he was going to speak sternly to me. With his elbow on the table, he held the left side of his forehead between the thumb and outstretched forefinger of his left hand, with the other three fingers curled underneath the palm, and transfixed me with the gaze of his big brown eyes. "You bastard boy," said Jim.

He had hurt his arm when he fell. He had only just evaded

Freddie's beam of light. There was a rumour it was him. But Jim could never be suppressed for long. "I nearly made it over the top," he said with enthusiasm. "Without a word of a lie, I think I would have got over if the pegs hadn't given way."

I didn't dare tell him the truth. He was still angry with me for beating him in the annual school cross-country race. We had agreed to stick together, but when Jim fell behind I pushed on over the three-and-a-half-mile course and came forty-sixth. After the race, Jim said he had done badly because he was hanging back waiting for me, wondering where I was. I couldn't convince him that I lost him among the hundreds of boys climbing the side of the Brisbane Grammar rubbish dump.

Anyway, I didn't think Jim had cause to worry about the tent incident. As far as Freddie was concerned, Jim could have knocked down every tent in Greenbank and been let off with a caution. Incredible as it seemed, Jim had won the Queensland schoolboys' science competition with his "no hands" refrigerator. Not only that, but the *Courier-Mail* had his picture in the paper in Terrace uniform with the refrigerator, and had put it in their window in Queen Street on display for everyone to see: together with Jim's drawing of a butcher in a blue-and-white striped apron carrying a large tray of meat in both hands and telling the refrigerator door to open.

Jim even got some days off school to arrange the display and talk to people about it, and I had even seen our headmaster, Brother Adams, standing outside the *Courier-Mail*, looking proudly in at Jim's handiwork.

What I couldn't understand was: why was everybody calling him a genius when he and I had such trouble doing our physics experiments together? Our recent attempts to count the vibrations sent out by tuning forks had turned into a farce. We had so much fun hitting them on various parts of our bodies that neither of us noted down any of the vibration figures—and Jim had to make them all up.

It worked, but not as successfully as the best ploy we pulled in all our years together.

To prepare us for the coming Senior exam, Freddie had been setting past exam questions for homework. Jim and I hadn't been doing any—we usually copied someone else's at little lunch. Freddie must have realised this, because he appeared to set a trap—especially for me: for weekend homework he set an algebra problem which, he said, no-one in Queensland had solved in the Senior exam the year it was set.

On Monday morning he looked around the classroom until his ever-broadening toothy grin settled on me, sitting down the back with Jim. "Master Lunn," he sniggered, "come up to the blackboard and do that algebra problem." He knew that—while I might have copied someone else's work—out at the blackboard I would be all on my own.

What a surprise for everyone then when I hit the blackboard like Freddie himself, and started covering it in numbers and letters—continuing right around the green roll until I met my beginning and wrote the answer in chalk: "Therefore A equals this; B equals that; and C equals this."

Hard luck, Freddie.

What he didn't know was that, because no-one in Queensland had managed to get the problem out in Senior, it intrigued Jim and I enough to spend the whole weekend on the phone working it out.

"Wrong!" said Freddie.

Wrong? It couldn't be wrong.

"Wrong!" he repeated.

Pleased with himself, Freddie turned his attention to the rest of the class: "Where is he wrong?" No-one except Jim moved, lest they might be asked. Not one hand went up, save Jim's.

Freddie couldn't believe it. Was it possible that the only boys in the class who had spent all weekend on this maths problem were Jim and me? "You must have attempted this problem. What answers did you get?" he asked the other boys.

I was standing on the raised floor in front of the blackboard and I could see by the blank faces staring at Freddie that they had no idea. No idea at all. And I could also see Freddie was getting really angry.

The class overflowed with prefects and boys with Vocations and editors and under-officers and cricket captains .... and not one had done as Freddie had directed. "Don't look at me," Freddie shouted at them. "The error's not on my face, it's on the blackboard"—and he pointed behind himself at me.

As Freddie harangued the class, he walked back to his desk and got his strap out of his briefcase: while with raised eyebrows I silently signalled to Jim at the back of the room. Any movement by him was fraught with danger. He mouthed something about "A". I shrugged my shoulders.

"I am now going to start counting to ten," Freddie told the class. "And when I get there I'm going to ask someone where the mistake is. And, if he doesn't know, he will regret it. And I will continue to do that until all those who don't know regret it. One ... two ... three ..."

The whole class was aghast. Could an entire class get the Tamer treatment?

Freddie set off for the back of the class and turned to face the front. As he did so, Jim held up a piece of paper with an A over a two. That was it! I had forgotten in the last line to divide A by two.

"It's on the blackboard," said Freddie to the class, calming himself. "Look at it and think. Four ... five ... six ..."

As Freddie turned to walk away from me, I slowly raised my right hand with the chalk in it, my eyes fixed firmly on Freddie's back, and quickly drew a line under the A and put a two beneath it .... and then rubbed it out again with the side of my hand.

"Eight .... nine ....." said Freddie, and an explosion of hands burst into the air, causing Freddie to swing around and look at the blackboard.

But nothing had changed.

Freddie was amazed that the whole class should suddenly realise the tiny mistake in such a long and difficult algebra problem. It was a miracle, but there was no way anyone could have told them all. And I couldn't have done anything: I was the one who had made the mistake.

"It's marvellous what a threat will do. It's marvellous what a threat will do!" was all Freddie could keep saying, over and over—as if trying to convince himself he had not been tricked.

And, when we broke for lunch, I found out for the first time what it was like to succeed, as dozens of grateful classmates surrounded me to give thanks for saving them from the cuts.

As the exams approached, each of the Brothers found his own way of saying goodbye.

Freddie called me out at the end of a lesson in the physics laboratory, as the others went upstairs for maths. His face turned ashen as I approached his big lab desk with its own sink. As he looked at me he seemed to develop a series of vertical wrinkles in his cheeks, like the top of an overcooked bun. "Are you deliberately trying to make me hate you, son?" he asked. I assured him that this had never been the case.

He got out his strap and was wagging it in front of him at my chest, clearly trying to control himself. The vein down the middle of his forehead stood out, and pulsated, as it always did when he was really angry.

In desperation I told him I had always done my best but that he had taken an inexplicable dislike to me from day one. He motioned with the strap for me to hold out my hand. As I did so, I noticed Rod's face bob up from behind a lab bench where he had been putting away some apparatus.

Now he was stuck there. He could see how angry Freddie was, and did not dare move.

As Rod bobbed up and down, I kept talking to Freddie: he was very nice to some boys who were worse than me. Yes, I did badly at his subjects—I didn't have enough brains to understand them, but I was doing alright under Doc and Brother Adams. I had done my utmost on the sports field and cheered for Terrace like no-one else; I had been misunderstood.

He said he had seen me in the cadets deliberately lead boys around a tree at camp. Was he talking about the sergeant stripes incident? If so, why did he let me escape at the time? I couldn't ask him, so I denied it. And he accused me of deliberately trying to disrupt his classes—which was rubbish.

Eventually, Freddie seemed to tire of the discussion and slowly lowered his strap and, as his anger ebbed, put it away. He would give me the benefit of what he called "a minuscule doubt". If I tried, and stopped mucking around, I could pass in his subjects in the coming exams, he said. I promised to try.

"I thought he was going to kill you," Rod said on the Tarragindi bus that afternoon.

Brother Adams's way of saying goodbye before the last exam was to bring both Senior classes together and plead for six more boys to apply to join Catholic law firms in the city—they wanted Terrace boys but couldn't get them. Then he warned us about the world: "Boys, when you go out into the world now, you will meet some wicked people. You will meet good girls but you will also meet some bad girls, wicked girls. Boys, remember there is to be nothing below the belt ... er ... I mean nothing underhand ... er ... I mean be good boys."

Luckily no-one so much as coughed.

And Doc—who always began addresses to large school gatherings, "Gentlemen of Terrace ..."—said: "Grow up with a sense of justice and rightness and always have a just perspective. Remember, it is stupid to assume that our cause is always just and nobody else's is."

Then, as we all stood up to leave the Catholic education system, he said: "You know, some of you will grow up and go and live in England and become Aussie con men."

20
Come blow your horn

Because I passed only three of the exams—including Doc's logic and English—I returned to Terrace the next year to try to get the necessary four subjects for a Senior pass.

It wasn't that I had any job in mind, it was just that there wasn't much demand at the start of 1959 for a seventeen-year-old boy who could play the trumpet, tap-dance, make meat pies, sort soft drink bottles and quote poetry. All of those things were on the way out as the electric guitar, rock-and-roll, the tin can, the hamburger joint and TV swept into Brisbane.

I suppose I could have got a job working with Fred as an apprentice cook, but Olive didn't want that—and I agreed with her after working as Fred's apprentice over the holidays. I got a new exercise book to write down how Fred made everything: with a series of columns for the ingredients, the quantities, the time in the oven, the mixing, and the secrets. But by the end of the first day I stopped, because my pad was full of useless instructions like: "add a small fist of salt", "use a handful of sultanas", "leave it proof and come back directly", and "stir until it feels right".

I felt very self-conscious going back to Terrace as a failure to mix with ninety new Seniors and, for the first time in nearly a decade, without Jim to sit next to.

Jim, thanks to Doc, had passed Senior English: filling his poetry paper, he said, with long quotations from "Peter Grimes"—probably impressing the examiners by being the only person in the state to answer that question. Thus Jim qualified to go to university, but he first took a job with Astor refrigeration in Spring Hill while he saved up to do engineering. So I was able to drop in and visit him on the way home from Terrace sometimes.

Doc had become headmaster, and he made me feel much better on my return. He put me in the A class and, turning seriously towards me, shook his ample jowls, and said as he squinted: "Remember son, there is no disgrace in being even the least when all are great."

That year I achieved what I had once seen as an impossible dream: I became fullback for the firsts and got the special black jersey—mine with a tall red leather "1" on the back. Each match was considered so important that the firsts gathered in a corner of the field and said the Our Father— no other team in the school prayed before a match. And the whole school chanted "come on Terrace—red, black, red" as we strove for the honour of "The Terrace", as Old Boys called it. Playing for the firsts made me someone, and numerous small Terrace boys gathered around me each week to ask how we would go in the next match. The other boys even had a nickname for me—"Q" (because it was easier to say than Hugh)—and, as I walked through town, I started throwing my tie over my left shoulder as if it had blown there.

I had learnt this from walking down Queen Street with Kenny Fletcher, who now had a job with Slazengers because he was a champion tennis player. He would always buy a *Telegraph*, which I thought was a very grown-up thing to do. Ken would read it out as we walked along, looking as if he owned Queen Street and all the trams in it. Or else he would roll the *Telegraph* up and practise his strokes as we walked down to the Palms cafe for a spider, or to a sandwich shop where the girl behind the counter refused to charge Ken anything.

Ken was the only person I knew who would tell you exactly what he thought, even admitting that girls affected him physically—giving him a horn, he called it. And, although he was very religious and went to Mass and Confession regularly—he also admitted that he was very interested in getting his hands on them. He didn't even mind if a girl knocked him back when he asked her for a dance. In fact, instead of walking away feeling lousy and deciding never again to ask another girl for a dance, he used to say: "Do you realise who you've just refused?" And then the girl would get up and dance with him. He kept telling me I'd be just as successful if I tried it, but he was very good looking and a champion.

I was relieved to know I was not alone in desiring both purity and girls in almost equal amounts, and Ken became the person I talked to about my inner life. I knew from experience he could keep a secret better than anyone else. But just as I made the firsts, Ken was sent on a world tour with the Australian Davis Cup team.

No doubt one of the reasons I had made the firsts was because Doc liked me. He often stopped to speak to me as he passed the corner where I sat. One day he showed me a letter he had received from one of his former students, rock-and-roll singer Johnny O'Keeffe, with "The Wild One" printed in blue on the envelope. Doc also told me he didn't like being headmaster because he had had to turn hundreds of boys away—"which is not many if you say it fast".

I had impressed him because, at the start of the season, I had stepped forward with the boys who wanted to get out of rugby. Usually you needed a medical certificate, but I told Doc the true story: that Fred thought football was like war, even though he was life vice-president of the Annerley Stars soccer club. (He only got this honorary position because he used to make big milkshakes for the boys who started the club.)

Doc said he understood Fred's objection, but my parents had chosen to accept the privilege of sending me to Terrace and, therefore, I had to obey the school rules and play whether I liked it or not.

A few weeks later, a Toowoomba Grammar centre broke through and I collided with him in a "tackle low", right in front of the form where the two headmasters sat to watch the firsts. On Monday afternoon Doc stopped me outside the college gate and said I had made him very proud when he saw the ferocity of the tackle—because he knew it was something I had done despite my feelings against the violent impact of football.

Doc seemed to like me more than ever after that. He let me play one Saturday even though I had stayed home from school the day before: a privilege he would never have allowed anyone else. But he could not resist my excuse: Olive asked me to stay home to help her lay some secondhand lino she had got from St Stephen's Cathedral for nix.

I was so popular with Doc that he went out of his way to talk to my parents at the football, and even patted our boxer dog "Droopy" who, with his jowls and dark eyes, bore a disconcerting resemblance to Doc. And he told me what a wonderful mother I had. Mum couldn't understand why Doc was always so concerned about her health: she didn't know that whenever I was late, I said she was sick: I had to, as this was the only excuse he would accept.

Fred had become completely captivated by the charm of Droopy. He taught Droopy to sit up on a chair, and then insisted on having him sit up at the kitchen table while we had dinner, where Fred would address him and say "look how he is trying to talk". He took Droopy everywhere we went in the Zephyr, despite the fact that the car would now barely hold us all. One day, when Fred was driving us all to the football, Droopy was complaining that he couldn't get his head out of the window, and Fred—who normally addressed Mum as "dear heart"—said: "For God's sake Olive, move over and give the dog some room." This became one of Mum's favourite stories.

Such behaviour might sound strange, but Fred was really just a bit of a scallywag. That was why he loved to mispronounce the names of sports people like Rod Larva (Laver) and Richie Renord (Benaud). One day, during a firsts' match, Fred was demonstrating Droopy's ability to shake hands when the dog—used to playing with the football in the back yard—raced onto the field .... with Fred chasing him .... and Olive running behind calling out "Fred get off the field. You will be killed!" Thirty big footballers were running in all directions .... including me—watching it all, absolutely mortified.

It was during the football season that winter of 1959 that my special relationship with Doc started to sour.

With Ken overseas with the Davis Cup team and Jim working, I was lucky: I had found myself a girlfriend—unfortunately, an Anglican girl in Senior from "the school on the hill". We met at a shindig and I immediately fell in love with her hair: which was the colour of ginger ale.

That was the night I wore my first, brand-new set of clothes, instead of Jack's hand-me-downs. Now that I was almost eighteen, Olive had taken me into Stuarts, the suit specialists, at North Quay and they made me a pair of dark blue strides. I was amazed when the tailor asked me which side of the trousers I "dressed"—and he indicated my balls—because the way people normally talked, it was as if we didn't have anything between our legs. The tailor also wanted to know if I wanted buttons or one of the modern zips for the fly: I opted for the buttons, which sounded safer. Then I bought a Guy Mitchell blue shirt with a horizontal black fleck and a white piece across the top of the pocket, and a long-sleeved Ming-blue jumper with two white stripes in the V neck.

And the new outfit worked.

The first time I took her to the football, she wore a pale blue sack dress and looked so beautiful there was no way anyone could say I was going out with a bat. She even wore stockings and white high-heeled shoes and lipstick and powder, and carried a gold compact. The only trouble was, being a Protestant, she didn't understand the difficulties of being a Catholic, and whenever she walked past Doc she would give him a big smile and say "hello Brother Campbell": causing him to shake his jowls like Droopy.

She was horrified when I told her I couldn't take her to the annual Seniors dance because she was a non-Catholic. She thought I must be making it up. But that was the rule. As Doc explained it to us, he was thinking of our own good: "The Church does not say it is against Mixed Marriage; the Church says it 'abhors' Mixed Marriage."

To ensure only Catholic girls were taken to the dance, those of us who were going were asked to write down on a piece of paper: the name of the girl we were bringing; the Catholic school she was attending; and the class she was in. I had a plan, and promised my girlfriend I would take her despite the rule, and she gleefully told her school friends that she was going to be the first St Margaret's girl to go to the Terrace dance.

I was fortunate in having a cousin, Imelda Laurie, at Lourdes Hill Convent and, without her knowledge, I wrote her details on my piece of paper. Each boy had to take his piece of paper up to the front himself and put it on Doc's desk. As I reached out nervously to put my paper down with the others, Doc looked up from under an immense frown and said: "Don't try it, son. Don't try it", and I crept back to my desk still carrying my lie.

When I finished sixth in the school cross-country, Doc did not congratulate me. "Lucky for the *Courier-Mail* you didn't come one hundred and forty-sixth," he said, because, thanks to Jack, they had carried the names of the first six place-getters. Then he sent me home from an athletics meet.

I had earned an Honour Blazer—by playing every match for the firsts—but no blazers had been awarded. So—instead of having a special red blazer with an embossed badge "First XV 1959" on the pocket to strut around in—I had only my secondhand, double-breasted, wide-shouldered suit coat to wear. It was almost summer, so I took my girlfriend to the Terrace-Churchie athletics wearing summer uniform. Doc called me over.

"Where's your coat, son?"

"I should have an Honour Blazer to wear. My coat is worn out and next week it's summer."

"Go home son", he said.

"But if.."

"Go home son."

I started to leave, then went back and pointed out that few Terracians had come, because we were bound to lose. But I had come to cheer our boys. Doc looked across at my girlfriend in her cinnamon dress, looked straight ahead at the athletics, and said without looking at me, "Go home son."

I took to meeting my girlfriend in Adelaide Street before school, in front of a long row of steps that led up to radio station 4BH, behind Allan and Stark's. Since we were doing

Senior together, she became my first real incentive to pass.

She never grizzled about the work-load or about the school authorities at St Margaret's, which insisted the girls wore singlets—and even had singlet checkers at the school gate. She was so great to talk to. Every flick of the eyebrow, every roll of the blue eyes, every touch to the red hair, meant something. Her hair was like a golden halo because it was tucked up under the edges of her dark blue beret—since St Margaret's girls weren't allowed to have hair as long as shoulder-length. She laughed so much, as we stood in the doorway, that she often put her leather purse—which was bigger than her tiny gloved hand—over her mouth to enjoy it all the more.

Even though we saw each other most mornings, we also wrote letters in which we quoted poetry. Since my only experience of life and girls came vicariously through poetry, I searched daily during lessons for any possible reference to her and got a special thrill from lines like:

What heart could have thought you?—
Past our devisal
(O filigree Petal!)
Fashioned so purely,
Fragilely, surely,
From what Paradisal
Imagineless metal,
Too costly for cost?
Who hammered you, wrought you,
From Argentine vapor?

It didn't matter to me that it was supposed to be about a snowflake.

That year I took her to the GPS athletics at the Gabba, despite an edict that there were to be no girls in the Terrace stand, on the illogical basis that the previous year we had the most girls and finished almost last. A prefect came and told us to leave, but we stayed. Freddie came and sat in the seat directly behind me for a bit of added pressure: but still we stayed, with her looking outstanding in another of her mother's creations—a strapless pink dress, tight at the

267

waist and above the knees, with an embroided white pattern.

TV had come to Brisbane that year. At first we could only see it by joining the large groups of people who gathered on Friday nights outside suburban shop windows to watch "Paladin" or "Seventy-Seven Sunset Strip", but her parents quickly bought a set and some Friday nights we would watch it together, and hold hands under a blanket.

When her father got free tickets, we went to see the Platters at Milton tennis stadium, and I listened avidly to the words they seemed to have written just for me:

Only you can make this world seem right;
Only you can make the darkness bright;
Only you, and you alone, can thrill me like you do.

But still I could not believe my luck, and I wondered when they sang "The Great Pretender"—might "I seem to be what I'm not, you see?"

Would she leave me to dream all alone?

She came over to our place from Toowong to see the shop and the house. I tried to re-paint the house before she came, but found some rotten boards and failed in my attempts to repair them. The front paling fence was leaning over so I knocked it down, but then failed to work out how to re-erect it. She was all dressed up, and carrying her small leather money purse and I asked why she had not brought a change of clothing. "I did," she said, and pulled a flimsy ruched bloomer suit from her purse. Nothing like that had ever been seen in Annerley Junction before.

Time passed very slowly between our weekend nights out, and so one day we agreed to wag school—"our little plan" she called it. We each got changed in the City Hall and went to the pictures and down to the Botanic Gardens on a trolley bus. It was a very dangerous thing to do and would have meant instant expulsion, excommunication, and death if seen.

Even though it wasn't a sin, I paid dearly for that wonderful day, when I had to take the false note I had written in my clumsy copy of Olive's handwriting out to Freddie—who examined it carefully and put it in his pocket, nodding his head knowingly up and down with a fiendish grin on his face, as if he knew it was a rort. All day I thought he finally had me, but he was only bluffing.

On our weekend night together I sometimes stayed so long at her place that I would miss the last tram, and we would have to rake up the six shillings between us for me to get a Yellow taxi home. It was on one of these nights—just a few days before Senior—when, as I was leaving, I walked under the house to look at her mother's Ford Consul which was parked, Queensland style, between the house stumps. We got inside and, in the dark, I began to kiss her and couldn't stop. "Pashing" was what other boys called it. It was so exciting that I felt like I had fallen off the City Hall tower and was floating.

I must have lost balance, because I put the palm of my right hand out to hold myself up, and was startled by a loud explosion which would not stop. It was the car horn: I had my full weight on this horn, right under her parents' bedroom—and I couldn't get it off.

Immediately her mother shouted her name down through the timber floorboards, and we leapt out of the car.

The world was rapidly catching up with us.

Postscript

I PASSED Senior and, after an eight-month false start in life, joined Jack as a cadet journalist on the *Courier-Mail*. I went to Hong Kong with Kenny Fletcher and spent seven years overseas, travelling through China and Russia, and working as a journalist in Indonesia and Singapore. For two years I lived in England, before being sent to cover the Vietnam War for Reuters.

FRED and OLIVE lost their second shop in 1962 after the Brisbane City Council forced the removal of Uncle Cyril's alcoves and a cake-shop chain opened a branch at 500 Ipswich Road—just four doors from our shop—and cut their prices until Fred was going broke. Olive found another shop on the other side of town at Chermside and they moved to a house nearby.

JACK married the girl he met while still at school, and went on to become general manager of the *Courier-Mail*. GAY taught dancing, compered fashion parades in Perth, and started her own radio program in northern Western Australia, Fred's home state. SHERYL raised her family not far from Fred and Olive's house near the new shop and, inheriting Olive's optimistic outlook on life, took a job on a newspaper. They each had three children.

OUR FARM was sold to pay bills when Fred got sick, and that area north of Southport is now called Paradise Point.

OUR HOME at Annerley was knocked down after it was sold, and a double-storey brick one built on its site. Ekibin creek and seven wells were eventually covered by Brisbane's southeast freeway. The timber Annerley Hotel was given a brick facade, the picture theatre knocked down, and the old tap-dancing hall next door became a secondhand car yard. An antique store occupies the site of Fred and Olive's first shop, and the Mary Immaculate church now calls itself by a nickname which once would surely have been a Mortal Sin: "Marymac".

FRED'S FATHER: After Fred and Olive died, I found from their papers that Grandpa Hugh had spent two years in jail because of his campaign to stop workers slaving away for the rich.

ROD, the smoker, died slowly of cancer in the chest after two terrible years of treatment.

KENNY FLETCHER went on to win five Wimbledon doubles titles, but lost three years in a row to the singles champion: though once he went within two points of victory. He made the winning Australian Davis Cup team of Laver, Emerson, Fraser and Fletcher, and now lives in London where he coaches tennis and is a member of the Wimbledon Club.

DOC never gave up on me. He wrote to me a few times, when he felt I had written something worthy. In 1967 he was put in charge of Christian Brothers in Queensland. In 1984, after sixty-four years in the Christian Brothers, he died. There was standing room only in St Stephen's Cathedral as the Rev. Dr Owen Oxenham preached the panegyric: "We still remember the shuddering jowls, the lowering eyebrows, the piercing eye." At the Brothers' Office of the Dead they said their farewell: "Pages will be written, volumes spoken

271

about J.S.C. We close with these words from one of his heroes, Hamlet:

> He was a man; take him for all in all,
> We shall not look upon his like again".

AND DIMA: Jim eventually moved to England, where he started an engineering firm which now makes golf carts, and where he kept on inventing things: including a "jump tank" which, instead of having a turret, jumps around to face the enemy. Though we knew nothing about swimming, Jim's nephew Tony captained and swam Terrace to victory, with great strength and style, at the 1988 GPS championship. A bachelor, Jim lives in a three-hundred-year-old house called "Frogholt" on seven acres near Folkstone, on the coast of Kent. He successfully fought before a House of Lords select committee to have the Channel Tunnel—planned to connect Europe with Britain—diverted around him.